Long-Term Success Building WordPress Websites for the Amazon Affiliate Program

RYAN STEVENSON

ISBN: 1493631861
ISBN-13: 978-1493631865

This publication is designed to provide accurate and authoritative information with regard to the subject matter covered. It is sold with the understanding that the publisher is not engaged in rendering legal, accounting, or other professional advice. If legal advice or other expert assistance is required, the services of a competent professional person should be sought. Any person acting on the ideas herein is responsible for his own actions, and acts at his own risk.

DEDICATION

To my beautiful wife, Sara, and our wonderful kids for tolerating the long work hours at home and my mindless ramblings about the internet that don't make any sense to them.
Happy 10th Anniversary Sara - I look forward to many more decades with you.

To my Mom for being a teacher and painstakingly correcting my grammar as a child.

To the coaching students from my original, live webinar series called Azon Master Class, which is likely referenced in this book.

Without any one of you, this book wouldn't exist, so you have my eternal gratitude.

CONTENTS

ACKNOWLEDGMENTS

This book is meant to be a guide for both new and existing affiliates of the Amazon Associates Program that are looking for reliable way to build websites to promote products to refer sales for commissions.

A single website will not make you rich, but building a series of sites can create a nice monthly recurring source of income. It is very important to remember that results will certainly vary from one person to the next, although success is typically proportionate to the amount of work you put into learning this strategy and putting it into action.

The other key thing to remember is that this strategy takes work, dedication and determination on your part to make it successful. Just reading this book isn't enough – you must actually do the work to build one or more sites.

About This Book
The content of this book was originally created for a live Amazon affiliate coaching webinar series that had 12 classes. Each of those 12 classes is now a main chapter of this book.

During that class, I walked trainees through my entire site building strategy while I built a site live for them on my screen.

That live training was done using online webinars where students could see my screen as I worked, hear me talk, and even ask their own questions.

This book is the guidebook from that live training, and it was meant as an easy way to follow along with the live training.

With that said, this book is intended as complete tutorial on how to build your own Amazon website without having technical knowledge or web design experience. However, it is also a first-hand guide on the construction of the website built for the live trainees, so you actually get real-life examples and have a real website you can visit to use as a reference.

Book Usage Recommendations
The 12 main chapters of this book are intended to be classes that you can work through at your own pace. There are numerous sub-chapters to each of the 12 main chapters (numbered as 1-1, 1-2, etc...).

Each of these chapters begins with an introduction, summary and a checklist. The checklist is excellent to use to ensure you have completed all of the main steps for that particular class with the construction of your own websites. There is also blank space after each checklist that you can use to make your own notes for that chapter.

Proceed through all of the sub-chapters for the first class. As you read through the lessons, try to work along with them on your computer. Complete the checklist for each class before going on to the next class.

After you are done with all 12 classes and this book, you will not only have the knowledge you need to build Amazon affiliate websites, but you will also have your first site completed and running already! Simply repeat the process to make more sites – the more sites you make, the better your monthly earning potential will be.

Watch The Coaching Videos & Amazon Advertising Software

The live coaching series for these 12 classes was recorded and is available for online viewing. There are 12 HD videos where you get to see this strategy being put into action – more than 26 hours worth of video training.

This book and the videos both feature (in class #8) the use of five WordPress plugins that create various types of advertisements for Amazon affiliates.

Those plugins are plugins that I have personally developed for use on my own Amazon affiliate sites and also make them available to my trainees to help them build advertisements for their own sites.

Although the ads could technically be built manually, I highly recommend the use of these plugins.

The coaching students of the live series received these plugins for free with this course. However, I am unable to do that with customers of this book because of the major price difference (live trainees paid up to $497 for this complete series).

The videos, plugins and also digital copies of the lessons from this book can all be obtained by purchasing option #3 of my home-study course for this series.

Visit my website below to get access to these videos and plugins:
http://ryanstevensonplugins.com/azon-coaching/

1 AMAZON PRODUCT & NICHE RESEARCH

In the first class, we will be focusing on Amazon itself to perform product research to help us determine some potential niches that we can target on our website. You'll learn how to navigate the Amazon website and research product information. Tips are also available to help you find the best products to promote, brainstorm niche ideas, and even select a potential niche to target.

Primary Lesson Objective

☐   Select a Potential Amazon Product Niche

Lesson Steps Checklist

☐   Explore Amazon Categories and Subcategories

☐   Browse Individual Products

☐   Look for Quality, Reasonably Priced Products

☐   Research Product Details and Customer Reviews

☐   Select a Potential Product Niche

☐   Derive a Specific Keyword Phrase from Selected Products

Chapter Notes

Chapter Notes

1-1 AMAZON CATEGORY EXPLORATION

Many Amazon affiliates will begin their search by hunting for a main keyword phrase or domain name, but I actually like to use a strategy that is a bit backwards: I hunt for Amazon products first.

Exact match domain names can give you a slight edge in search engine rankings (where the domain name is the same as your main keyword phrase). However, the strength of these domains has diminished over time. As a result, the domain name should not be the deciding factor of whether you target a niche or not – the niche and the products in the niche should decide that. If you can get an exact match domain for a good niche, then that is an added bonus.

Amazon Shop By Department

To get started, simply visit the home page of Amazon. I'll be using Amazon.com throughout this tutorial, but feel free to use one of the other Amazon sites if you will be trying to build a site to target consumers that are more likely to buy from those sites (ie, someone in the UK would be much more likely to buy from Amazon.co.uk – some products niche may be unique to those areas, so they would make excellent choices for a site using that Amazon locale).

In the top-left of their website, you'll see their logo and the words **Shop by Department** below it. Under it are many of the main categories on the Amazon website. This is pictured below.

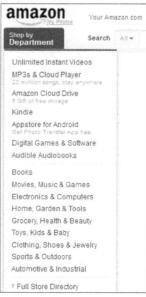

Simply hover your mouse over one of these categories to show even more related categories. I'm going to hover over the **Home, Garden & Tools** category (pictured below).

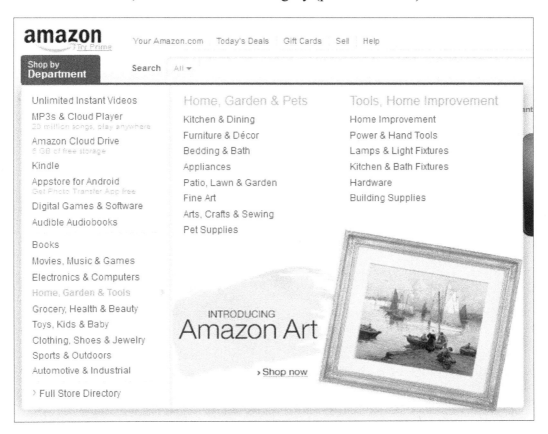

If you do not know what product niche you want to target with the site you are going to build, this simple interface can help to give you some initial ideas to explore.

The most common dilemma that people have at this point is whether to build a site revolves around a product or niche that is already familiar to them. Unfortunately, there is not a simple answer to provide for you here because it will heavily depend on the type of product knowledge you already possess.

In general, if you want to build a site about products you already know, you will want to target something that is highly specialized in some way.

For example, basically everyone in the USA might feel like they are fairly knowledgeable about modern televisions. However, that would actually be a bad niche choice because of the vast amount of products in the niche and the high competition because of the common nature of the product.

By comparison, if you have some advance knowledge about a specific type of television that is brand new on the market, this might be more realistic because of the age of the product (less competition initially) and it's specialty (not everyone will know about these new products yet, so they will be looking for information about them).

The key is to get as specific as you possibly can while still leaving yourself enough room to build a website around the idea and teach people something useful about the products and/or the niche.

For this tutorial, I am going to look in the Bedding & Bath category found under the Home, Garden & Tools department.

Even more categories can be found from the Full Store Directory link at the bottom of that list. This page actually provides a full list of the main categories on the site.

This link takes you directly to the Full Store Directory on Amazon.com:
http://www.amazon.com/gp/site-directory/

On the Bedding & Bath category page, there are a number of things worth pointing out. On the main part of the page, you have a listing of featured categories:

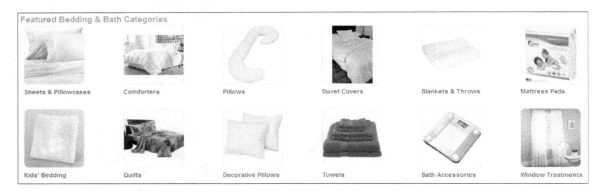

There are even more listings of bestselling brands along with numerous product types listed for each.

Towards the bottom of the page, there listings of Bedding & Bath Markdown items, for peoplelooking to drive sales with bargains/discounts.

There is also a listing of various Bedding types from Pinzon by Amazon.com. This is Amazon's bedding brand that is exclusive to their website.

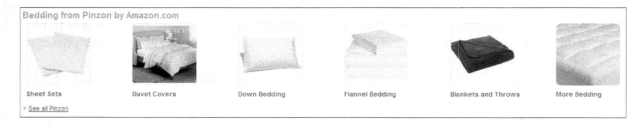

Whenever you can find these products in a niche that seems like it should have decent demand but not an excessive amount of competition, they can be worth looking into more.

Amazon will often have these products manufactured by some of the leading makers of the same products for other brands, except Amazon will sell the products for less because their operating costs are lower than traditional retailers. They are also good quality products because Amazon pays attention to fine details and has their products manufactured by top companies that already have experience making those products.

Amazon Browse Menus

I am actually going to go into the Down Bedding category under Pinzon for this tutorial, but I want to discuss one more thing before I proceed with that.

On the left-hand side of the page, you'll find a long list of menus that are excellent to use to help you find the products you are looking to find. At the top (pictured below), there is a list of subcategories that are available.

Bedding
   Bedding Collections
   Bed Pillows
   Bedspreads & Coverlets
   Blankets & Throws
   Comforters
   Decorative Pillows
   Down Bedding
   Duvet Covers
   Feather Beds
   Inflatable Beds
   Kids' Bedding
   Mattress Pads
   Memory Foam
   Quilts
   Shams & Bed Skirts
   Sheet & Pillowcase Sets

 > All Bedding
Bath
   Bathroom Accessories`
   Bathroom Hardware
   Bath Rugs
   Bath Sheets
   Bath Towels
   Hand Towels
   Shower Curtains &
    Accessories
   Showerheads
   Towel Warmers
   Washcloths
   Wastebaskets

 > All Bath

If you continue to scroll down the page, you'll also find ways that you can browse products based on a variety of options (they vary depending on what category you are viewing), brands, price points, average review ratings, and more.

One of my favorites here is the New Arrivals section (pictured below). Go here to find products that may be brand new to Amazon, which could present an excellent targeting opportunity because of low competition.

New Arrivals
   Last 30 days (140,482)
   Last 90 days (192,989)

The categories and other options available to you here will change as you navigate through categories. With the above example, there are nearly 200,000 products that have been released in this category in the last 90 days.

You could try browsing through some of them, but it would be really hard to find something specific here. However, you can drill-down into subcategories to lower the product numbers to a more realistic number that you could browse.

Also take note of the Sort By drop-down box in the top-right of search results. Use this to change how Amazon sorts products to help you find what you want. I commonly use this to look at low and/or high priced products in the niche and to find the highest rated/most popular/newest items.

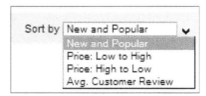

1-2 AMAZON PRODUCT RESEARCH

After going into the Down Bedding category under Pinzon, I am actually shown a search for the term **pyrenees**, which does include some Pinzon products (which are **pyrenees**).

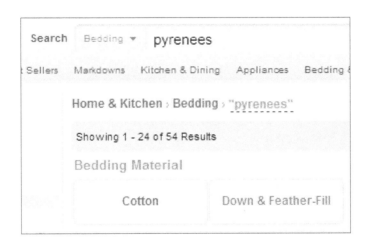

I am now going to click on the Down & Feather-Fill button here to narrow my results even more.

This provides me with just six results. Five of them are Pinzon products – two down comforters and three pillows.

These five Pinzon products are all sold by Amazon, so they are eligible for Amazon Prime (free shipping for Prime members).

In an ideal situation, your website will target some type of product niche that will provide you with good commissions, so we're talking about $100-$200 products. I also like to promote lower priced products on these sites, as long as they relate to my main products – this helps to boost your commissions per customer and also increases your sales volume on Amazon. For these reasons, I am more inclined to look into the two down comforters here as a potential niche to target.

Take a look at all six of the results from this search – the Pinzon comforters are in the top-right and bottom-left.

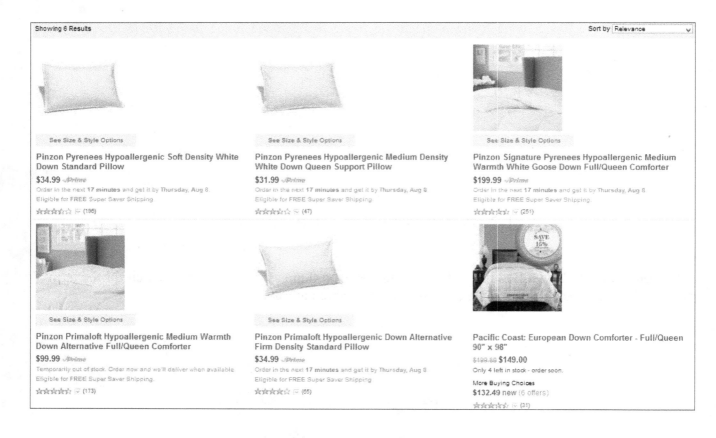

This is a good start – five products, that should be Amazon exclusives, all with good reviews and eligible for Amazon Prime's free shipping.

Investigate Individual Products

At this point, it is time to investigate a few of the primary products that have drawn in our interest for the niche.

The first one will be the $200 goose down comforter. Before I even visit the actual product page on Amazon, I scan the basic listing information.

I am interested in the average reviews as well as the shipping and/or availability information here.

First, notice the yellow check with the word Prime next to it. This indicates the product is eligible for free shipping with Amazon Prime (two day shipping in most cases). It is also eligible for free Super Saver Shipping. Seeing these is definitely a plus because this provides more value for the consumer.

The sentence that says **Order in the next 4 hours...** indicates that the product is in stock.

The review count on the product is at 251 and looks to have close to 4.5 stars average. This is an excellent indication that it is a quality product that has also seen some decent sales numbers on Amazon because only a small percentage of buyers will actually leave a review.

I also consider products that have good reviews but a low total count or even products that do not have any reviews at all (especially if they are newly released products).

Instead of taking a close look at this product, I am going to go ahead and move on to the next product, which will be shown in more detail. The previous product looks to be a great choice, so I do not see a big reason to research it more yet (I will eventually before deciding to promote this product).

For now, I will go ahead and copy the product name and the URL for the product. I simply save this information in a Notepad file on my computer for easy reference later.

The second Pinzon comforter in the results is a down alternative comforter. Again, I will review the basic product information here.

See Size & Style Options

Pinzon Primaloft Hypoallergenic Medium Warmth Down Alternative Full/Queen Comforter

$99.99 *Prime*

Temporarily out of stock. Order now and we'll deliver when available.

Eligible for FREE Super Saver Shipping.

☆☆☆☆☆ (173)

With this product, almost all of the information is very similar to the previous product with one major exception – this product is listed as being out of stock!

This brings me to a critical decision point – is this product worth promoting or not? To answer that, I ask myself more questions like 'Who is selling the product?'.

If a product is an Amazon Exclusive, it could be worth promoting anyways because they will be in stock again or removed from the site if discontinued. In fact, them being out of stock could simply be a good indication of the demand for the product.

If another vendor is selling, you will really have to make your own judgment call on whether you think the product will be back in stock again.

Try looking at recent reviews to see how long ago the last purchase seemed to be, look at review ratings for the vendor, or even research the actual product being sold in terms of whether it is discontinued or not.

I am going to look at the actual product page now to try to get more information. The main product information at the top of the page has been shown below for this product.

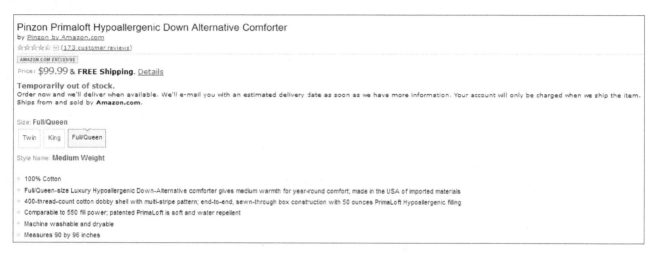

Here are a few important things to point out here:

1. Directly below the product name, notice the smaller text that says **by Pinzon by Amazon.com**. This tells you the vendor, and this is obviously sold by Amazon itself (not just shipped by Amazon).

2. Below the review rating, notice the yellow box that says **Amazon.com Exclusive**. This is a clear indication that this product is something produced by Amazon itself and sold exclusively on their website. These are excellent products to promote because they often have very competitive prices and good quality too.

3. Next is the obvious red text that says Temporarily out of stock. If you continue reading the text here, you can see that people can still order and simply have it shipped when it is ready – they won't even be charged until it ships (which is also when you would receive your commission for referring the sale). Always consider why it is out of stock. For this particular product, it has the best sales in the cold months of the year, and this product information page is viewed in the middle of the summer. For this reason, combined with everything else, I think this product will be back in stock soon, especially as the summer ends. With the high review count, it could also be a popular product and simply sells out often.

4. Finally, take note of the Size choices. This product is selected as a Full/Queen but Twin and King are also available. Some products may even have many different options to choose from here. Technically, every option here is a separate Amazon product (and has it's own

Amazon ASIN that can be used to directly link to the page with that option selected). This is very important with an out of stock product because it may just be that one option that is out of stock. Below is a picture of what the same part of the page looks like if I click on the **King** option here – notice that this option is in stock and that the price changed because of the option selection!

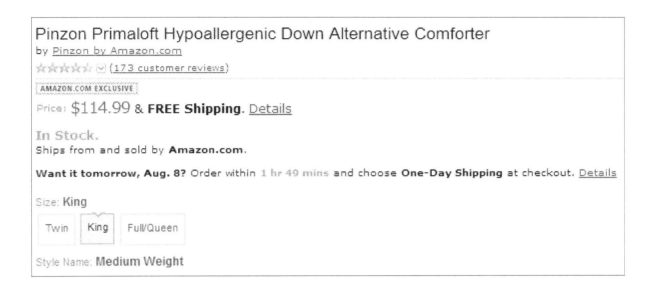

Explore Related Products

Below the product information, Amazon displays other information that is intended to help boost sales with other related products. As an affiliate, you can take advantage of this information because this is actually free research for you! Use this to find other related products that could be good to promote alongside the same product or even on other pages of the same website.

Below you can see two sections of products: **Frequently Bought Together** and **Customers Who Bought This Item Also Bought**.

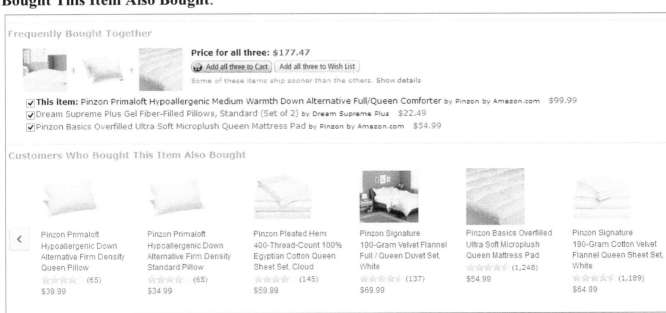

The first shows additional products that are purchased with the main product being viewed. This information is actually based on real-time stats from Amazon sales.

The second section shows even more products that have been bought by the same customers that bought the main item. These may be products that were purchased in the same transaction or they may have been purchases from separate transactions. Arrows are provided to show lots of products in this section – sometimes 100+ products can be found here.

You don't have to go explore these additional products right at this moment, but it is an easy way you can continue your research after you are done investigating this particular product.

Utilize Additional Product Information

Most Amazon products also have a Product Description. This is customized information provided by the vendor that tells more about the product. Sometimes this may just be a couple of sentences worth of information and other times it is a more complex description that can even include images and HTML code.

Here is the Product Description from this particular listing:

Product Description

Size: **Full/Queen** | Style Name: **Medium Weight**

Enjoy a great night's sleep with a Pinzon comforter just right for your needs. For sensitive sleepers who want to enjoy the benefits of do fiber. It's called PrimaLoft, The Luxury Down Alternative, and it has many of down's amazing properties, like lightness, warmth, and loft. B

Full/Queen Comforter Buying Guide

PINZON
Luxury Comforters
Pick the perfect comforter to get a great night's sleep.

Full/Queen

	Pyrenees White Goose Down	Pyrenees White Down	Pyrenees PrimaLoft®
Size Dimensions	Full/Queen 90" x 96"	Full/Queen 90" x 96"	Full/Queen 90" x 96"
Fill			
Light Warmth	N/A	29 oz.	N/A
Medium Warmth	40 oz.	40 oz.	50 oz.
Extra Warmth	N/A	50 oz.	N/A
Fill Power	600	550	Comparable to 550
Construction	14" Baffle Box	14" Baffle Box	End-to-End Sewn-Thru Box
Comforter Shell	400-Thread-Count Cotton	400-Thread-Count Cotton	400-Thread-Count Cotton
Pattern	Dobby-Woven Stripe	Dobby-Woven Stripe	Dobby-Woven Stripe

This full/queen comforter is filled with 50 total ounc and quickly passes body heat and moisture vapor t what would be 550 in a down comforter. Fill power is high quality.

The Pyrenees PrimaLoft comforter is made with a s filling, and the layers are stitched together all the v evenly distributed.

The Pyrenees PrimaLoft comforter will look great in compressed, to quickly regain its loft. PrimaLoft also percent cotton in a 400-thread-count dobby weave

Safe to clean at home in the washer and dryer, Pinz

A lot of affiliates will actually use this information directly on their website as the content of the page that promotes the product. This is OK to do if you intend on providing additional, unique content of your own, but you don't want to solely rely on Amazon's content to power your website.

Instead, use Amazon's product information as a way to learn about the product, and then try to present that information to your users in an informative and helpful way.

Another way that you can learn about products is by actually reading Amazon's Customer Reviews. Again, some people will try to use this content on their own website, but this is actually not allowed by Amazon. However, you can read them to learn about a product, and present that information in your own words on your sites.

Here is the initial Customer Review section on this page:

At the top, take note of the bar graph that shows you how many people have left reviews at each level. Seeing most of the reviews towards the top is the best – you just don't want to see a lot of 1 and/or 2 star reviews.

Most Recent Customer Reviews

★★★★★ **Perfect**
I've never bought a duvet insert before and I knew I was taking a bit of risk ordering one online but this is really perfect for me.
Read more
Published 1 day ago by Madeline Reicher

★★★★★ **Warm comforter for cool bay area nights**
This is a nice comforter for the cool Pacifica nights. I'm very much enjoying it and have no complaints so far.
Published 11 days ago by Jon Passki

★★★★★ **Down alternative king comforter**
This is a very nice comforter which looks nice even when the duvet cover is being laundered. The loft doesn't seem to pack down and it's light weight is very comfortable to sleep...
Read more
Published 12 days ago by R. Hurst

★★★★★ **Love this comforter and have ordered it several times**
This comforter is a perfect weight for summer or winter in the northern states. The filling stays in place which is wonderful. Read more
Published 14 days ago by Wendy

Below that, you can actually read the reviews that were left. I like to read a variety of reviews, both good and bad, to get an overall sense of the product.

On the right side of the page, you will also find the most recent customer reviews. Always look at these to ensure the product quality and service is still good. I also use this when looking at out of stock products to get a general idea of when the product was in stock last.

For this product, notice that most of the recent reviews were from roughly 2 weeks ago, so I would estimate that this may be the timeframe of this product being in stock last.

Another excellent way to find out about a product is through the Customer Questions & Answers.

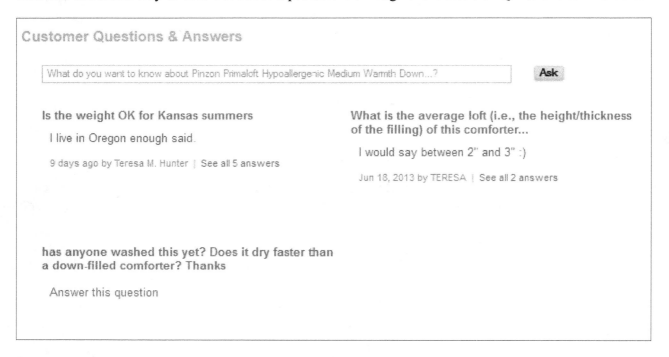

Some products on Amazon will have existing questions and answers about the product, all direct from actual customers that have these products and are using them or customers that are interested in buying them.

Some of these may be common questions that people wonder about a product before buying it, so always be sure to investigate this area, if there are existing questions. They could be great selling points that you can use on your site to promote the product.

1-3 SPECIAL AMAZON PAGES

Beyond browsing Amazon categories to find products, there are a variety of other Amazon pages that you can use to help research new niches. I have discussed the best of these here.

Gold Box & Lightning Deals

Back on the home page of Amazon, look for the **Today's Deals** link in the top-left:

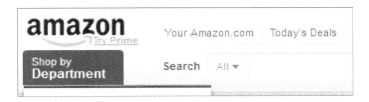

The **Today's Deals** link takes you to the Gold Box page on Amazon.

There are four sections that I want to point out here...

1. **Deal of the Day** – In the top-left you will find the deal of the day. This is the featured Gold Box Deal, which changes daily.
2. **Lightning Deals** – In the top-right you will find the Lightning Deals. These are limited quantity deals that are also time sensitive. This page is the only way to find these deals to promote (ie, you won't find Lightning Deals in software, like my plugins).
3. **Best Deals** – Towards the bottom of the page is a section of additional Gold Box deals that you can browse through using the arrow buttons on the left and right. You can also sort them using the provided drop-down box.
4. At the bottom of the page are the Gold Box Deal Categories. Just click on one to narrow the results in the Best Deals section if you are hunting for something related to a specific niche.

All of these products, except the Lightning Deals, can be added to your Amazon WordPress sites using my plugin Daily Deal Azon. This will be covered more in-depth once we get to adding advertisements to our sites.

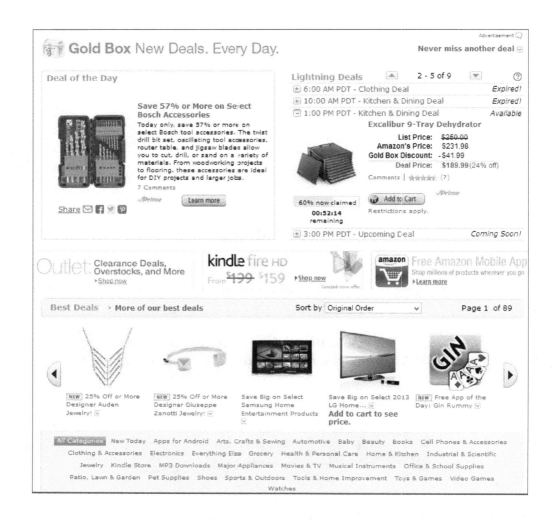

At the top of the Gold Box page, look for the menu links to get to some of the other special Amazon pages. I've shown these links below.

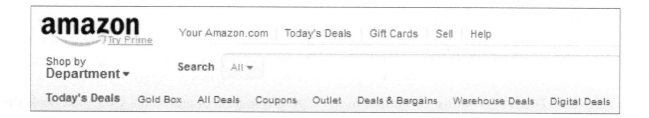

Feel free to browse through some of these other pages to see what else Amazon has to offer – they even do outlet and warehouse deals.

Amazon Coupons

One particular link that I want to explore here is the Coupons page.

This special page on Amazon actually provides coupons that you can use as an affiliate with products you promote. A ton of different categories can be found in the menu on the left, and available coupons show up on the right.

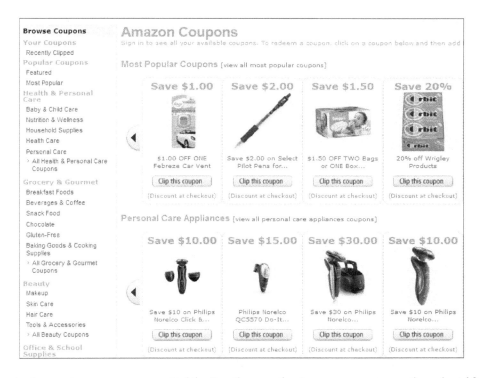

There may not always be coupons available for the products you are promoting, but if you are working in a niche that contains commonly purchased products, it may at least be worth a look here to see if there are indeed coupons available cause they can be helpful to boost conversion rates.

I was not able to find any coupons to use for the product niche that I am using for this tutorial, so I will not be using them in this series. However, I still wanted to mention this in case you are targeting a niche that has coupons available.

Product Category Special Pages

This next type of special page actually has a few different pages included. Whenever you are viewing a product category, look for menu links at the top of the page. I have shown some of these below.

This picture is from the Bedding & Bath category. Not only can this menu give you some more ideas for niches and/or relational products that you can promote but it can also help you get to more of Amazon's special pages.

The Best Sellers link is one of these that I want to discuss more here.

Category Best Sellers

Amazon provides a list of best selling products in any category. Best of all, these lists are updated hourly from real sales data on Amazon.

Here is the top of this page for the Bedding & Bath category:

This page can be used to find the 100 most popular products from the entire category! While this is great research information, do not get blinded by it and try to solely promote best sellers.

I recommend using this page as guidance to figure out what people are buying from the category. It can
also help you to figure out common buying price points for relational products (ie, are people buying the expensive or cheap products from the category).

If products in this list fit my target niche, I will definitely make a note of them – just add them to the Notepad list that you're creating while browsing product categories and doing other research on Amazon.

Towards the bottom of the page, you will see a listing of numbers grouped together:

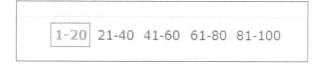

Just click on another set of numbers here to see more results – you'll be able to look at the top 100. In some categories, you may even be able to drill down into another subcategory to look at the best sellers there (it really just depends on the category and how many different kinds of products may be in it – there is also a best seller list for the whole site, for example).

-

Other Category Lists
In addition to the best sellers, there are even more top 100 lists that Amazon provides for most categories. These can be found on the right side of the best sellers page, as shown below.

There are four additional lists here, which have been briefly explained below. Just click on the See Top 100 link to the right of each name to see the full list, just like the best sellers list. I use these lists for research in the same manner as the best sellers list too.

Hot New Releases – These are new arrivals in the category but also sorted by sales volume. This is a good list to use to find new products that are already showing good sales records on Amazon – a decent indication that it could be a good niche to target.

Top Rated – These are products in the category that have received the highest average review rating from actual customers of the product. This is a good way to find high quality products that are more likely to have low refund rates and/or higher conversion rates.

Most Wished For – These are the category products that are most commonly added to Amazon Wishlists and/or Registries. Some of these products may be best sellers while others may just be products that a lot of people want others to buy for them. This can be helpful to use to figure out what kids or future parents want to buy, giving you the chance to position yourself to earn on those sales before they actually start.

Gift Ideas – These products are best sellers that have been designated as a gift to someone besides the buyer on Amazon (during checkout). These can be great products to target because people will often buy things for others with less research and decision time than they will for themselves, making the products easier sales.

1-4 AMAZON NICHE SELECTION STRATEGIES

I've already discussed a number of my niche selection strategies in this guide while showing you the research for my own niche, but there are some additional recommendations that I wanted to provide for you.

Targeting Products vs Targeting Niches

Once you have actually found products that you think could be good to promote on Amazon, you'll then need to figure out how you want to target those products.

This is really where a lot of affiliates have a problem translating all of the research into a functioning and useful website – it's success either made or broken at this point. Unfortunately, I also cannot tell you exactly what to do here because it can vary from one product/niche to the next.

The key thing that you want to think about now is how to take a good product on Amazon and turn it into an affiliate website.

For my examples that I've been using in this tutorial, I found two comforters as potential main products for the site. Obviously, I could try to build a site about comforters, but that is pretty broad reaching. Instead, I want to try to narrow my focus down to a smaller selection of products that is more realistic for me to research, review and promote on my own.

One of the comforters is a down alternative comforter and the other is a goose down comforter, so down comforters would be a more specific niche that relates to these products.

Since one product is real down and the other is a down alternative, I may also want to use this in how I build my site and target the products. I could try to educate my website viewers on these types to help them figure out which one would be the best to buy for their needs, so I may be creating some type of guide for these products to accomplish this aspect.

That is essentially how you should think about your own products when you are trying to derive a niche from them.

Alternatively, some affiliates will solely focus on targeting actual products, model numbers, and/or brand names. You can try to take advantage of these tactics in some situations, but I really don't recommend making this the focus of your entire site (ie, building a site revolving around a single product/brand instead of a niche or idea).

For example, some people might want to try to build a website targeting the Pinzon brand as their niche, but this isn't a real niche to target. Instead, try to pick an actual niche to target and then perhaps build a section of your site dedicated to the brand or whatever else you want to target.

This strategy also helps you avoid trademark violations. NEVER target a trademarked name (brand or product name) as your primary keyword phrase and as part of your domain name. The domain name is the important part of this, which I will be sure to cover more in the next class when we proceed to this step. However, you should already begin thinking of possibilities for domain names for your niche at this point.

Ebay Pulse

There is one source that I sometimes use for Amazon niche research that is actually located outside of Amazon, and that is eBay Pulse. Technically, eBay Pulse doesn't exist anymore, but I still refer to it as that because it is familiar for many people. The new version of this page is the Popular Items page on Ebay.

You can find this here:
http://popular.ebay.com/

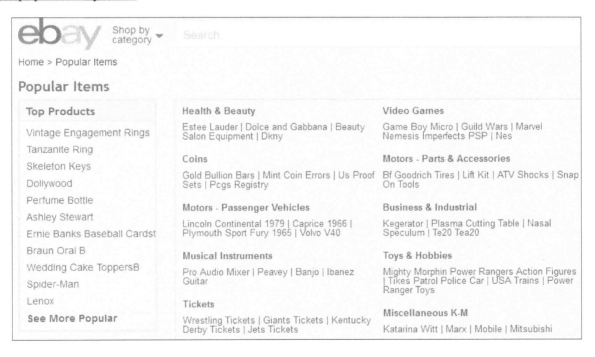

This is a listing of the most popular products on eBay. They provide you with general categories, more specific niches and even specific product and/or brand names.

On the left, they give you some specific niches of top selling products. On the right, you have a massive listing of general categories, more specific niches, and even specific types/brands of products.

Clicking on some of these items will take you to even larger lists of niches and/or products. Once you click on a specific niche, brand or product, you will likely be taken to an eBay page showing some of those products (this is intended to be used for customers of eBay and not necessarily marketers).

If you have already found a potential niche, see if you can find it here to get more ideas or to verify that it is a popular product type online (don't worry if you cant' find it though – eBay doesn't list everything here, just the most popular products).

If you find yourself stuck trying to come up with an idea for a niche, try to pick out a specific product from this page, and then perform research on that product on Amazon to see if it could be a good possibility.

I have personally used this eBay feature to come up with ideas for numerous good Amazon niche sites, so it is something I always recommend to others.

2 GOOGLE RESEARCH

In the second class, we will take our potential Amazon niches to Google to perform additional research. This will be keyword research to find a potential keyword phrase that we can target on our website. You will also learn competition research to ensure that we can build a reasonably sized site to target that phrase and obtain decent search engine rankings without a ton of ongoing work.

Primary Lesson Objective

☐ Pick a Primary Keyword Phrase and Domain Name

Lesson Steps Checklist

☐ Use Google Keyword Planner to Research Phrases for your Niche

☐ Use Google Search to Gauge Competition for Keyword Phrases

☐ Use Google Trends to Research Long-Term Niche Trends

☐ Select and Register a Domain Name

☐ Create a Website Hosting Account (or Use Existing Account)

☐ Research Other Relational Keywords for your Site

Chapter Notes

Chapter Notes

2-1 GOOGLE KEYWORD RESEARCH

Once I have a potential niche to research, which I have obtained from researching Amazon products, I can then proceed to Google for more research.

This time I am looking to find out whether people are searching for my niche and/or products on Google. I am also looking to find a primary keyword phrase that can summarize my entire website as well as a variety of other keyword phrases that relate to that primary phrase and can be used on individual pages on my site.

Google Keyword Planner

To start your keyword research, you'll need to go to Google Keyword Planner. It requires a Google Adsense account to use – if you do not already have one, it is free to join (no need to set up any ads or billing information there to use the Keyword Planner).

Go to this address to access it:
https://adwords.google.com/ko/KeywordPlanner/Home

On the Keyword Planner page, just look for the **Search for keyword and ad group ideas** link, as shown below.

Keyword Planner
Plan your next search campaign

What would you like to do?

▸ Search for keyword and ad group ideas

After you click on that link, enter a keyword phrase under **Your product or service**. For this tutorial, I will be using the niche that I picked out in the Amazon Research class.

I could search for a very specific keyword phrase here, like alternative down comforters, but for now,

I am going to stick with something fairly basic, down comforter, so Google will provide some additional ideas for me.

Also take note of the Targeting options that are provided in this search box. The first of these options allows you to specify search countries (or you can remove them to search all locations). This option will end up controlling the search traffic volume that Google shows you for the keywords.

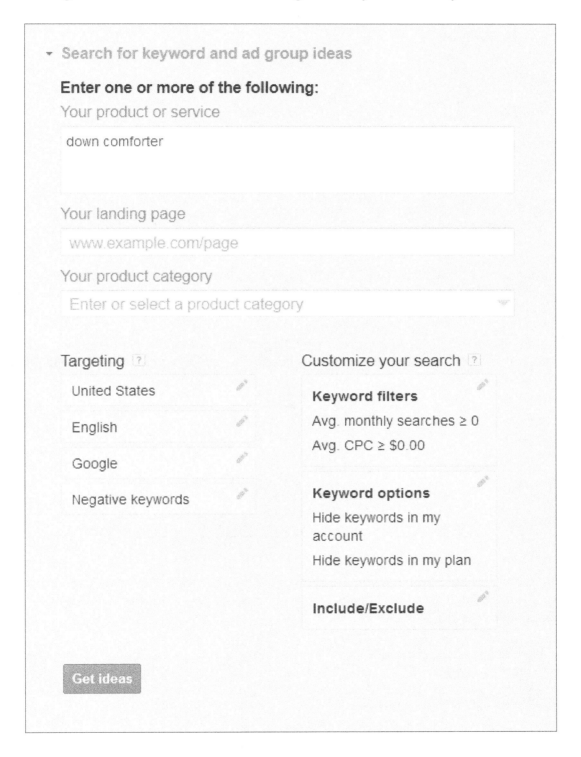

Once you have provided a keyword and have the country targeting set, click on the Get ideas button to proceed.

At first, you'll see a page that has two tabs, with the **Ad group ideas** tab automatically selected (shown below).

Your product or service			
down comforter		Get ideas Modify search	

Ad group ideas Keyword ideas		
Ad group (by relevance)	**Keywords**	**Avg. monthly searches** ?
Keywords like Best Down Comforter (14)	best down comforter, black down comforter, down comforter guide,...	14,920
Goose Down (47)	goose down comforter, goose down comforters, white goose down ...	10,000
Alternative (43)	down alternative comforter, alternative down comforter, down alter...	10,020
King (29)	king down comforter, california king down comforter, cal king down ...	18,200

The Ad group ideas are basically categories of keywords that Google has organized and considers relational. Each of the Ad groups could potentially be a topic for your entire website or even for a specific page on your site.

You can click on one of these Ad groups to see a larger listing of keyword phrases that have been organized into that group. This larger listing shows you the actual keyword traffic for each phrase listed.

Keyword (by relevance)	**Avg. monthly searches** ?
best down comforter	2,400
black down comforter	720
down comforter guide	480
down comforter reviews	880

This is the same type of listing that you are shown if you click on the Keyword ideas tab, except that tab will have all of the keywords listed together instead of being organized (but you may be able to get more keywords out of the Keyword ideas tab).

If you go back and visit the Keyword ideas tab, you can attempt to sort through the keywords on your own. Initially, these keywords will be sorted by relevance to the phrase you searched, but you can also change this by simply clicking on one of the header titles (like Keyword, to sort by name, or Avg. monthly searches to sort by search traffic volume).

The data that Google provides for each keyword phrase includes a few different pieces of information. You may notice that I left out the Competition and Avg. CPC columns from the screenshots that I have provided here – this was done because I actually don't use those columns at all (they really apply to Google Adsense competition and cost, so they are useless for organic search information).

I have shown another picture below, this one from the Keyword ideas tab (showing the top few results along with the search traffic volume).

This really looks just like the previous keyword list viewed from the Ad group ideas, except many more keywords are listed at once here.

The main thing that I am interested in here is the Avg. monthly searches column. There are a few things I want to talk about involving this column of data.

First of all, if you ever used the Google Keyword Tool (which is currently being phased out as I am writing this), you may remember two different numbers provided for each keyword phrase: Global and Local Monthly Searches.

In the Keyword Planner, the Avg. monthly searches can CHANGE depending on the country targeting that you have provided for the search. This is how Google has reduced two data columns into one – because it can actually show either of those numbers. If you have selected to target all locations, you'll see a Global monthly search average here, but if you target one or more countries, you'll be shown a Local monthly search average for your targeted countries.

These numbers can actually vary from Google Keyword Tool numbers for one major reason: Keyword Tool didn't include mobile search traffic but Keyword Planner does! In this regard, I believe Keyword Planner is actually a better tool to use, even though it may initially appear to have less features than the Keyword Tool.

One more thing worth mentioning is that search volume traffic shown here is the Exact Match traffic. Keyword Planner no longer offers data for Broad and Phrase searches. Personally, I was more interested in the Exact Match data in the Keyword Tool anyways, so I believe this change just simplifies the Keyword Planner to make it show the data I want (without having to do anything). Exact Match traffic basically just means that the search volume shown is for people that searched for the exact keyword phrase being shown, which is what you want to know to target a particular phrase.

The second thing that I want to talk about concerning the Avg. monthly searches column is the little graph icon that shows up to the left of the search volume number for each keyword. The search volume number is the average number of monthly searches that phrase has received for the last 12 months, but this graph icon gives you access to better and more useful data for the search traffic volume.

By simply hovering over the graph icon for a keyword phrase, you will be shown the monthly traffic for each of the last 12 months that has gone into the calculation for the average monthly search number shown for that phrase.

This graph is known as the Search Trends graph because it can show you the monthly trending patterns of a keyword over the past year. Take a look at this picture below:

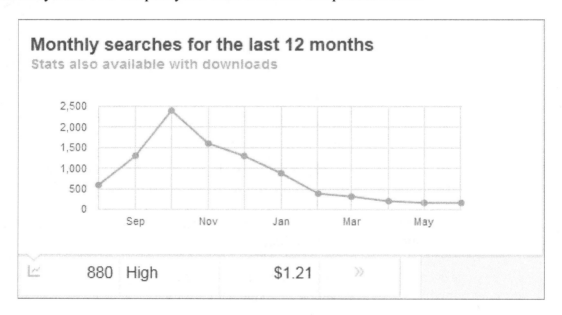

This is the Search Trends graph for the keyword phrase "down comforters". If you look at the bottom of the picture, you can see the average monthly search volume, which is 880 searches per month.

Now, if you look at the graph for the past 12 months, you can easily see that the months of February through June all have less than 500 searches each. However, the month of October has nearly 2,500 – that is quite a big difference from the 880 average! You can get an exact number for any month there by hovering over the dot on the graph for that month.

This Search Trends graph in the Keyword Planner used to be available in the Keyword Tool but only as as spreadsheet data. It was one of the other major aspects of the Keyword Tool that I relied on to help me find niches that others had missed, so I was happy to see it easily available in the Keyword Planner.

There are a couple of reasons why the information in this graph is VERY important to me:

1. It tells me if a keyword phrase may be trending or on the decline. A trending phrase may show a low monthly average but actually much higher numbers in more recent months. When the average person is searching through these keywords, they're judging a keyword instantly by the average monthly search count, so the lower numbers will immediately be dismissed by them. As a result, if you can find a phrase with a low average monthly count that is trending upwards and has a high count for recent months, you may find that the competition for that phrase is considerably less than expected.

2. It tells me if a keyword phrase may be seasonal. The data is based on my country targeting (important to remember), so I can look to see if certain seasons or perhaps holidays may have higher traffic for a particular phrase. It is also VERY important to consider whether a phrase could be seasonal or trending. If you were to look at the Search Trends graph above during the month of November, you may mistakenly think that the phrase is trending upwards when it is actually just a seasonal phrase. In most cases, simple common sense can often be used to determine which is which. In this example, down comforters can often be hot in warm months of the year but are excellent for cold months of the year, so this would obviously indicate that it is most likely a seasonal phrase and not a trending phrase. I'm not necessarily against seasonal phrases though because they can be very rewarding during the peak season and may still make money during the off season (just make sure some type of traffic exists for the phrase in the slow months of the year to ensure a site can still make something all year).

In general, I am searching for a keyword phrase that has an average of about 500 monthly. I will sometimes go above or below that number depending on trending and competition for the phrase (in the organic search results, which I'll cover in another chapter in this guidebook).

Obviously, it would be great to be able to get the traffic from a phrase higher than 500, but I have found that most phrases at 1,000 or above simply have too much competition to overcome without a ton of work. The idea with my strategy is to not pull my hair out trying to get traffic to the site. You also have to consider that there will be other phrases besides the primary phrase that will be targeted on the site, so the entire site will definitely be targeting more than 500 monthly searchers.

In general, the lower the average monthly search count, the lower the competition will be on Google in the organic search results. This is why I like to look out for trending or sometimes seasonal keyword phrases – because they can offer traffic levels above 500 but without the competition typically associated with those traffic levels.

In addition to the search traffic volume, I am considering whether each keyword phrase could summarize an entire site for my intended purposes and whether I could actually build an authority site to cover that subject.

I also consider what type of site would be expected out of that keyword phrase. For example, a phrase like "down comforter reviews" would likely have a lot of competition and be expected to be nothing more than a site reviewing a variety of down comforters.

I like the looks of a phrase more like "down comforter guide", because it implies an informational and helpful approach to selling a specific type of product. This is my preferred approach to these affiliate sites because a useful website will be much more appealing to a visitor than a purely sales oriented website.

Here is the Search Trends graph for "down comforter guide":

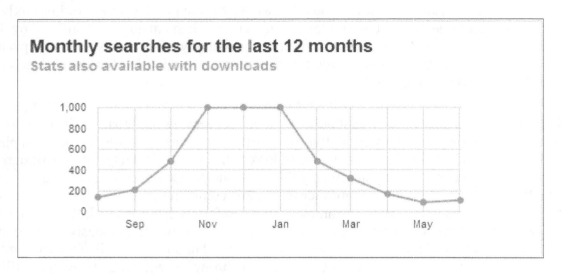

This graph looks somewhat similar to the one for "down comforters", except the peak season looks to be more extended and the down season looks to be shortened.

The average monthly search traffic for this phrase is 480, so this is around my target number, but when I consider that it is a seasonal phrase, I know that I will have a number of months above that number and also some months below it.

From November until January, the monthly search count is at 1,000. This would give me more than twice the average for a full 25% of the year, even extending past the Christmas buying season when sales of many other products may decline.

February and October look to be right around the average count. March is also below the average count but not as low as the down season (this looks to be the end of the peak season).

May looks to be the lowest month of the year but traffic still exists, which I like to see if I am targeting a seasonal phrase (this just means that I can still make something from the site, even in the worst month of the year for the niche). Other months of the year look to be either declining or inclining months heading towards a peak or down season.

Overall, I like the looks of this phrase, especially if I plan to build a variety of seasonal sites that can provide me a strong income all year. It is fairly easy to find a niche that is seasonal based on the Christmas holiday, especially in the USA, but other seasonal niches will be less common, so I like targeting them when I can find a good one.

If you plan to build many different Amazon sites, having a decent variety can really help you develop a more stable income because it makes you more resistant to market changes (ie, if one niche starts to decline, it wouldn't kill your business because that one site would just be a portion of your entire business that covered many different niches, seasons, etc).

2-2 GOOGLE SEARCH RESEARCH

Now that I have a potential niche, I am going to go to Google Search to do some additional research on the keyword phrase.

This research is going to help me gauge the level of competition for the phrase. If it turns out to be too high, I can simply find a different phrase to use for the same niche and try again until I find the right one.

Doing the Google research after the Amazon research allows me to stay focused on the same niche (or a couple of niches) until I find the right phrase to use to target it. Once I find the right phrase, I can be very confident that I have made a good niche selection because I already looked into the Amazon products for the niche ahead of time.

Quick Competition Gauge

One of the first things that I will do in this phase of my research is to perform three different searches using the primary keyword phrase. I have shown pictures of each of these searches and described them below.

The first search is simply for the keyword phrase itself. I'm looking for the total number of search results that are provided for this phrase – 883,000 in this case.

I do not have a specific number that I am looking for here. I have been able to easily rank sites when there are 5-10 million results available but had trouble with some phrases with even less results. For this reason, I use this number as a general gauge and also use it in combination with the other two search methods I'll discuss in just a moment.

If you get a phrase that has billions of results, you will probably want to avoid it – you likely have some words in your keyword phrase that are too widely used on the internet for them to be considered a good target phrase.

This number tells you how many other pages on the internet use this exact phrase somewhere in their content or use another phrase that is considered to basically mean the same thing.

I will revisit this particular search in a bit, but for now, I am going to continue with a few other searches to gauge the overall competition of this phrase.

For the second search, I enclose the keyword phrase in double quotes. This will tell me how many pages on the internet use this exact phrase somewhere in their content.

For this search, I am again looking at the number of results, but this time I am looking for this number to be much lower than before.

19,100 results here is excellent to see – this tells me that only 19,100 other pages on the internet use this exact phrase. In general, I want to see this number below 100,000 (for the lowest competition). However, I have also ranked in the top 10 with more than 1.5 million results for this exact phrase search.

Finally, I am looking for the number of pages on the internet that use this exact phrase in the title of the page. This is done by adding the word **allintitle** and then a **colon** to the front of the exact phrase search that was previously used.

With this search, I am typically looking for a very low number. In general, anything under 1,000 could be considered to be very low competition. I often consider anything above 10,000 here to be high competition unless the other two numbers are significantly lower than expected. This could indicate that there are a decent number of people targeting the phrase with a page on their site but not many sites that are actually covering a lot on this subject overall.

For this particular situation, the number of results is definitely higher than I usually like to see, but this is still a phrase that I am going to go for because of the other numbers and also to test the limits of this strategy.

I still feel confident about getting a top 10 ranking on that phrase, but it is hard to say how much time it will take to make that happen (especially if I want the #1 spot). I have built sites that target a phrase with nearly 75,000 results for the allintitle search and managed a #8 spot, just to give you an idea of the potential upper limits of this strategy (that result could still be improved with more work and time though).

More In-Depth Competition Research

Google is not only a great tool to use to gauge the overall competition of a keyword phrase, but it is also excellent to use to conduct research on specific competition for a niche. To do this, I will be revisiting the first search I made for my target keyword phrase. I've shown the first few results from that search below:

These results, as well as the others in the top 10, are all for larger websites that simply seem to have a page or possibly a section of their site devoted to this particular topic.

Some people may look at the results and think 'How can I ever expect to beat Overstock.com and/or BedBathAndBeyond.com?', but I see it more like 'These guys don't stand a chance because there aren't any dedicated niche sites for this subject in these results!'.

As I continue to look through the results, I want to find a site that seems to be solely devoted to this subject. I was able to find a couple of these sites towards the bottom of the third page of results, which I have shown below – the top 3 results in this picture all look to be sites that may be devoted to this subject.

Down Comforter Guide. DownStore
www.the**downstore**.com/**down**bed**cingguide**.htm ▾
DownStore's **guide** to buying a **down comforter** that is perfect for the way you sleep.

Types of Bedding - **Down** Buying **Guide**
www.**downbuyingguide**.com/content/types/types.html ▾
The '**Down** & Feather Buying **Guide**' is a great resource of information for ... Comforter construction can include anything from a wide-open 'bag' filled with **down** ...

Vintage Bedding | The **Down Comforter Guide** ⑦
www.the**downcomforterguide**.com/vintage-bedding-reviews/ ▾
Vintage bedding is the kind that never goes out of style and is still highly popular especially with the younger set. There are a number of vintage bedding.

TLC "How to Clean a **Down Comforter**"
tlc.howstuffworks.com › ... › Cleaning & Organizing › Laundry Guide ▾
Before tackling the task of cleaning a **down comforter**, check the care labels to find out what cleaning method the manufacturer recommends. If there are no care ...

Searches related to **down comforter guide**

down comforter **reviews**	down comforter **sale**
down **alternative** comforter guide	down comforter **cleaning**
hypoallergenic comforter	down comforter **care**
down comforter **weight** guide	**bed bath and beyond**

‹ Goooooooooogle ›

Previous   1 2 **3** 4 5 6 7 8 9 10   Next

If possible, I am looking to find a site where the home page is ranking for this term, but I have still not been able to find one of them in the top three pages, so I will stick with one of these sites that looks to be devoted to this subject.

I have selected DownBuyingGuide.com to use for this competition research.

I then want to take that domain and use it for a Google search to find out how many pages the site contains. This is done by adding the word **site**, then a **colon**, and then the domain name to the Google Search bar, as shown.

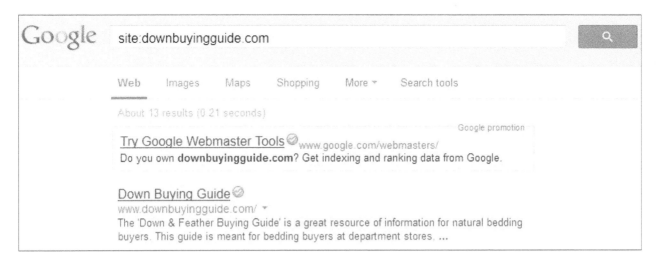

This search shows 13 results, which tells me that this site has 13 pages on it that are indexed in Google, so it took them 13 pages of content to reach a rank of #28.

This looks to be a good indication, since I'm not 100% convinced that the site is really devoted to the exact subject (I could look at the site itself to find out more) and it wouldn't be hard to build a site with more than 13 pages of content, especially if that content is targeted better.

Again, this is just research that you can do to get a general indication in terms of the amount of work you may need to do to be able to rank for your primary keyword phrase.

You can also replace the word **site** in that search with the word **link** to find how many indexed backlinks there are for this site in Google. Google does not show all links to a site – just ones that it considers to be legitimate and/or important.

If you find that a site has a lot of links, especially from respected websites, it could indicate higher competition (depending on where that site is ranked).

I am typically not looking to rely on backlinks to rank my websites though, so I am mainly interested in ensuring that an enormous amount of backlinks won't be needed to rank for this term (you can always add more content to a site to make up for a lack of backlinks though, which is my preferred method of building rank for a site).

2-3 GOOGLE TRENDS

Yet another Google tool that I use for my research to verify the potential profitability of a niche is Google Trends. The same or similar features used to be available as Google Insights (something I taught in my first Amazon training course a couple of years ago).

Think of Google Trends like the Search Trends graph that I showed you in the Keyword Planner, except that Google Trends is a more general gauge (doesn't give you exact search numbers) but lets you see a longer period of time.

You can use the tactics with Google Trends discussed in this chapter to simply verify the long-term health of your niche to help you decide if it is the right choice for your website.

Access Google Trends here:
http://www.google.com/trends/

On that page, just type in your keyword phrase at the top.

You will then be shown a time-based graph for the popularity of searches on that keyword phrase – I've shown this below for the phrase **down comforter guide**.

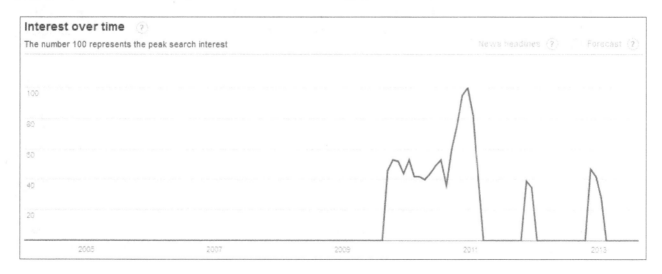

Before you get too wrapped up in the results for the first graph shown, make sure the Limit settings on the left are set as desired. In particular, pay attend to the country setting – the Worldwide results for a phrase may be quite different from the results for the United States (if that is the country you are targeting on your site).

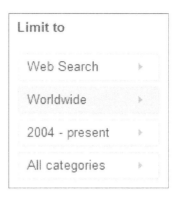

By simply changing Worldwide to United States in the Limit settings, my graph data looks to be a bit different:

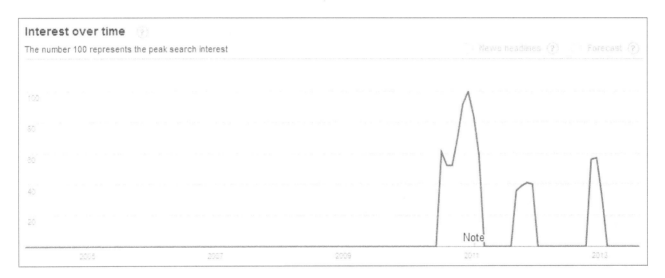

Initially, you may be thinking that this niche is on the decline over time, but you really can't make that judgment based on a single graph for one keyword phrase (especially when it is a more targeted phrase).

You can hover over various points in the graph to find out the month and year as well as a number that relates to the peak interest level for that search phrase, with 100 being the peak level. By doing this, you can see that the spikes in traffic on this graph are the seasonal spikes each winter (which we also saw in the Keyword Planner Search Trends graph).

Now, what should we make of the fact that winter of 2010 looks to be the peak year with a sharp decline the next year?

First, winter of 2012 looks to show decent recovery over the previous year.

You also must consider other factors, like the recent economic recession, which does seem to be slowly recovering now.

On top of that, always think about whether your target keyword phrase actually represents the niche itself or just something specific about the niche. In this example, my phrase is about the products "down comforters" but I am also using the word "guide" on the end to target my site more. For this reason, I cannot simply look at the traffic for my phrase and gauge the health of the whole niche.

If I change my search to just the basic niche name, "down comforter", I can get a more accurate picture on the health of this niche.

I have shown the graph from this below, which is targeted for just United States traffic:

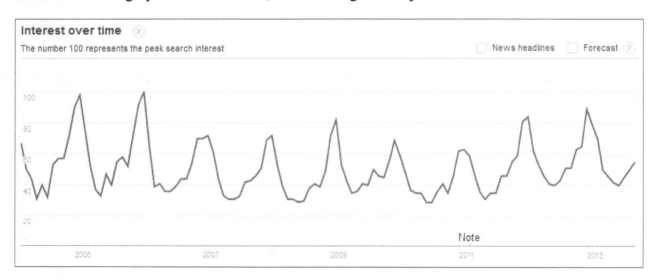

This time, you really get much more information that you can use than with the previous search (although it is still good to know how your actual phrase is doing). This happens because Google Trends works off of search traffic volume, and it won't show any data unless the volume is high enough. Blank graphs, like at the beginning of the previous few graphs I have shown, could simply indicate lower volume and not ZERO volume!

When I get more general with more search phrase but still staying closely related to my target niche, I get access to high volumes of search data to give me a better picture of the overall health of the niche.

Now when I look at the graph above, I get a much different picture of the health of the down comforter niche overall.

This graph shows the seasonal tendencies of this niche with much more clarity.

Up through 2006 looked to be strong years with some declining years after that. By itself, that may be a negative sign, but those were basically the same years of the declining economy.

In the winter of 2011 and 2012, the niche looks to be on the rise again and even looks to be just 10%

short of historic levels before the economic decline. I believe this to be a good sign that the niche is regaining traffic (and likely sales) to previous levels as well. This coming winter (of 2013) could indeed see levels very close to old levels, which would obviously be great for any site targeting this niche.

Below the graph, you can also see a map that shows the level of interest in various countries (or states, if you have selected a country for your search). There are also related search terms provided for you here, which you could use for even more research or ideas for targeting your site.

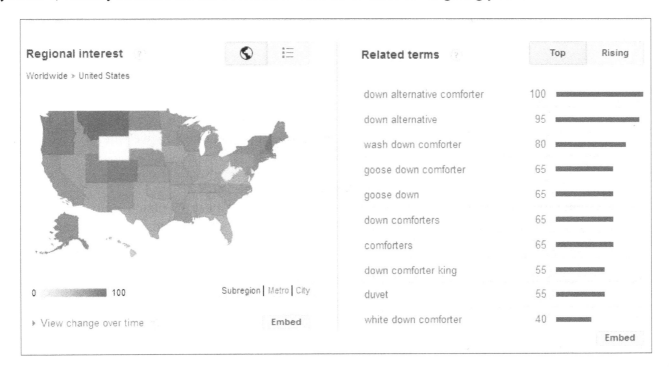

On the left, you get to see which USA states have the most interest for this niche and more options are available. This can be excellent information to use if you decide to do any advertising in your niche.

On the right are the related terms but you can also view the rising terms in that same area to try to find trending products or sub-niches.

2-4 DOMAIN NAME HUNTING & SELECTION

Picking a domain name is a major choice for most people looking to build a new website, so I wanted to be sure to talk about a few approaches that you can use.

Exact Match Domain (EMD)

The most commonly used strategy to pick a domain name is to get an exact match .com, also called an EMD, for your primary keyword phrase. Using the phrase for my niche site, that would mean using the domain name downcomforterguide.com.

This is a strategy that I have used repeatedly for more than a decade with excellent results. Even though most people believe that the power behind an EMD is dead these days, I still debate that they maintain at least some power and always will.

I definitely agree that EMDs do not have as much power as they used to. For this reason, it is really up to you what type of domain name you would like to use for your site.

If you can find an EMD .com for your target keyword phrase that looks to be a great phrase with all of the other research you have done so far, then you should probably get it because it certainly won't hurt and you also don't want someone else competing with you using that domain.

If the EMD you want is not available, that is still OK, but I do recommend making sure that particular domain isn't ranked in the top 10 for your target phrase. If this is the case, you could be eternally competing with that particular domain.

Branded Domains

The other option is to go with a branded domain, which would essentially make you look more like a business. With this option, you really have unlimited choices in what you could pick, making it a viable option for any site. However, I still like to make sure that someone with the EMD is going to be a major competitor for my site.

You can go for a completely branded name or a mix of a branded domain and an EMD. For example, I could make a site called RyanDownComforter.com or RyanDownGuide.com – both of these contain a word completely unrelated to my niche and then two words that are from my target keyword phrase.

You can even do the same and only use one word from your target keyword phrase, like

DownEmporium.com – the key is to use a word or combination of words that still has some type of relation to your target phrase because it will help you with search rankings.

Available Domain Name Hunting

If you only have one or a few potential domain names that you may want to use, searching to find out if they are available may not be a big deal. However, if you have a large keyword list and want to find out if you can get an EMD .com from that list, you may find that this could take forever to do.

I want to take just a minute to show you my personal strategy for hunting for EMDs that I have been using for years.

First, go back to Google Keyword Planner and search your target phrase and/or a general phrase for your niche to get a large list of keywords.

In the Keyword ideas tab of the Keyword Planner, look for the downward pointing arrow button in the top-right:

Just click on that arrow to open a window to download an Excel CSV file with those keywords – this is just a spreadsheet file.

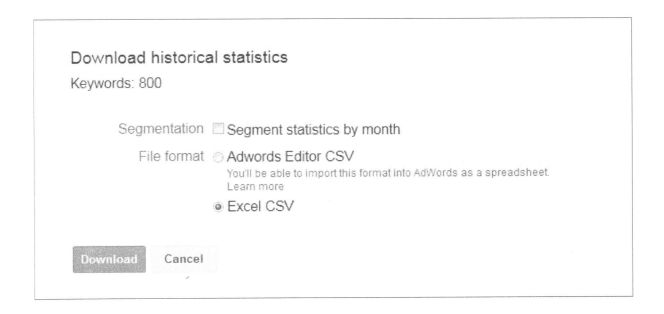

Then open that file to get access to the full keyword list that you can copy and paste. If you don't have a program that can open a CSV file, like Microsoft Office, try OpenOffice.org (free, open source - remake of Microsoft Office basically).

This Excel CSV file uses Tabs as the delimiter – if you're importing the file into Open Office, you will need to select the checkbox for Tab to get the file to open correctly. Take a look at the picture below to see how this should look. Once you click on the checkbox for Tab, the field information will split correctly into columns.

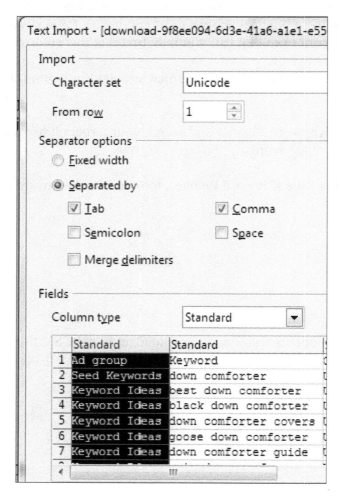

Now when I open the file, I can see all of the information for those keyword phrases that includes a column for nothing but the keywords.

	A	B	C	
1	Ad group	Keyword	Currency	Avg. mont
2	Seed Keywords	down comforter	USD	
3	Keyword Ideas	best down comforter	USD	
4	Keyword Ideas	black down comforter	USD	
5	Keyword Ideas	down comforter covers	USD	
6	Keyword Ideas	goose down comforter	USD	
7	Keyword Ideas	down comforter guide	USD	
8	Keyword Ideas	twin down comforter	USD	
9	Keyword Ideas	down comforter reviews	USD	
10	Keyword Ideas	down comforters	USD	
11	Keyword Ideas	queen down comforter	USD	
12	Keyword Ideas	king down comforter	USD	
13	Keyword Ideas	colored down comforter	USD	

If I click on the second row under the keyword column (which says down comforter), I can then scroll down the page to find result number 501. Then just hold down the SHIFT button and click the keyword for row number 501:

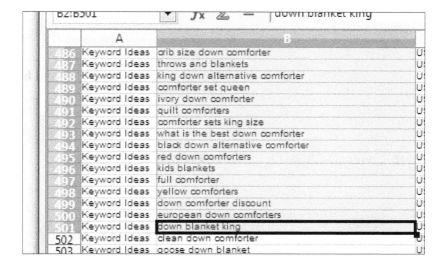

This highlights a total of 500 keywords for me. Now just press CTRL + C (to copy those keywords).

Next, open the program Notepad and paste all of those keywords into it – these steps could also be done in the spreadsheet program, but by default, the CSV file will be read-only, so it won't let you perform these operations on it without saving it to a permanent file first.

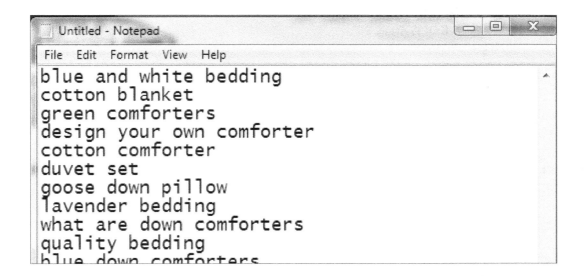

All I want to do here is simply delete all of the spaces in these keywords. To do this quickly, click Edit and then Replace from the menus at the top of Notepad.

In the Replace window, just type in a single space into the Find what text box, and then click on the Replace All button.

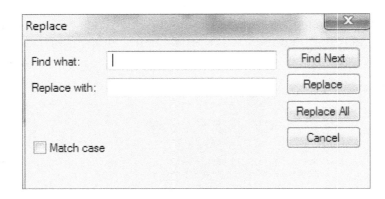

Once you have done this, you should see a list of keywords without spaces:

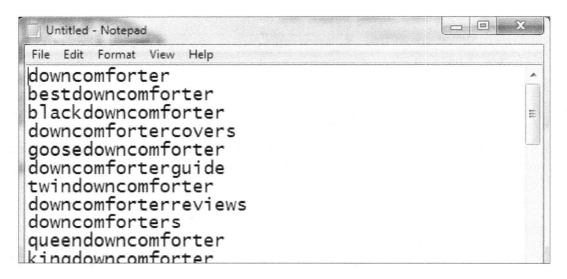

Select and COPY all of the keywords in Notepad now.

Then open a browser window for GoDaddy to look to see if there is an available EMD for one or more of these keywords.

I have picked out some discount coupons that are available for GoDaddy and my recommended hosting company, HostGator:

http://supertargeting.com/domain-name-and-website-hosting/

If you begin your GoDaddy domain name search by clicking on the banner on that page, you can get your initial registration purchase of the domain for a steep discount. You can also get a discount on HostGator hosting by originating a purchase through that page.

On the GoDaddy home page, look for the Bulk Search text link to the left of the large domain search bar.

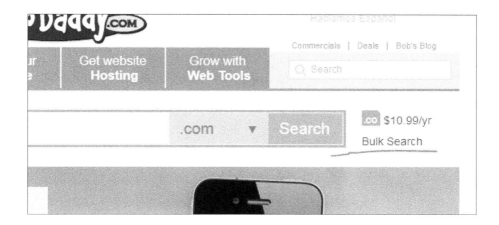

Now PASTE (CTRL + V) all of the keywords without spaces into the Bulk Search box for GoDaddy – also be sure to click on the .com checkbox to the right:

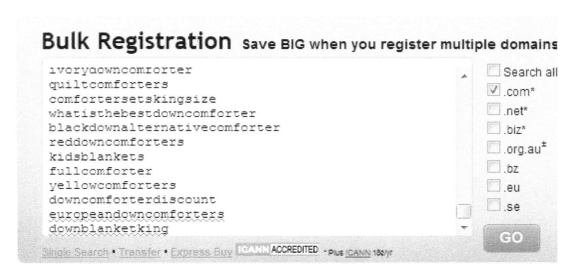

Now all you need to do is click the GO button and GoDaddy will do the rest of the work for you to check the availability on 500 EMDs all at once! 500 is the max amount they will search with each attempt, which is why I only had you select 500 of the keywords even though 800 were in that CSV file. You could then return to that file to get the other 300 keywords to search for even more.

From that one search of 500 keywords, I was able to find 186 EMDs:

Again, this is just a strategy that I will use if I want to hunt through a large list of keywords to find an

EMD, but if I already have a preferred primary keyword phrase that I want to use, I may just search for that by itself instead of doing a bulk search.

For the purposes of this tutorial, I will be building DownComforterGuide.com, which was one of the keywords in that list.

2-5 ADDITIONAL RESEARCH & SITE PRE-PLANNING

Once you have picked out your niche, primary keyword phrase, and domain name, you can still do additional research with Google to help you target additional keywords and even to help you start planning your site.

This process simply involves using Google's Keyword Planner to help you find additional keywords relating to your primary keyword phrase, most of which can easily be used as topics for additional pages on your site.

Site planning will be covered more in-depth in the next class, so the purpose of this additional research is not to plan out every page of your site – it is simply to get an idea of other potential keywords and topics that could be used on the site.

If I revisit the Google Keyword Planner and search the phrase "down comforter", I can easily get a summary of potential topics for the niche from the **Ad group ideas** tab.

By simply browsing through that list of Ad groups, I can pick out numerous potential topics that I could use within content of pages or as the topic for an entire page (or even a section of pages) on the site.

For example, I can quickly pick out various comforter sizes listed here: **King, Queen, Twin, XL & Oversized**.

I can also tell that some people are searching for information about colors with these topics: **Color, Purple, Pink & Brown**.

Some people are searching for **Cheap** or **Discount** down comforters, while others want **Luxury** comforters.

You even have people searching for **Lightweight** or **Summer** down comforters, which is a strong indication that people like these comforters but think they are too hot during the warm months of the year (which is also backed up by the seasonal tendencies of this niche). Even more people want to know about **Washing** or **Cleaning** these comforters. Any of these points would make excellent informational pages for the site because they are obvious selling points or points of concern for consumers of these products.

I have shown the various Ad groups that are displayed for this search.

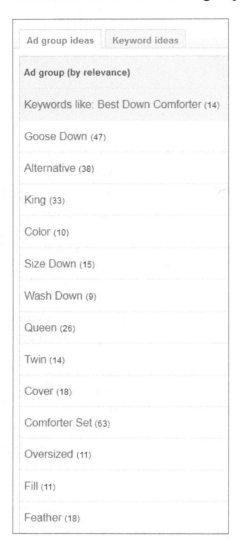

Any of these topics could be used as topics for an entire page, a portion of a page, or even an entire section of pages on the site – it really just depends on how much information could really be covered for each topic and how you want to present that information to your site visitors.

Open up a text editor program on your computer, like Notepad in Windows, and simply make a list of some of the potential topics that you've been able to find for your site. You can even expand this list more by searching for these topics (to find subtopics) or even searching for additional keyword phrases related to your niche and/or the products you want to promote.

For now, just making a list and at least considering how you might try to cover some of the topics in your website content is a great start because it gets you thinking about the niche and the products.

3 SITE PLANNING

In the third class, we will plan out the website. This process involves taking keyword research to plan topics for each of the pages that will be on the site. We will then learn how to organize potential topics to come up with a more finalized planned page topic list. After that, you must do research to learn about the niche, the products, and your planned page topics to make final plans for the site. This provides you with a roadmap that you can follow as the site is built.

Primary Lesson Objective

☐ Plan 20 Page Topics & Provide a Summary for Each Page

Lesson Steps Checklist

☐ Gather Keywords, Product Names, and Customer Info to Create a Potential List of Page Topics

☐ Organize and Group Page Topics Into Categories

☐ Decide on Roughly 20 Page Topics (Including Home & Categories)

☐ Research Page Topics & Write Summary Plan for Each Page

☐ Plan Product Advertising Locations and Include in Summary Plans

Chapter Notes

Chapter Notes

3-1 PAGE PLANNING STRATEGIES

Now that I have a domain name picked out for my site, the next thing that I need to do is figure out what I will build on the site. It is very important to do this step to ensure that your site content is both useful and targeted to attract search engine traffic.

The key to this process is to create pages for a variety of purposes but still be sure to keep everything relevant to your main keyword phrase. As you move through this planning process, try to continually think about how everything will connect together on your site to make it easy to understand and use for your site visitors.

I'll be discussing the different page types in this chapter and also talking about where I come up with the ideas for the pages.

Keyword Pages

The easiest way to come up with ideas for pages on your site is to use the Google Keyword Planner. Although you could likely come up with enough ideas to fill an entire site using that, it is still important to use other sources for page ideas and be sure to carefully choose your keywords.

First, you obviously want to make sure that the keywords you are targeting are relevant to your primary keyword phrase. Many phrases may be relevant in some way, but ask yourself if they are truly a good fit for the overall purpose of your site.

I am building DownComforterGuide.com for this tutorial, so I want to keep my page topics in line with that basic idea. I could obviously cover tons of different things about down comforters, but I am really more interested in the topics that consumers are interested in before they purchase one.

In addition to relevance to my primary topic, I am also interested in finding the keywords with lower competition, so I will generally go for keywords that are under 1,000 monthly searches.

Since many of these topics for secondary pages on my site will be even more specific than the topic for my overall website, there is even a decent chance that search engine traffic for your target phrases may be very low. This is quite alright though, as long as they fit your site and offer some type of traffic potential that should be easy to obtain (after all, there won't be many people competing for these very low traffic phrases).

Another thing to consider is that these keywords may actually be valid for the other two types of pages that I will talk about next: product/brand pages and question/informational pages. It can be good to have some of those other page types that are targeting a keyword phrase that gets traffic, although not all of those pages need to target keywords (in fact, I believe it is good if some of them do not).

To start your keyword page research, simply search your primary keyword phrase in Google's Keyword Planner.

Once Google provides results for you, look at the ad group ideas. I briefly showed this to you at the end of the last lesson, but this time, I am looking to get some specifics and take notes.

I have shown pictures for all of the listed ad groups in my search so I can explain my thought process to you.

This list contains the ad group ideas, so these are just basic keyword ideas that Google has organized for me.

With that said, I'm not looking to make a final decision here. Instead, I merely want to use these as the initial research to find the actual keyword phrases that I want to target.

The first thing that I do is to browse the ad group ideas and try to imagine all of them grouped together and organized even more.

For example, many of the initial ad group ideas like King, Queen and Twin are obvious references to bed sizes because comforters are sold in various sizes for different beds.

Google actually has a Size Down group here, which should contain more references to those same keywords and other common size search phrases.

The comforter sizes are definitely a possibility for a page topic as part of my down comforter guide. However, if all of the comforter products that I promote on my site are available in all sizes or even the most common sizes, then I might not want to use this as a basis for organizing my site – this could simply be a footnote for each comforter promotion page. I could still build an information page about sizes for the site though and simply link to it from the size footnotes.

Other ad group ideas that stand out as great candidates for this site are Fill, Thread Count, Alternative, Hypoallergenic, Summer and Lightweight. These all sound like topics that consumers may be interested in learning more about before they decide to buy a comforter, which obviously makes them match my primary keyword phrase.

Beyond those obvious ad groups, most of the remaining ad groups seem to occupy one of a few general categories: Pricing/Cost, Brands, Colors and Accessories. These could be additional points that I address in my buying guide on my site.

As you go through keywords for your own site, simply open up Notepad (if you use Windows) and take notes.

Instead of simply planning your pages based on the ad group ideas, it is actually a good idea to drill down a bit deeper into the actual keyword phrases that Google provides for those ad groups. This will tell you the phrases that people actually use in their searches for those ad groups, which can then be used on your own website to target pages to those phrases.

For example, if I go through the Alternative ad group, I'll find many different keywords that all reference basically the same thing.

With all of these keywords available for essentially the same subject, how do you pick one to target?

Personally, I will try to pick one out of the list to make it the primary keyword phrase of a page of my site or the content I'm writing. I will also take a look at the other keyword phrases in case some of them could work as secondary phrases or variations of my main phrase, which could simply be used within the content of the page.

Here is a picture of just some of the words provided under this ad group:

Ad group: **Alternative**	
←	
Keyword (by relevance)	Avg. monthly searches ?
down alternative comforter	⊵ 4,400
alternative down comforter	⊵ 720
down alternative comforters	⊵ 480
alternative down comforters	⊵ 110
down alternative	⊵ 590
down comforter alternative	⊵ 70
down alternative bedding	⊵ 40
down alternative vs down comforter	⊵ 30

When I am trying to select a primary keyword phrase to target for a specific page on my site, I will use the same selection strategies that I used to select the main keyword phrase of the entire site. This means that I want something that is low competition, which will likely be a lower traffic number (often 500 or less).

For this particular phrase, I like the look of "down alternative comforters". That specific phrase receives 480 average monthly searches. However, within that exact phrase, you can actually find other phrases from this same list: down alternative comforter and down alternative.

Combined, those additional two phrases offer 5,000 monthly searches. I know the competition will be high on those phrases, so I don't expect to get a ranking anytime soon, but this could at least give me the possibility of ranking for those phrases in the future.

I also take notice of informational based search phrases that could appear in this list like "down alternative vs down comforter". Even though the search traffic for this phrase is very low, it could still be worth making a page based on this phrase or even just devoting a section of my "down alternative comforters" page to target this additional phrase.

If you find that you need more information on a topic, feel free to search additional phrases on Google to try to get different results or more in-depth results on a particular topic. I did this for the colors and also for the Pinzon brand to try to come up with some additional targeting options and/or ideas.

Product / Brand Pages

Although you may be able to find some keyword phrases for products and/or brands in your niche, it doesn't mean that your site should only be targeted to those phrases. Don't be afraid to build pages on your site to target relevant brand names and/or products in your niche, even if you can't find any search engine traffic for related phrases.

One of the easiest ways that you'll be able to find these phrases is by looking on Amazon for them because you won't want to focus on brands and/or products that you can't promote on Amazon. In fact, you may already have this research done from your previous Amazon research on your niche.

I actually already mentioned one of these phrases. Pinzon is a brand that wasn't provided to me in the Google ad group ideas, but I knew it was a brand that I would want to target because of the products I want to promote on Amazon through my site. I searched for it on Google Keyword Planner to see if there was search engine traffic for it and to try to pick a decent phrase to target, but I can do more extensive research on Amazon itself for their products.

Beyond the actual products and brands that you can find there, you may also be able to come up with keyword phrases and page ideas simply based on information in the product listings. Obviously the comforters have size options on Amazon, but some of these even have Style options, like one of the Pinzon comforters. Targeting these weight names, even as a secondary phrase on my product pages and/or informational pages on my site, could help to bring in targeted consumers.

Here are the Style Name options from one Pinzon comforter that uses "weight" names:

Another example that I was able to easily find in a Pinzon listing is the comparison chart in their vendor product description:

There are tons of great keywords here that I could reference in pages of my site or even as complete topics for pages. Pyrenees and PrimaLoft are two examples, but I could even go into vocabulary used in the chart itself – especially the left-hand column. Most of the items in the left-hand column were actually found in the Google ad group ideas too.

Again, just add any of these to your Notepad list. You can even search for them in the Keyword Planner to try to come up with some type of Google phrase to target for these topics, but it is quite alright if you cannot find relevant phrases because not all of your site pages need to target a specific phrase.

Question / Informational Pages

The other type of page I am looking to build is to target questions that potential consumers may have or other information that they may be interested in researching before they purchase my targeted products.

For the down comforter niche, some of these topics were addressed through keyword phrases that I was able to find, but other topics may only be found through customer reviews and/or customer Q&A on Amazon (or at least this is one good source to find these questions, as I had mentioned in the Amazon research lesson).

Here is the Customer Q&A from a Pinzon comforter (not always available with every product but often with the popular products):

Customer Questions & Answers

Q: Corner Loops: Are there corner loops so the comforter can be held by a duvee cover?
A: On the one I have, yes it does. Mine is the Queen sized, medium warmth. One on each corner.

Q: is this 100% goose ? is this product 100% goose down ?
A: there's a photo provided that reads minimum 75% down.

Q: Have you had any problems with feathers coming out of the comforter?
A: Yes yes and yes! Look at the picture I uploaded. I ended up returning the comforter. Get a pacific coast comforter.
See all 10 answers

See all 8 questions & their answers

First of all, these are great selling points for this product and potentially for the niche in general.

Make sure you take a look at all of the questions and answers available – there is a link at the bottom to view them all. Under each question, you may also see a link to additional answers, since more than one customer can provide an answer to each question.

There are also customer reviews that you can read through for most products. Not only can you figure out if products are worthwhile to promote or not, but you can also figure out excellent selling points for your products using the Amazon reviews.

Here is one review that I was able to easily find for a Pinzon comforter:

☆☆☆☆☆ **Fantastic Value** January 29, 2011

By M. Rees

Style Name: Medium Warmth White Goose Down | Size Name: King | Amazon Verified Purchase

I spent a great deal of time looking for a good quality comforter. As such, I read many reviews. While many were somewhat helpful, none of them really helped me zero in on whether or not this particular comforter would suit the needs of my wife and I. How warm is your room when you turn in for the night? Do you generally run hot or cold as a general rule? Are people reviewing this w/ other blankets involved? What exactly is WARM? So, I will address a few points that might help the rest of you out because for the life of me I couldn't find a review that laid out the important pieces.

A. Temperature - we go to sleep at 65 degrees F. Our thermostats roll back at 7pm so I am quite comfortable saying its actually 65 degrees when we go to bed.

B. Personal preferences for warmth - my wife is almost always cold. I am almost always hot. During the night, we flip flop. I cool down and become comfortable, she warms up and starts to sweat.

C. We only sleep w/ this comforter and a sheet. Haven't bought a douvet (sp?) yet.

****

This comforter is fantastic. We are kept comfortably warm all night, neither too hot nor too cold. Our temperatures remained stable through the evening into morning. Its a pleasure to go to sleep underneath one of these.

As mentioned in other reviews, its filled very evenly, lofts nicely when out of the box, and the comforter material is very soft.

Very happy we purchased this item - would not hesitate to recommend to a friend or family member.

4 Comments | Was this review helpful to you? Yes No

This particular review quickly points out a few great selling points – comforter warmth, softness, and filling evenness.

Here is a second review:

☆☆☆☆☆ **Best comforter I ever bought!** June 5, 2008

By Moanakai

Style Name: Medium Warmth White Goose Down | Size Name: Full/Queen | Amazon Verified Purchase

I have owned many many comforters over the years and this is by far the best. The previous one I was using felt too heavy and was way too hot except for the coldest of winter nights. The current one I was using was way too thin and the down clumped in the middle and left the perimeters bare (it was an expensive one bought at a high-end well-known department store too); I returned it after 6 months since it had a 4 year warranty and exchanged it for another one which supposedly was stitched thru to prevent the down from shifting. Wrong advertising, returned to department store again! After reading the reviews on this one, worth a try since my options were so limited. Extremely happy: it is plush enough to give that "comfy" feeling but not so heavy as to weight you down. The covering material has the feel of silk; the pattern is gorgeous. Most importantly, NO shifting of down whatsoever, so it is advertised correctly. And also importantly, if it has to be machine washed, it can be. The price also beats sales at high-end department stores. If I had another bed to buy for, I'd buy another one.

Comment | Was this review helpful to you? Yes No

This identifies a number of great points – warmth again, thickness/fluffiness, weight/heaviness, down filling shifting and stitching, machine washing ability, and pricing.

It is important to remember to also take a look at negative reviews, if you can find them, in addition to the positive reviews. This helps to give you a better overall picture of the quality of a product, and it can also give you some excellent selling points that are major concerns of consumers for your niche.

Here's a negative review from the exact same product as the positive reviews I listed before:

73 of 82 people found the following review helpful
★☆☆☆☆ **NOT Leak-proof = Feathers EVERYWHERE** November 24, 2008
By Swoop
Style Name: Medium Warmth White Goose Down | Size Name: Full/Queen

Buyer Beware! The item was indeed excellent quality, at least for about the first 30 days. Unfortunately, shortly thereafter, I started finding more Down feathers on my floor than in my comforter. I have always used a duvet cover (300 thread count), but feathers constantly leaked. There are no obvious holes or weak seams. The feathers simply come directly through the fabric. I just purchased an $80 "comforter protector" that will hopefully resolve the problem, but if I knew this was going to be an issue, I would have spent $80 more on a better quality comforter in the first place.

2 Comments | Was this review helpful to you? Yes No

This identifies a common flaw with down comforters and/or this one in particular. It basically says that the feathers leak out and seemingly straight through the fabric.

We can actually investigate this customer complaint more through the Comments link available here. I've shown that page below:

Comments
Track comments by e-mail

Showing 1-2 of 2 posts in this discussion   Sort: **Oldest first** | Newest first

Initial post: Jun 19, 2011 1:03:19 AM PDT
☑ Bumblefish says:

Did you ever find a leak proof down comforter? I've been searching forever but alas...I don't think they exist. At some point, all down comforters start to leak feather balls

Permalink | Report abuse | Ignore this customer
Reply to this post   7 of 14 people think this post adds to the discussion. Do you? Yes No

In reply to an earlier post on Nov 8, 2012 9:03:39 PM PST
☑ scott says:

LL Bean's are down proof unless they rip. I agree that the Pinzon does leak some feathers. Ours mostly leaks just tiny floaty feathers.

Permalink | Report abuse | Ignore this customer
Reply to this post   4 of 4 people think this post adds to the discussion. Do you? Yes No

‹ Previous 1 Next ›

By taking a look at the comments, we can get more information to use for our content on this topic and also help to determine if the product is worth promoting or not.

As you can see, the first person basically believes that all down comforters will do this. The second persons says that LL Bean has ones that won't leak, although it also mentions that their Pinzon just leaks tiny feathers.

This topic is definitely worth investigating more, but I would suspect that down leaking has something to do with the thread count and/or fill power. A higher thread count should produce a tighter weave, essentially squeezing tight the tiny holes that allows the down to escape over time.

I also want to be sure to address questions about washing and/or caring for down comforters.

Pyrenees was listed as the type of down fill for the Pinzon comforters on Amazon, so I have also included the potential for an informational phrase based on the fill type. I was able to find a related keyword phrase that looks to be related to a question about this topic.

After I have gone through all of these ad group ideas and their keyword phrases, here is my list that I have come up with – again this is not a final decision to build a page for all of these topics but merely research and a nice reference guide to use for myself throughout this site building process.

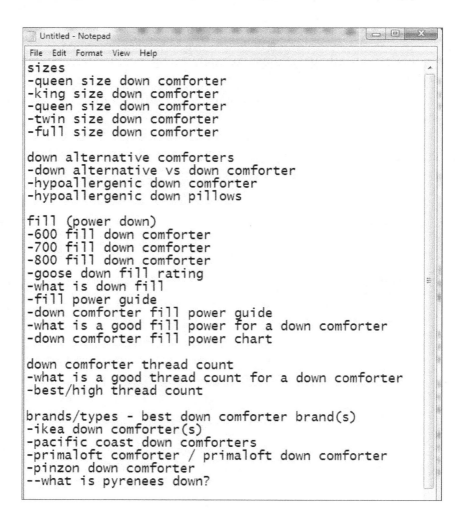

```
sizes
-queen size down comforter
-king size down comforter
-queen size down comforter
-twin size down comforter
-full size down comforter

down alternative comforters
-down alternative vs down comforter
-hypoallergenic down comforter
-hypoallergenic down pillows

fill (power down)
-600 fill down comforter
-700 fill down comforter
-800 fill down comforter
-goose down fill rating
-what is down fill
-fill power guide
-down comforter fill power guide
-what is a good fill power for a down comforter
-down comforter fill power chart

down comforter thread count
-what is a good thread count for a down comforter
-best/high thread count

brands/types - best down comforter brand(s)
-ikea down comforter(s)
-pacific coast down comforters
-primaloft comforter / primaloft down comforter
-pinzon down comforter
--what is pyrenees down?
```

```
care/wash
-can i wash a down comforter

summer weight down comforter
-lightweight

accessories
-down comforter duvet cover
-down filled pillows / goose down pillows
-down quilt|
-down throws

colors
-red down comforter
-blue
-brown
-purple
-pink
-navy blue
-black
-white
-gray
-orange
-green
-plaid
-yellow
-chocolate
```

With just this information alone, you can already start to get a general picture of what the site will be about, and the best part is that Google did a lot of this research for me! You definitely don't want to solely rely upon their keyword phrases to plan your entire site, but this is a really easy way to get a jump-start and figure out what people are searching in your niche.

3-2 PAGE ORGANIZATION & STRUCTURING

Now that you have a list of potential page topics, the next step is to go back through these topics to organize them.

The idea here is to try to organize them in a manner that will make sense for your website and also make it easy for visitors of your site to find the information they want.

I've sorted through my list of potential topics to try to organize everything in a way that make sense, allows for easy product targeting, and produces a website that will actually be useful for your visitors.

Here is my new list of topics:

```
home page - down comforter guide
-sizes
-fill power guide & chart
-thread count
-down shifting/comforter stitching
-leaking feathers
-brands
--pinzon
---primaloft
---pyrenees|
----what is pyrenees down?
--ikea
--pacific coast
-care/washing
-summer/lightweight
-colors
-down alternative comforters
-hypoallergenic down
-about page
```

This is a total of 19 different page topics for my site, which is right around the 20 page total that I usually shoot to hit (give or take a few pages is quite alright).

Notice how many of these page topics are indeed targeted for keyword phrases, but then there are also some other random informational pages thrown in that are simply meant to help consumers reach a decision and address their common concerns.

Also notice the hierarchy and structuring that is taking place here. Everything is listed underneath the home page, but then relational parts of my list are also grouped together, such as the brand pages. I've grouped all of those brands under a single brand page, which will essentially act as a category page for the various brand pages on the site.

Depending on how I choose to display all of this information on my site, I may even want to try to group together more of these page topics. For example, I could have one section devoted to consumer concerns like shifting down feathers, leaking feathers, washing down, summer heat, etc, while another section was devoted to more buying guide relevant topics like sizes, colors, fill power, thread count, down alternative and hypoallergenic.

This would essentially give me three main points to talk about on my home page, and then those three points would become category pages and link to the rest of the content on my site (doing this would put me up to 21 pages total, since I would need 2 new category pages beyond the brands page).

I often wait to make a final decision on this until I decide what content I will build for the site and how I decide to display that information.

If you browse through all of the topics I currently have planned for this site, you should be able to get an idea of what the site will really be about now. You should be able to tell that this site will be heavily informational, although there are obvious places/pages where I will be able to promote relevant products on the site and even funnel traffic to those pages on my site through the content of the informational pages.

This is the entire idea behind my strategy – create a useful website for the target niche. I could definitely build a complete website based on my niche and the planned topics I listed above WITHOUT actually advertising any products. If this holds true for your site, niche and planned topics at this point, then you should be all set to proceed. If not, try to come up with more informational topics that you could use for your site and reduce the amount of product based topics.

Also, make sure you keep your previous page topic research, especially where you have listed actual keyword phrases. The page topic summary that I provided below is only loosely based on keyword phrases from my list, so I will still use the previous list from last chapter when it comes time to actually build those pages (I just put all of this in one Notepad file, so the information is all in one place and easy to access later when you need it).

3-3 CONTENT RESEARCH & PLANNING

Now that you have all of your page topics planned out, you need to do more extended research for your niche and your exact page topics so that you can actually write relevant and helpful content on your site.

The goal here is to simply learn about your niche and products. If you happen to already have this knowledge, you may be able to skip along to the bottom of this chapter to the Content Planning section. However, it could still be worthwhile to learn this information because you will likely need to perform this type of research for sites you build in the future.

In general, if you do not consider yourself to have above average on your products and niche then you should be doing additional research until you reach that point. After all – how can you expect to build a useful site about a topic unless you know more about it than the average person? The good news is that the effort put into this step does not go wasted because you will be building a great site that has long-term earning potential, assuming it is done correctly.

There are tons of sources of information that you can use for this research. The way you go about the content research for your site can actually depend a lot on your niche choice and product targeting.

Instead of walking you through the exact research that I will do for this website, I want to talk to you about this step in more general terms so that you can have a variety of ideas to use for your own content research.

Research with Amazon

The most obvious place to find information about your niche, on Amazon itself, is something that I already discussed in previous lessons. However, I still wanted to be sure to mention it here.

By simply browsing through listings for products that you may promote on your site, you can really learn quite a lot about them and your niche.

Vendor provided information here is always a good source, but be sure to pay special attention to actual customer reviews as well as the customer question and answer section (when available). This customer information is VERY important, especially when you see multiple customers that essentially say the same thing about a product (good or bad).

This type of research is great to learn about your niche in general or the products that you will want to promote on your site. You will also be able to learn about special points of interest for your targeted consumers.

Research with Google

When it comes to learning specific information about a keyword phrase that you'll be targeting on a page of your site, you may be best going to Google itself.

Go through each of your page topics for your site, search for each on Google, and then read through the pages of the top few listings to see what type of information they are providing for the topic. Here are some questions to consider about the listings as you read:

Do they contain different information on each page/site or is it essentially the same information?
-With different information on each page, you could simply learn all of the information and create your own, unique page that essentially offers all of it in one place.

Do they briefly talk about particular things without explaining much about them?
-If so, you could easily do additional research about other relational topics to be able to provide even more information all on one page.

Do these pages seem user-friendly and/or do you feel like they could be done better?
By seeing what your direct competition for a particular keyword has to offer, it is much easier to gauge how to beat them. Think about the user and the search engine rankings will follow, so all you need to do is make a better page than your direct competition. When I say "better" here, I'm really talking about the actual, useful information being provided on a subject and/or the way it is presented – this has nothing to do with the flashiness of a page, so don't feel like you need to have better graphics than the competition or something like that.

This research alone on Google can often be enough to be able to write about your site topics in a way that will actually help your site visitors.

However, still consider other options to try to gauge what may work best for your niche. After all, if you can come up with additional information on the topic that isn't found on the competitor sites, then you can truly set your site apart from all of them.

Phone/Email/In-Person Research

The next research tactic that I want to discuss with you is a bit sneaky but really quite an easy way to obtain information that you may not be able to quickly find with a Google search.

This simply involves taking advantage of helpful customer service and/or sales representatives at various companies.

The great thing about this tactic is that it can be done with online companies from the comfort of your own home or you can even do it with real brick and mortar companies in person.

For online companies, simply find some kind of major retailer online that is selling the product you want to know more about. Then email them, call them on the phone, or even use live chat agents on their websites.

For brick and mortar companies, this is best done in person but can sometimes be accomplished over the phone (just depends on the company and who ends up answering the phone really).

The trick here is to pretend to be a real customer that is interested in the products you want to promote on your site. Ask specific questions you may want clarification on or even ask them to tell you some of the important things about the product(s).

If you go into a retail store in person, you can even bring a pen and notepad with you.

For my niche, I could simply go to a department store that has real beds set up. Start looking around at some of the down comforters and wait to be approached by a friendly sales person.

I could even just approach someone with my pen and notepad and say something like "Hi, I'm interested in finding out more about down comforters. I've never bought one before, so I don't really know anything about them, but my wife wants to get one and wanted me to come check them out."

Then, you can easily sit there, take notes, and ask a lot of questions without them thinking twice about it. You also have an easy excuse to not actually buy anything, since you need to discuss it all with your wife/husband/girlfriend/boyfriend/etc before making the actual decision (don't claim to be married without a ring on your finger, lol). After an in-person visit like this, you could easily soak up and/or have notes on tons of great information for your site.

Content Planning

Now that you have all of this great information about your niche, products, and the topics you've planned for your site, you need to figure out a plan to present that information to your site visitors in the best way possible.

The key here is to think of easy navigation to find the information they want to get to on your site and learn. You also want to consider how you will work all of that into promoting products on your site, which I'll be discussing more next.

My best recommendation for you that could apply to any niche is to revisit your planned page topics and add more detail. Go through each topic and essentially give a summary or brainstorm of the information that you would like to discuss on each page. If you already know how you want to present the information on each page, you could simply write a note about this for each topic.

Once you have the summaries for each topic, go back through the list to try to visualize this information laid out on a page on your site. Would the information be best presented as an article with a few different headings, pictures, graphs/charts/tables, lists, videos, or even a combination of all of these? Ultimately, it is impossible for me to simply tell you to do this a specific way, but you should be able to get a general idea of what may work best for your topics at this point (since you will know a lot of information on these topics now).

I have gone through and done this in my Notepad file that I showed you previously. Note what I've done for each of my planned page topics here. There are five different pictures to show you here, which actually contains quite a bit of information, but I thought it would be worthwhile to show you all of it so you can see my thought process behind planning DownComforterGuide.com.

home page - down comforter guide
this will be the front page of the website and will be the "down
comforter guide". since brands is really the only category that
i have picked out here and there are a lot of other subpages for
the site, i should organize the other subpages to display them
here in a manner that is easy to use.
by grouping them, i could feature and link to a number of the
subpages under a description and picture for each group.

-sizes
general information on picking the right size comforter and/or
bed size
since there are 5 main sizes with information and specific
recommendations for each, a comparison chart may work on this
page to present this information

-fill power guide & chart
provide general information about fill power - what it actually
means, how it changes the price of comforters, what difference
it makes for the consumer
a comparison chart would also work here to provide some
information about common fill powers

-thread count
general information about thread count for comforters in a
similar manner to the fill power topic. may also be worth making
a chart to provide specific information on common thread counts.

-down shifting/comforter stitching
this will be a page targeting a big consumer concern for these
products. for many consumers, this concern is only realized
after buying a cheap comforter that isn't designed in a way to
prevent the shifting/bunching of the down fill. the stitching of
the comforter itself is the real reason this happens, so this
will be the main point to address on this page - especially
stitching that works to prevent this problem.
an article would likely provide most of the information here,
but some pictures may also be helpful to show some stitching
patterns.

-care/washing
many down comforters need to be dry cleaned, or at least they
state this on the tags for many. this is because down comes from
a real animal. once it isn't on the animal anymore, water will
cause it to break down, which degrades the quality of the fill
power. in general, they should only be professionally cleaned
once every few years, unless there is a need for it (but not
more than once a year). surface cleaning is ok if the down fill
isn't getting wet. alternative down is usually fine to wash and
dry like a normal blanket because these alternatives are usually
cloth or synthetic fiber. pinzon pyrenees down says it can be
washed, which could partially be a result of the pattened box
stitching.

-summer/lightweight
heat is a major concern for consumers of down comforters because
many believe them to be too hot to use in the warm months of the
year. there are actually different weights of these comforters,
so some are actually meant to be used in the summer. some
companies label their products with a weight word (light,
medium, heavy) while others will use a number gauge. geographic
location, weather, and personal preference can all affect the
need for a particular down comforter weight. either use an
article with subheadings here or possibly a comparison chart to
present the various weights.

-colors
i'm not sure how helpful this page can really be except to
possibly direct people to products for various colors,
especially since there is a lot of search engine traffic for a
wide variety of down comforter colors. possibly present this
information in a comparison chart.

-down alternative comforters
address the reasons for the popularity rise of down alternative
comforters lately. hypoallergenic properties are obviously a
major point to this, but cost also seems to have a lot to do
with it because they cost less than real down comforters. the
primaloft fill is a particular down alternative that is popular
and a topic for this site, so definitely link up to that page
here (and likely vise versa).

-leaking feathers
this is another page targeting a consumer concern. it is common
with real down feather comforters. manufacturing quality,
feather type, fill rating, thread count, and usage habits can
all affect this problem. an article with some subheadings would
likely work best here - possibly with a list and/or pictures
too.

-brands
this will be a category page that will briefly talk about down
comforter brands, summarize the brands that will be covered on
this site, and then link to the brand pages. since pinzon will
have some subpages, those pages should also likely be linked
from this page so people do not have to hunt for those pages
(especially since they will be some of the main pages of the
site that promote products).

--pinzon
this is amazon's brand, although i am really just focusing on
their down comforters for this page. this will have a total of
three subpages, so i will be summarizing each of them here and
linking to them. i also want to talk about the brand some here,
especially in reference to the fact that they are an exclusive
amazon product that is actually manufactured by a leading
company that makes quality down comforters for some other major
retailers as well. this also makes amazon competitive for this
type of product when it comes to pricing, since their expenses
are lower than brick and mortar retailers - this could be used
to target the 'discount' keyword for this niche as a secondary
phrase.

---primaloft
this is a popular fill used for down alternaitve comforters,
which is not exclusive to the pinzon brand. pinzon's
hypoallergenic down alternative comforter uses this fill. it is
considered to be a luxury down alternative fill and is supposed
to mimic the premium quality of goose down. the US Army actually
contracted it to be developed as a synthetic replacement for
goose down that is also hypoallergenic. the fill is actually
ultra-fine fibers and not real feathers, so they can be easily
machine washed and dried.

---pyrenees
these are the real down comforters by pinzon, even though the
primaloft comforter is also listed under this name in amazon's
comparison chart (and pyrenees is actually a fill used by other
companies, like pacific coast). they offer a white goose down
and a white down version of these comforters. the goose down is
more expensive and has a higher fill power, while the
unspecified down is cheaper with a slightly lower fill power.

----what is pyrenees down?
this is a type of goose down that is commonly used in a variety
of bedding products. down types are based on their geographic
origin, so this is the pyrenees mountains between spain and
france (making this european down). pinzon uses this for their
down comforters but other companies, like pacific coast, also
use it, so it is not exclusive to pinzon. down quality seems to
be based on the fill power, which is actually based on the
goose, their health, and their molting process. lower quality
down thus has a lower fill power. pyrenees down is offered by
pinzon at 550 and 600 fill power, which is considered decent in
the industry (with 850 being a maximum).

--ikea
another brand that produces a line of down comforters. ikea is
well known overall and is also popular for this particular
product, so there is some search engine traffic for the phrase
to make it worth targeting in addition to the fact that their
products can also be promoted on amazon. discuss some general
information about the brand and their bedding/comforter line
here.

--pacific coast
pacific coast seems to have similar products to pinzon, at least
at their heart. they also use european pyrenees down for their
comforters and have search traffic for this product line.
discuss the brand here in a similar manner to ikea and also link
up with the pyrenees down informational page that will be under
the pinzon brand (it can be linked up from both brands, since it
is relevant).

-hypoallergenic down
down alternatives are hypoallergenic, but there is a major
market for hypoallergenic keywords, so this is worth targeting
separately. discuss typical allergies to real down comforters
here and present solutions. likely best done in an article
format.

-about page
this will simply be a general page about the website. i like to
put a mission statement here to essentially summarize the site -
just an article is fine.

Once you have completed the content planning for each of your page topics, you really start to get to the point where you have an excellent guide that you will be able to use as you progress through building the site and writing the content for each page. In addition to that, since you are thinking all of this out ahead of time, you'll really be in the best position to present the information to your visitors in a way that is best for them and also for your purposes as an Amazon affiliate.

3-4 PLANNING FOR PRODUCT ADVERTISING

The final step for this lesson is to plan for your product advertising. Since I will actually be creating my Amazon product ads using my WordPress plugins, I do not actually need to have a specific list of products for this step.

The main purpose of this step is simply to plan where you will promote products throughout your site pages and ensure that there are relevant products for those pages.

You DO NOT need to have product advertising on every page of your site. In fact, I actually recommend against it because I believe this is a good indication to Google if your site solely exists for those products ads or not.

Instead, try to use advertisements where it is relevant to do so on your site. For the pages where you will not have advertisements, try to funnel traffic from those pages to pages that do promote products (either directly or possibly through another page that then links to pages promoting one or more products).

Some pages of your site may work best with by promoting a single product while others will be more useful when you promote multiple products. There is really no right or wrong answer here – it just depends on the topic for your page and/or what is available on Amazon (you don't have to promote everything just because it exists on Amazon though).

Once again, I will go back through the topics in my Notepad file and continue to make more notes for each page. When relevant, you can list specific products here that you want to promote, but you can also be more general and simply say what type/brand you want to promote there (since we will create these ads by searching for products in my WordPress plugins after we have built the site).

When you reach a page topic in your list that you feel like is a relevant place to promote a product, go over to Amazon just to ensure that there is something there that you actually want to promote for those topic. There is really nothing worse than planning a page topic and actually building the page only to find out that Amazon doesn't have a good product to promote for that page.

Also keep in mind that your informational pages on your site may be best simply linking to another page on your site that promotes a relevant product instead of filling those pages with ads. This will make it seem like you are not trying to push those advertisements upon people that do not wish to see them, which will help you to convert sales from those that are actually interested in buying.

I won't go back through and provide another five page list for you here. To avoid repeating that same list with small amounts of new information, I will simply talk about some of my ad plans for this particular site.

My main advertisement pages for this site will be the brand pages: Pinzon Primaloft, Pinzon Pyrenees, Ikea and Pacific Coast. Products can be found for all of these on Amazon.

Primaloft and Pyrenees pages will just be promoting a single down comforter, although I will also be including some accessories on these pages.

Ikea and Pacific Coast pages may promote more than one product. Depending on the variety of decent products that I can find for these two brands, I may create comparison charts on one or both brand pages to promote a few different down comforters instead of just one.

I may potentially be promoting a variety of products on the colors page too, which would likely be best done in a comparison chart since there will be many different colors and at least one product to go with each color (will just depend on the availability on Amazon). I may also link this page up with other pages on the site, if I have promoted a product on other pages that fit a color here.

The remaining pages of my site will all funnel to those product pages in relevant places. The about page on the site is really the only one that I probably can't target to a specific product page in a very relevant manner.

This may not seem like a ton of advertising for this whole site, but the site topics should help to bring in a lot of relevant traffic. It is also doing so in a way that isn't pushy and won't be perceived as affiliate spam by Google (and especially their independent relevance rankers).

I can also gauge the popularity of products that I promote and various pages of my site once it is receiving traffic and generating sales to help to make changes and/or additions to my product promotions.

4 WORDPRESS INSTALLATION & SETUP

With the fourth class, we will set up the actual website, although we will not actually begin to build the site until the sixth class. For now, the domain name must be properly connected to the web hosting account. Then we can install WordPress and begin to prepare it so our site can be built. Preparation of WordPress involves initial settings, installing a theme, and installing plugins.

Primary Lesson Objective

☐   Install WordPress & Prepare for Site Building

Lesson Steps Checklist

☐   Add Domain to Web Hosting Account

☐   Add Hosting DNS Records to Domain Name

☐   Install WordPress using QuickInstall

☐   Provide Initial WordPress Settings

☐   Install Plugins & a WordPress Theme

Chapter Notes

Chapter Notes

4-1 ADD DOMAIN TO WEB HOSTING ACCOUNT

The first step to creating your Amazon affiliate website is to add your domain name to a website hosting account.

If you do not already have a website hosting account that you can use to add another domain name to, you will need to create a new account.

I recommend using HostGator. You can get 20% off your initial hosting purchase with them through a link on this page:

http://supertargeting.com/domain-name-and-website-hosting/

When you create the new hosting account, simply specify your new domain name to have it set up as the primary domain for your new account.

For those of you that are adding a domain to an existing account, I will be showing you how this is done. Even if you aren't doing this step right now, it will be something you'll need to do eventually when you decide to create additional websites.

First, login to the Control Panel for your hosting account. This is accessed through your primary domain name with a **forward slash** and the word 'cpanel' at the end – ie, **http://example.com/cpanel**

Find the **Domains** section of links in the Control Panel, as seen below:

The link we want to use here is called **Addon Domains**.

Fill in your domain name and passwords, then click **Add Domain**. This creates the domain name on your web hosting account, but we still need to have the domain name itself pointed to the server.

4-2 DOMAIN NAME SERVER (DNS) MANAGEMENT

Now we need to get the Name Servers from our hosting account.

Go back to the cPanel Home and scroll all the way to the bottom of the screen. In the bottom-left box called **Account Information**, look for the **Name Servers**, as shown below:

```
Name Servers
  ns2229.hostgator.com
  ns2230.hostgator.com
```

If you're using HostGator, it should look very similar to this, except the numbers at the beginning of each Name Server will likely be different.

I need these two name server addresses to take to my domain name registrar.

I typically use GoDaddy to register my domains these days, and DownComforterGuide.com is registered with them.

The exact process to do this may look different with other domain name companies, but the basic principles should still be the same.

Login to your domain name account, get to the list of registered domains that you own, and then edit information for that domain.

In GoDaddy, this is done by visiting their home page. Look for the **All Products** menu in the top-left – just select **Domains** and then **Domain Management** from this menu to get to the right page.

On that page, click on the domain name that you want to point to your web hosting account.

This opens the **Domain Details** page in GoDaddy. On that page, look for the **Settings** tab with the **Nameservers** section.

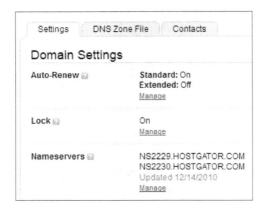

Click on the **Manage** link under **Nameservers** to open the **Nameserver Settings** window.

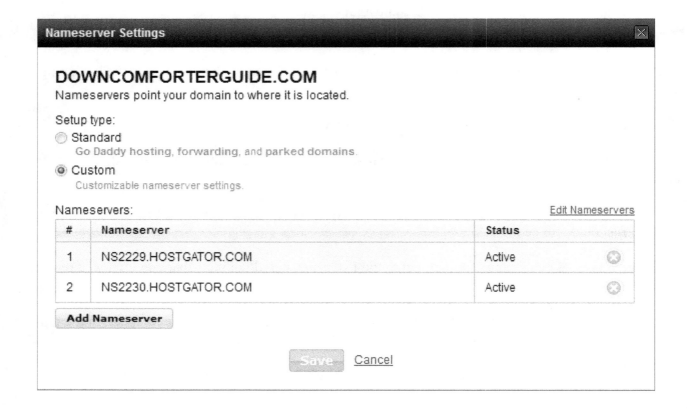

We'll be using the **Custom Setup type** here, which allows us to set our own nameserver settings. If you have existing Nameservers set here already, be sure to remove them with the **red X** on the right. To add your new nameservers, just click on the **Add Nameserver** button.

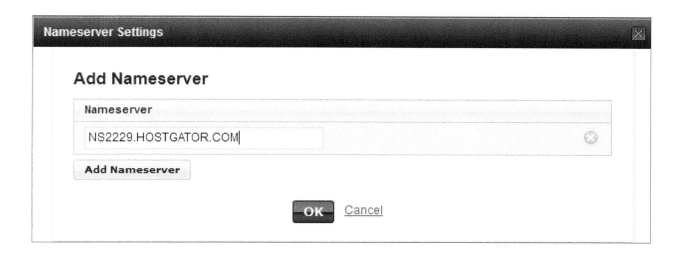

When you add a new nameserver, be sure to use both that are provided in your cPanel Account Information. Click **OK** when you are done. Then be sure to click **Save** on the previous window.

4-3 INSTALLING WORDPRESS

At this point, you should be able to type your domain name into a web browser and reach the site (even though there is nothing installed on it yet).

Sometimes it will take your domain name registrar up to 24 or even 48 hours to completely transfer the name server settings, but you will often be able to reach the site immediately or within a couple of hours.

To be sure, try visiting your cPanel through your new domain name (it won't work if it isn't transferred to your server yet).

When you can reach the Control Panel through the new domain name, you can proceed with installing WordPress.

Look for the **Software/Services** section of icons in cPanel, and click on **QuickInstall**:

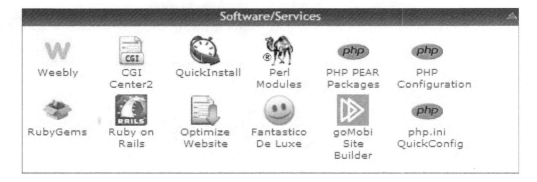

In the top-left of the **QuickInstall** page, look for the menu called **Blog Software**, and click on the **WordPress** link:

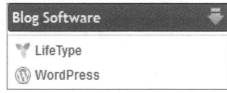

Next, click on the **Continue** button:

You will now need to provide some initial information so WordPress can be installed. Start by selecting the domain name from the drop-down list. The text box to the right of the domain should remain blank, unless you are trying to install WordPress to a subdirectory on that domain.

I typically choose to disable Auto Upgrades and simply perform them manually with each new version release (to ensure new upgrades do not cause conflicts with old plugins on the site, which could break the site without me knowing about it). As of WordPress 3.7, bug fix and security upgrades are now performed automatically without this setting – only major updates need to be performed by you (upgrading from 3.7 to 3.8, for example).

Provide a title for your site, which I often set as my target keyword phrase for the whole site. Then provide an admin username as well as your first and last name. Click the **Install Now** button when you are ready to proceed.

Install WordPress
Application URL (where you will find the app in your browser):

| http:// | downcomforterguide.com ▼ | / | |

Enable Auto Upgrades:	☐
Admin Email:	ryan@ryanstevensonp
Blog Title:	)own Comforter Guide
Admin User:	admin
First Name:	Ryan
Last Name:	Stevenson

☐ Install Now!

You will then see a progress bar start at 1% and build up to 100%. Once it is done, WordPress is installed and running on the domain name.

You will also be provided the link for the administration area and your login information. You will need the password provided here to be able to login to the site for the first time. In case you close that page, the password is also sent to you in an email using the admin email address you have provided for the installation.

Other notes and/or important information may be included by WordPress here as well. Currently, they are packaging WP-Super-Cache with WordPress to increase performance, but this information could easily change as new versions of WordPress are released (this is current as of version 3.6 of WordPress).

I've included a screenshot of this page from my installation. I've still included all of the login information below, just so you can see the important parts that you'll need to retrieve from your own installation (I didn't want to blur this out for this picture). With that said, the login information below won't work to login to my site – I've simply changed it after logging in for the first time, which you should also do with your own site (ie, don't use the default password).

Once you have WordPress successfully installed and running on your domain name, just login to the **Admin Area** using the information provided here. We'll be working directly on the site starting with that page in the rest of this lesson.

4-4 INITIAL WORDPRESS SETTINGS SETUP

Now that WordPress is running on our domain name, we can begin work on the site.

However, before we begin building content, we will actually need to set up settings and then other software to get WordPress prepared for this site.

The first thing that I want to mention is that WordPress is intended to be a blogging content management system, but I don't use it that way.

With that said, there are some default WordPress settings that I change, so I need to discuss these with you in addition to other important settings that even bloggers would need to change for their new sites.

Jetpack & Other Default WP Plugins

When you first login to your WordPress dashboard, the first thing that will likely draw your attention is a big blue banner across the top of the page for Jetpack.

> **Your Jetpack is almost ready** – A connection to WordPress.com is needed to enable features like Stats, Contact Forms, and Subscriptions. Connect now to get fueled up!
>
> Connect to WordPress.com

This allows you to connect your blog to a WordPress.com account (where you can have a blog hosted by WordPress instead of self-hosted).

However, this isn't something I'm interested in using for these sites, so I simply deactivate and delete the plugin.

To deactivate and delete the plugin, we need to go the installed plugins list in WP.

Along the left-hand side of all of the administration pages, you'll see a long menu, as pictured here.

Look for **Plugins** in this list.

If you hover over it, it will open up a sub-menu containing even more links.

Either click on the word **Plugins** in the main menu list or click on **Installed Plugins** in the sub-menu list – both will bring you to the same page.

Even though I have just installed WordPress and haven't done anything on the site yet, there are already four plugins installed. However, I don't have any use for three of these four plugins.

I have shown the Installed Plugins page here from my site.

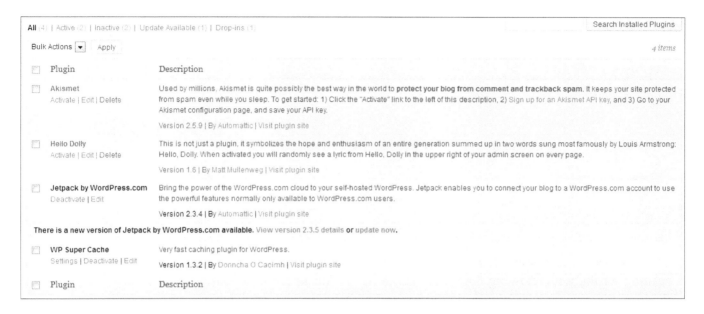

Akismet is used for controlling comment spam, which is absolutely out of control on WordPress sites. However, don't be fooled, it doesn't even work good! I have actually been able to figure out that some old WordPress sites of mine got hacked using a security vulnerability in Akismet itself, even with it deactivated on the site, so be sure to delete this plugin. It has been a couple of years since that happened (at the time of this writing), but I still won't trust it and really don't have use for the plugin.

Hello Dolly is completely worthless, maybe whimsical at best. Delete it. Jetpack that I mentioned before is the third plugin that I delete – you'll first need to deactivate it before you can delete it.

Any of these plugins can always be obtained again by simply searching for them through WordPress and installing them again (it downloads directly through WordPress).

WP Super Cache is worth holding onto. It can help make your site run faster when you start to get regular traffic coming to your site. However, if you are building your site and find that updates you've made are not appearing to show up on the main site, try deactivating this plugin just until the site construction is completed. When the site is set up how you want it to look, turn it back on if you did deactivate it. If it doesn't cause you any problems though, try to leave it activated.

User Profile Settings

My next stop is to visit the User Profile. Look for Users in the left-hand admin menu. Hover over it and click on Your Profile.

Going down the left-hand side of your profile page, you can see four sections that use **bold** text to indicate each section of settings. I want to skip down to the second set of settings, **Name**.

Some WordPress themes will show your username on various parts of the public website. While there is nothing wrong with showing that your username is **admin**, it could be more useful for people to see a real name or even some type of pseudonym that you want to use for the site.

For this site, I could call myself **The Down Expert**. It is better for those viewing my site than showing **admin** and it is also relevant to my targeted niche, down comforters.

Put your public name in the **Nickname** field, and then select that name in the drop-down box below:

Now I want to jump to the fourth section of settings – **About Yourself**. Here, you can set a New Password for your account so that it is something you can remember instead of the auto-generated password that WordPress sets for you.

Be sure to type your password twice here – in the **New Password** and **Repeat New Password** text boxes.

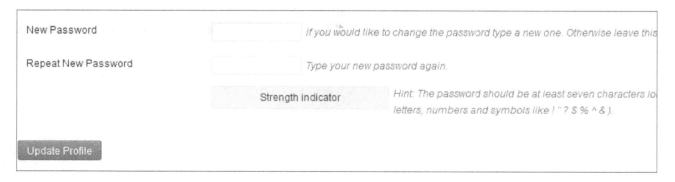

After you are done with your changes, be sure to click the **Save** button at the bottom.

Default Post & Page

A fresh WordPress installation contains a default post and a default page. These are just intended to be examples for new WordPress users, so we do not need these pages. I always delete these from the site.

Look for **Posts** and **Pages** in the admin menu.

First click **Posts**. You'll see the default post, **Hello world!**. Hover your mouse over the title of the post to get links to show up below the title. Then just click on the **Trash** link to remove it from the live site.

It still keeps a copy in the **Trash** that can be restored, but this at least takes care of what we wanted to do. It can be permanently deleted from the **Trash**, if you want, but this isn't something that has to be done.

Repeat the same process with the **Pages** link. A default page, **Sample Page**, will be found there.

WordPress Settings

There are a number of different settings pages available in WordPress that need some attention to change some of the default settings.

All of the pages I'll be discussing for the remainder of this chapter will be found within one of the admin menus, **Settings**, which is all the way at the bottom of the list.

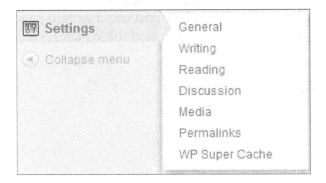

First, I want to point out the **WP Super Cache** link here. This was actually created and added by the WP Super Cache plugin, so the link isn't technically part of WordPress itself. This simply means that other plugins may add a settings page to this particular menu list. I will be discussing most of the other links here with you today.

General Settings

The first settings link is for General WordPress settings. I've shown the top portion of this page below:

The part that I am interested in here is the **Tagline** that says "Just another WordPress site". Obviously, this is just a default setting and not something I want to use on the live site, so I want to change this to something related to my site and niche.

My recommendation here is to avoid using any of the same words in your site title (main keyword phrase) but still try to summarize what your site is about in a short sentence.

For my site, I have come up with "Helping you pick out the best bedding products for your personal needs" - not technically a sentence, but it will do. Come up with something for your site (this really isn't too important, so don't spend too much time on it). Add it to the **Tagline** text box and then click the Save Changes button at the bottom of the page.

Reading Settings

The next step is to change a setting on the Reading page. This setting is at the very bottom of the picture on the follow page and labeled as **For each article in a feed, show.** The picture shows the default settings here.

94

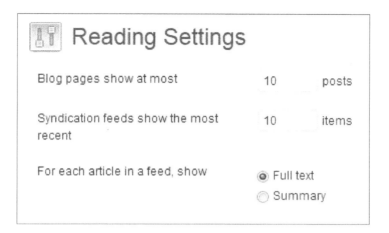

Simply change that setting to **Summary**, and click the **Save Changes** button at the bottom of the page. My reasons for changing this are purely precautionary – I don't want others to be able to retrieve all of my site content using a feed for this site (all WordPress sites have a feed that lists the content, which can be all of the content or just summaries of that content and a link to the full content). If someone is going to grab my content, I would prefer to use the summaries and hopefully get a backlink to my site in the process.

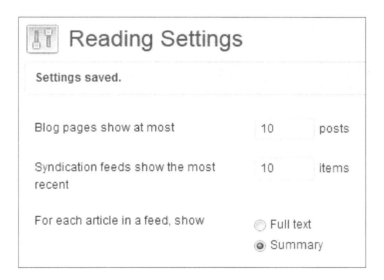

Discussion Settings

Next we need to go to the Discussion settings page. This page controls the WordPress commenting system, which allows your public site visitors to leaves comments.

If you remember me talking about Akismet, I mentioned that WordPress sites get a lot of spam comments. As a result, I simply disable commenting on these sites, especially since they are not blog-style websites that commonly receive visitors that leave comments.

I have shown a picture here that shows the default settings on this page.

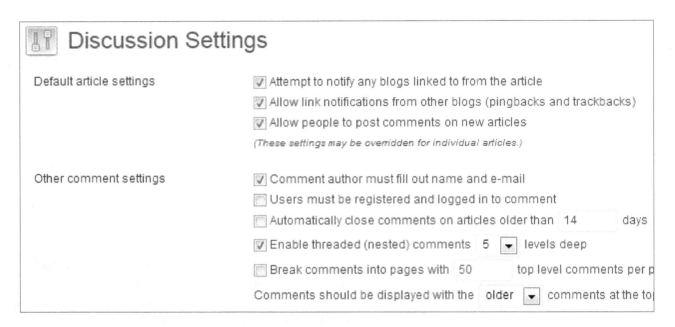

The main thing I want to change here is the setting that disables comments – **Allow people to post comments on new articles**. Simply uncheck the box next to that setting.

If you already have content on the site, the existing pages will not have commenting disabled when you have only used the above setting. The sixth setting on this page, **Automatically close comments on articles older than 14 days** can be used to take care of those existing pages on the site. Just check the box next to that setting and change the number **14** in the text box to a **0**.

I have shown these changes below:

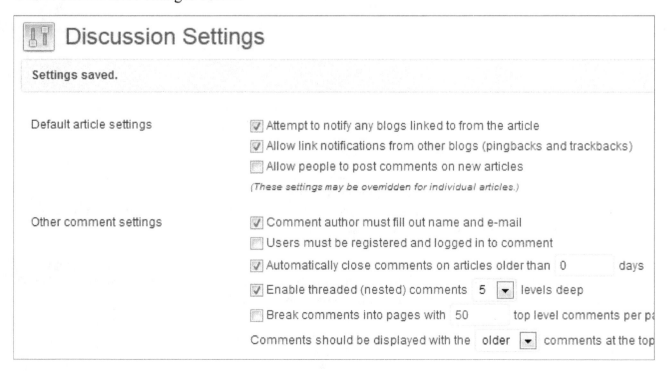

Permalink Settings

The last settings page that I want to talk about is the **Permalink Settings** page.

Under Common **Settings** on this page, I want to ensure that **Post name** is selected and not **Default**. This ensures that WordPress uses the post title as the URL address instead of referencing each page on the site with a PHP variable in the URL and a number for the value. To make a long story short, this will help with search engine rankings.

Here is what this setting should look like:

Permalink Settings

By default WordPress uses web URLs which have question marks and lots of numbers in them, howev archives. This can improve the aesthetics, usability, and forward-compatibility of your links. A number of

Common Settings

○ Default	http://downcomforterguide.com/?p=123	
○ Day and name	http://downcomforterguide.com/2013/08/26/sample-post/	
○ Month and name	http://downcomforterguide.com/2013/08/sample-post/	
○ Numeric	http://downcomforterguide.com/archives/123	
⦿ Post name	http://downcomforterguide.com/sample-post/	
○ Custom Structure	http://downcomforterguide.com /%postname%/	

Optional

If you like, you may enter custom structures for your category and tag URLs here. For example, using to /topics/uncategorized/ . If you leave these blank the defaults will be used.

Category base

Tag base

Save Changes

4-5 WORDPRESS THEME SETUP

For this step of the setup process, we will be installing a theme for our WordPress site.

I don't like to use the default theme for these Amazon affiliate sites because it really seems to be more for bloggers.

Although I have a particular theme that I like to use for these sites, you are more than welcome to choose your own theme if there is a particular one that you already like to use or if you are going for a particular look for your site.

However, my recommended theme actually allows for a lot of customization. It includes a number of sub-themes that each feature a different design and/or layout.

You can also take any of those designs and alter a variety of different aspects, especially colors, making it an easy theme to use for a wide variety of website designs.

My recommended WordPress theme is completely free and can be installed directly through WordPress. It is called **Weaver** (actually **Weaver II** now).

Look for **Appearance** in the admin menu in WordPress:

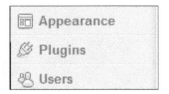

When you click on **Appearance**, you'll be taken to the **Manage Themes** page. Here you'll be able to see the installed theme, which is Twenty Thirteen.

Now click on the **Install Themes** tab to start looking for a new theme to install.

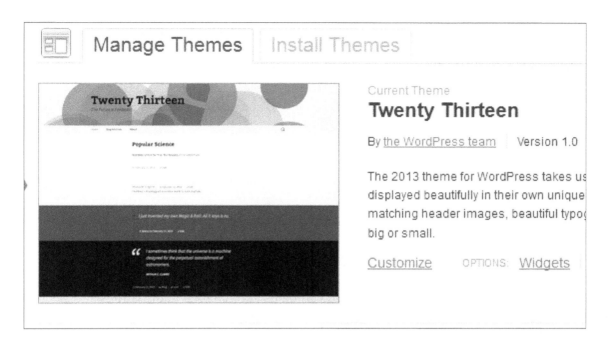

On the **Install Themes** page, you'll be able to search through the WordPress repository for free themes that you can download and install directly through your site. Although there are a lot of different options that you can use here to try to find a particular theme, I'm looking for a specific theme here, so I will just type in the name **Weaver** into the search box. Click **Search** once you are done to fetch results from WordPress.

After searching, **Weaver II** should be the only theme displayed in the results – just click on the

Install Now link at the bottom to automatically download and install this theme on your site.

Next, click on the **Activate** link after the theme is installed:

Downloading install package from http://wordpress.org/themes/download/weaver-ii.1.3.8.zip...

Unpacking the package...

Installing the theme...

Successfully installed the theme **Weaver II 1.3.8**.

Live Preview | Activate | Return to Theme Installer

After activating the theme, you'll be taken directly to the admin page for Weaver II.

At the top, you'll see a series of menus. These can be used to change many different aspects of the theme, including fine-tuning of colors throughout the various parts of the site. Some of the options are restricted to the Pro version, which isn't free, but I have honestly never purchased it and simply find the free version to have enough features for my needs.

I have one thing to show you on one of those menu pages, but first I need to select my subtheme to use with Weaver II.

The subthemes and the ability to customize individual parts of the live site are the main reasons why I like this theme.

On this main page for the theme, you'll find thumbnails for all of the subthemes at the bottom. Simply select the circle next to the name of a subtheme and click the **Set to Selected Subtheme** button.

Personally, I like to use **Twenty Eleven Light** for many of my sites, unless I am going for a particular look that might require the use of colors. I can then fine-tune various parts of this subtheme to make it look however I want for the site I'm building.

Now I am going to go to one of the menu pages in this theme. Look for **Main Options** in the menu across the top of the theme page. On that page, click on the **Footer** link in the secondary menu that appears across the top.

At the bottom, look for the **Site Copyright** header. I want to check the checkbox below the large text box here – it says **Hide Powered By tag:** right in front of the checkbox.

When that change is done, be sure to click the **Save Settings** button.

Now that Weaver is installed, the left-hand menu of WordPress is a bit different. The Appearance menu is expanded, as seen below:

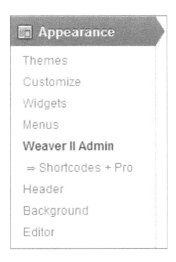

You can see that we're currently on the **Weaver II Admin** page – this is where you will want to go if you want to make style/design changes to the overall look of the site.

The **Header** link here is also useful and something I use for basically every site I build. This allows me to add my own customized header image to the site, if I want to. Instead of using an image, I can also choose to simply remove the image – just click the **Remove Header Image** button on the **Header** page.

This leaves a blank space at the top of my site, which is filled by the title and tagline that was set on the General Settings page, which you can see below:

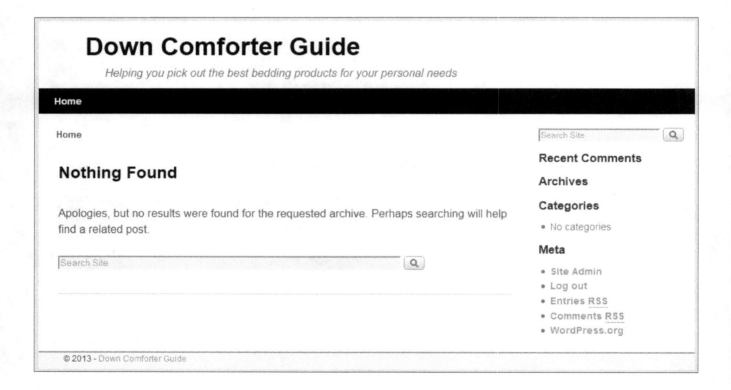

At this point, we have a fairly basic site, which is what I'm trying to achieve (this keeps the focus on the content you build on the site and not the design itself).

The site says **Nothing Found**, because there isn't any content on the site yet – this will change once we move on to start building the actual site.

4-6 WORDPRESS PLUGIN SETUP

The last step to setting up a WordPress site is to install WordPress plugins.

My own Amazon plugins can be installed on the site at this point, but that is not the purpose of this stage in the training because advertising won't be put on the site until it is built. For this reason, I will be waiting a few lessons before I actually go through all of this for my plugins.

This chapter is really about the other plugins that I use on my Amazon affiliate sites. These are actually free plugins that can be installed directly through WordPress, just like I did with the Weaver theme.

If I am looking to achieve something particular on one of my Amazon affiliate sites, I will definitely attempt to search the free plugins to see if something is there that can do the work for me. However, beyond those types of plugins, there is really one main plugin that I will use on all of my Amazon affiliate sites, so that is the plugin I would like to have you install now.

This plugin is **SEO Ultimate**, which takes care of all of the backend SEO for us on the site. Many people may have tried this plugin or already use **All-in-One SEO** – either one is really OK but SEO Ultimate is just my personal preference (and what I have used for years with good results).

To start, look for the **Plugins** link in the left-hand WP admin menu. Hover over it and click on **Add New** in the list of sub-items.

Now, type **SEO Ultimate** into the search text box on the **Install Plugins** page.

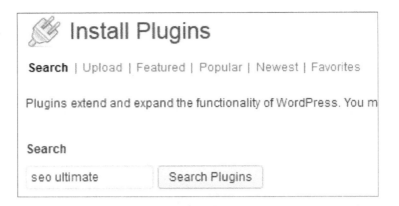

You should then see SEO Ultimate as the first plugin listed – just click on the Install Now link under the name of the plugin:

After the plugin is installed, click on the **Activate Plugin** link provided:

After the plugin is activated, you'll be taken to the list of active plugins on your site. Look for SEO Ultimate listed there. Then find and click on the Title Tag Rewriter link, as shown below:

On the Title Tag Rewriter page, I am looking for this: **{blog}**

I want to remove all instances of **{blog}** that can be seen in the picture above, EXCEPT FOR THE

FIRST! I also want to remove keystroke symbol (a vertical line), as well as the space before and after it.

This prevents the primary keyword phrase for my site, the blog title (which is represented here as {blog}), from being repeated in the title of all of the pages throughout the site – just the home page. I believe using the main keyword phrase in that regard on all pages of a site could be viewed as keyword spam.

I've shown what this looks like afterward below:

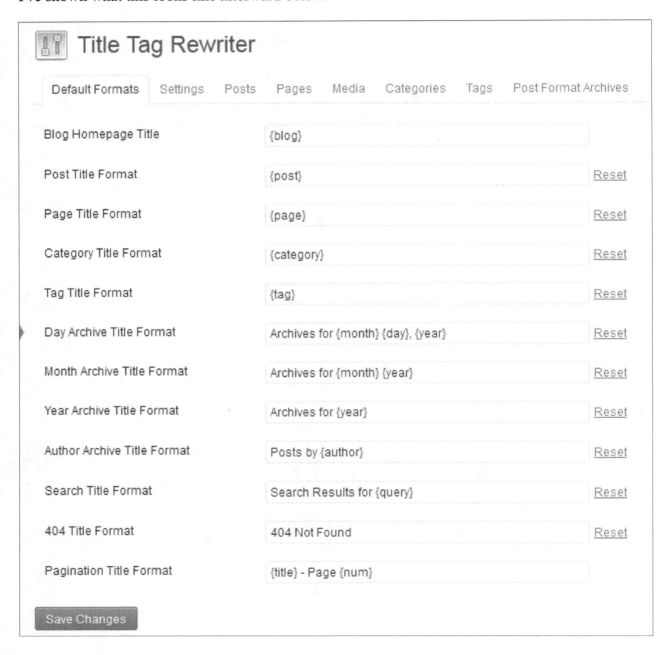

More free plugins will be getting installed on this site as this course progresses, but for now, this is the main plugin I want to have installed on the site initially.

5 HOW TO USE WORDPRESS

Before we move on to begin building our site, it is important to understand how WordPress works. The fifth class is devoted to teaching you the essential things about WP that you will need to be able to build these sites. This is one of the few classes in this book that is really just educational and not designed to accomplish anything towards the progress of building out site. You'll learn the differences between the post and page systems in WordPress, how to use WP Widgets, and how to keep WP, plugins and your theme up-to-date.

Primary Lesson Objective

☐   Learn How to Build Your WordPress Site

Lesson Steps Checklist

☐   Creating and Using WordPress Widgets

☐   Creating and Using WordPress Custom Menus

☐   Learn about WordPress Posts, Categories & Tags

☐   Learn about WordPress Pages

☐   Keep WordPress Core, Plugins & Theme Up-to-Date

Chapter Notes

Chapter Notes

5-1 WIDGET SETUP & USAGE

On a WordPress site, the actual content of a post or page that you create doesn't take up the entire web page with most WordPress themes.

There is often other information or links above, below, and/or on the sides of the post/page content.

One of the most common examples of this is the sidebar, often found on the left or right hand side of a page.

This sidebar will generally contain links to other pages on the site and other information that will show up on every page through the website.

WordPress Widgets allow you to control these sidebars and some other parts of the site that are not part of the post/page content.

To get to this page in WordPress, look for the **Appearance** menu on the left. Hover over it and click on **Widgets**.

On the right-hand side of the Widgets page, you should see a section at the top, called **Primary Sidebar**, filled with Widgets (as shown below). Each of the items listed here is a widget and can show up on the public website.

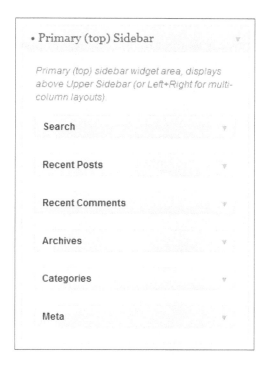

By default, these widgets are setup in this theme and get displayed in the right-hand sidebar of the public website. I've shown a picture below of what this is creating on the public site:

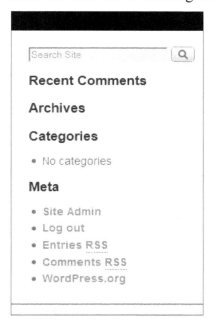

You may notice that the **Recent Posts** Widget doesn't display here – this is happening because there are no posts on the site at the moment (it would appear if I created one).

For blog-style websites, this widget setup may work just fine, but for the Amazon affiliate sites that I build, it doesn't work because I don't use posts or comments. This immediately removes the need for 4 of these 6 widgets: **Recent Posts, Recent Comments, Archives & Categories.**

There are two ways you can remove a Widget that is already in place:

1. Just click on it and drag it to the **Inactive Widgets** bar in the bottom-left of the page. This keeps the settings for your widgets, in case you may want to restore them later. You can also just drag them off the sidebar to delete them entirely.

2. Click on the down arrow in the top-right of a Widget, then click the **Delete** link:

You can also see that when I clicked the down arrow in the top-right of the Widget, it offers me options. Not all Widgets will have options here but many do. If you make changes here, be sure to click the **Save** button when you are done.

For my Amazon affiliate site, I am actually going to remove all of the widgets except for the **Search** bar, as seen below.

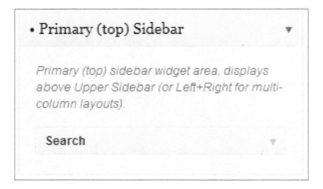

I will be revisiting Widgets when I am actually building my site to add something useful here, but for now, I simply want to discuss how to go about adding Widgets.

On the left-hand side of the Widgets page, you have a large list of **Available Widgets**. Simply click one and drag it into a Widget position to add it to your site. You can then click the down arrow for the Widget to change settings for it.

Some widgets may be automated and work without any input from you, while others are simply designed to let you add your own custom content to the site as a widget.

Be sure to read the description that comes along with each widget to see what it will do.

I've shown just a couple of the **Available Widgets** below:

Custom Menu

Use this widget to add one of your custom menus as a widget.

Recent Posts

The most recent posts on your site

Text

Arbitrary text or HTML

Custom Menu is one that I actually use a lot, but it requires you to create your menu first. I'll be using this once I proceed with building the site, but I at least wanted to point it out for now.

Recent Posts was the widget that I removed from this site.

Text is a custom widget that allows you to set your own content, which can be plain text or even HTML code (something else I find myself using on many sites).

In addition to the **Primary Sidebar**, most WordPress themes will also offer other Widget areas on the site. This allows you to place your widgets where you want them to show up on the site (ie, you could place a widget in the Footer to get it to show up at the bottom of the site instead of in the sidebar).

I have shown some of the possible Widget areas available in the theme I use, Weaver II.

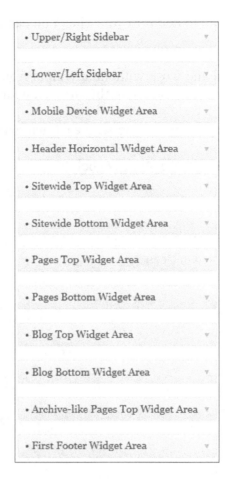

- Upper/Right Sidebar ▾
- Lower/Left Sidebar ▾
- Mobile Device Widget Area ▾
- Header Horizontal Widget Area ▾
- Sitewide Top Widget Area ▾
- Sitewide Bottom Widget Area ▾
- Pages Top Widget Area ▾
- Pages Bottom Widget Area ▾
- Blog Top Widget Area ▾
- Blog Bottom Widget Area ▾
- Archive-like Pages Top Widget Area ▾
- First Footer Widget Area ▾

To get familiar with your WordPress theme and the available widget areas, try this exercise:

1. Add a **Text** widget to each of the available Widget areas.

2. Edit the settings for each of those **Text** widgets. Set the text to the name of the Widget area, and Save your changes.

3. Visit your live site to see the Widgets in action. This will give you a very clear idea of what is designed to show up where.

If you try this exercise, be sure to remove all of the Widgets you created once you are finished and have an understanding of your Widget areas.

5-2 WORDPRESS MENU SYSTEM

The next part of WordPress that I want to talk about is the menu system.

I briefly mentioned creating a custom menu widget before – this menu system is what is used for those widgets. Beyond being used for custom menu widgets, this menu system can also be used to control the main menus displayed on your public website.

By default, most WordPress themes will add all of your new pages to the main menu of the site (often shown directly below the site title/logo).

For blog-style sites, that design may work just fine, since most of their content is created in posts.

However, since I am building sites entirely out of pages, I simply don't want all of those pages to show up in that menu. The menu would actually take up multiple lines on the site, which isn't very useful or attractive for your site visitors.

To use the menu system, look for the **Menus** link in the **Appearance** menu:

Here is the **Menu** page – nothing is going on here yet because we have not created a menu and there aren't any pages on the site.

WordPress has actually changed this menu system recently, so it may be slightly unfamiliar, even to experienced users, if you have not used it in a while.

To get started, enter a **Menu Name**, then click on the blue **Create Menu** button on the far right (that button isn't pictured above).

I like to call this menu **Top Menu**, because it is the menu that I use at the top of the public website.

Once you give the menu a name and click the **Create Menu** button, you'll then need to build the menu.

On the left-hand side of the page, you can simply select existing pages on the site or even add your own custom links. I will often add the main pages of my site to this menu. However, since I don't have pages on this site yet, I'm just going to create a custom link for now.

I've shown this custom link being created, which is for my home page.

I could ordinarily create this home page link by simply selecting the home page from the **Pages** list but again, there are no pages on this set yet (even a home page technically).

Provide the custom URL and the text for the link here, then click the **Add to Menu** button.

This immediately adds the menu item, which is reflected in the main screen on the right. Here, you can set the main settings for the menu and even edit existing menu items.

If you click on the down arrow for the menu item you just created, you can see the **URL** and **Navigation Label** text boxes already filled out with the information you provided. However, the **Title Attribute** box is still blank. I actually like to go back through my links and provide text here.

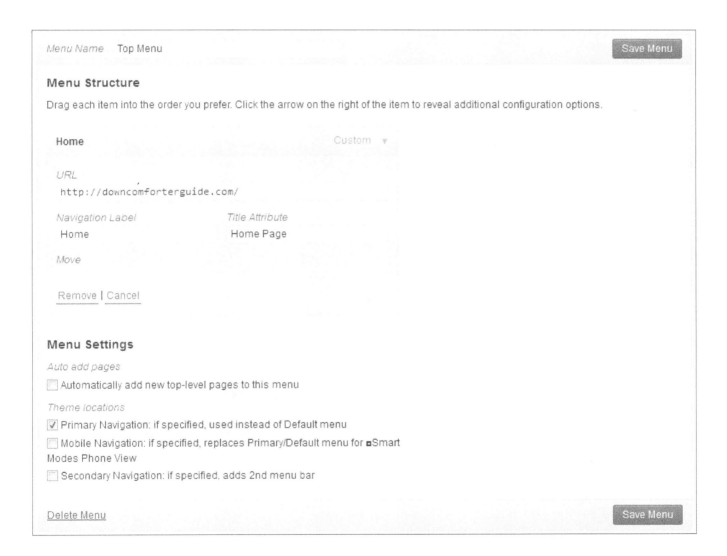

The **Title Attribute** is text that the website visitor will see when they hover over your link, so I use this to explain the link a bit more.

If you can rephrase the title of the page or the link text here without getting spammy with your keywords, I feel like this is the best choice.

However, with the home page of the site, I try to avoid keywords completely here – I think this is a key sign of a keyword spam site and even Google may look to make sure your Home links aren't spamming keywords.

At the very bottom of the page, look for the **Menu Settings**. There are two sections of settings here.

The first, **Auto add pages**, has one setting.

This setting makes the menu behave like a default WordPress menu – where new pages (not posts) added to the site will automatically get added to the menu. This was actually the setting I wanted to avoid by creating my own custom menu, so I definitely do not want to select this.

The next set is called **Theme locations**.

The three settings here control where the menu is displayed on the site. Depending on the theme you are using, the settings available here may actually be different. However, all themes should have a **Primary Navigation** setting, which allows you to override the default main menu on the site.

I want to select **Primary Navigation** for this menu, to get it to become the main menu of the site. When you get done with yours, be sure to click the **Save Menu** button.

If you visit the live site after this change, you may notice that the main menu isn't that different.

I still have a **Home** link that goes to the front page of my site. However, if I hover over that link, I can see the text **Home Page** being displayed.

The real difference becomes apparent when new pages are added to the site because they will not automatically show up in this menu – I'll have to add them myself.

I can simply return to the menu page at any time during my site construction to add new links to this menu. Just look in the **Pages** list to find the page you want to add as a link.

As I begin to build pages on my site, I will be revisiting this menu system with you to show you exactly what I do for my menus.

5-3 CATEGORIES, POSTS & TAGS

There are really two different ways that you can build your WordPress site – with posts or pages. Even though the decision to pick one may not seem very important, after many years of building WP sites, I have figured out that there is actually a big difference.

Ultimately, WordPress works different depending on whether you are creating a post or a page.

Personally, I prefer to build all of my sites using only WP pages because it gives me complete control over the site. However, I still wanted to discuss WP posts so that you have a complete understanding of these two ways to create content on your site.

I'll be moving on to WP pages in the next chapter, so I'm going to get started by teaching you about posts.

The main thing that you need to understand about WP posts is that they are not standalone pages. They are actually connected up with other WP posts through two kinds of associations: a category grouping and a keyword/tag grouping.

Take a look at the **Posts** menu in WordPress, shown below:

At the top of this menu, you have two links for the actual posts: **All Posts** (which will show you existing posts) and **Add New** (which allows you to create a new post).

The bottom two links, **Categories** and **Tags**, are for the category and keyword groupings.

Post Categories

Before I show you how to create a WP post, I need to talk about the Categories page first.

The WordPress Category system is used to group together posts.

Whenever I talk about using Categories on my Amazon sites, I AM NOT talking about these Categories – I actually create WP pages as my Category pages.

On the **Categories** page, you can add a new Category on the left-hand side of the page or edit existing Categories on the right.

There is already a default category in the system, called **Uncategorized** (pictured below).

However, I am going to create my own Category to show you how this system works, and so I can point out why I don't like to use it.

On the left-hand side of the page, I am going to add a new category.

Notice how I have only provided a **Name** for the Category here.

The **Slug** (controls the URL where the category is accessed) is automatically generated based on the **Name**, but you can customize this if you want.

The **Description** box can be filled out. However, I have actually found that a large majority of WP themes don't use this at all, so it is often a waste of time.

After I click the **Add New Category** button at the bottom, the Category is created in the system and added to the list on the right:

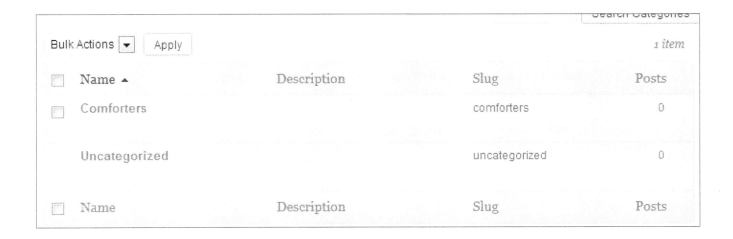

At this point, I am going to proceed on to creating a new Post, so you can see how all of this works. I'm going to click on the **Add New** link in the **Posts** menu (shown at the beginning of this chapter).

I am now shown a page that allows me to create the content for this new post. Here is the main part of the page, where you provide a post title and the actual content:

First, I need to point out the two tabs here on the right-hand side: **Visual** and **Text**.

The **Text** tab is used for HTML code input, although you could still simply enter text here to write an article for the page.

The **Visual** tab actually shows you a visual representation of what the page should look like, which completely avoids any HTML coding.

This Visual tab is excellent for those that do not have any HTML knowledge because you can simply select text, and then click one of the toolbar buttons to apply various HTML styles to your site.

SEO Settings

If you continue to go down the page from there, you should run into the SEO Settings section.

This actually exists here because of the SEO plugin we installed. It gives us a way to set various SEO settings for this particular page.

In general, I always recommend providing a **Title Tag** and **Meta Description** here, although you can leave out the Title if you want it to simply be the Title you provided above for the post.

The **Social Networks Listing** tab allows you to specify some information to be used if someone references this page on a social network, like Facebook.

The **Miscellaneous** tab allows you to request that the site not get indexed by search engines.

In general, you'll want to avoid doing this, but I still wanted to point it out in case you want to create a special page on your site that isn't shown to users, even in search engines, unless they actually have the link for it (could be a link you provide in a newsletter, for example).

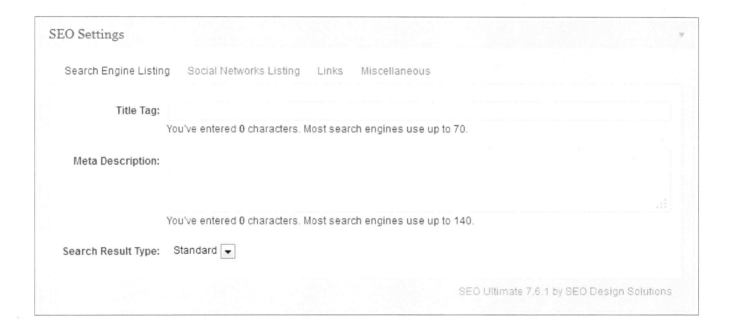

Weaver II Post Options

Even more down the page are options available through the Weaver II theme that I am using.

These options are very handy, especially if you want to change the way one specific page on your site looks. I will often use these settings to completely disable the header and footer on a page, when I am creating a sales page for example.

A good practical use for average site builders is to use the **Hide post title** option here, if you didn't want to show the title of the post at the top (WordPress tends to repeat this title a couple of times at the top of the page – once for a link and another time for the title itself).

Publish Post

On the right-hand side of the page at the top, you have a box with a blue **Publish** button in it. This is what you click when you are done creating the post and ready to make it live on your site.

You can optionally **Preview** the post here or even **Save Draft**, to avoid publishing it (if you want to come back to it before making it live).

The **Edit** link next to **Publish immediately** can also be used to schedule the publishing of a new post. This can be handy if you have a lot of content to build but want the site building to appear natural and not done all at one time.

Categories and Tags

There are also boxes for Categories and Tags on the right-hand side of the page.

The **Categories** box is used to select the Category that you want to use for the site (multiple can be selected).

The **Tags** box is used to provide keywords for the post, but these keywords should be words that would also relate to other posts on the site. This is basically a secondary grouping system used to connect similar posts together.

I'm going to select the checkbox next to **Comforters** in the Categories box. I will also add a new Tag to this post: **Alternative**.

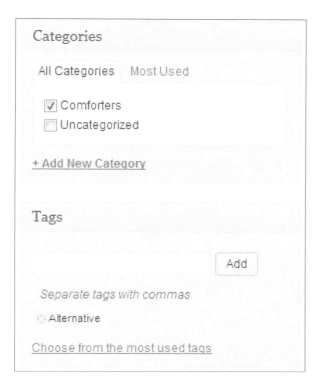

Featured Image

Some WP themes will show image thumbnails next to each post when they are listed on a category or tag page, but a Featured Image needs to be set for each post for this to happen.

Just click on the **Set featured image** link, which will open up the WP Media system. You can select existing images or even upload your own.

You can actually reach this Media window by clicking on the **Add Media** icon at the top of the page.

This system can be used to upload images and place them on your page.

Posts In Action

I am now going to **Publish** my post so you can see how this system works. I have shown a picture below so you can see what this post looks like on my live site:

Home→Comforters→**Pinzon Down Alternative Comforter**

Pinzon Down Alternative Comforter

Posted on September 1, 2013 by The Down Expert

Here I will add the content and other information about this subject/product.

This entry was posted in Comforters and tagged Alternative by The Down Expert. Bookmark the permalink. Edit

A few things to point out here:

1. At the top of the page, notice how there are breadcrumb links going from this page back to the category page and then to the home page. This isn't necessarily bad (good for SEO). I'll come back to this in a second.

2. Next, below my post title, notice how there is another line of text that states a post date and the author name (the custom name I set in my admin profile). This typically only shows up for posts. Although this could be beneficial for people that see your posts quickly (they would know it is new content), it can also be bad once your site content becomes a bit dated. How many consumers will really trust content that is a few years old, for example.

3. At the bottom of the post content, there is a sentence that contains a few links. It mentions the Category for the post, along with the tag and author name.

First, I'm going to visit the **Category** page link – this can be either link (the one from #1 or #3).

Home→Categories **Comforters**

Category Archives: Comforters

Pinzon Down Alternative Comforter

Posted on September 1, 2013 by The Down Expert

Here I will add the content and other information about this subject/product.

Posted in Comforters | Tagged Alternative

First, notice the text used at the top of the page now, Categories **Comforters**, and the text below it, **Category Archives**: **Comforters**. That information is essentially the base content of the category page. Obviously this doesn't allow much room for customization, since I don't even have control over this content here or any way to add additional information to this page.

This is actually the number one reason why I don't use the WP Category system. WP spits out the category pages but doesn't offer a way to customize them. As a result, I feel like the pages aren't horribly useful for website visitors because they are simply a list of the posts in that category.

You can see the actual content of this category page is the simple summary list of the post I just created. It also shows links for the categories and tags used for each post.

If I now click on the Alternative link, I will go to the Alternative tag page:

Home→Tags **Alternative**

Tag Archives: Alternative

Pinzon Down Alternative Comforter

Posted on September 1, 2013 by The Down Expert

Here I will add the content and other information about this subject/product.

Posted in Comforters | Tagged Alternative

As you can see here, this page looks almost identical to the previous page, except **Comforters** is now replaced with **Alternative** and **Categories/Category** is now replaced with **Tags/Tag**.

Again, this doesn't make for a very useful page, and I also don't have an easy way to customize the content of this page.

In addition to all of that, the actual content of the Category and Tag pages essentially end up being identical unless you have a lot of content on the site sorted into numerous Categories and Tags.

What is important to consider here is that Google will index all of these pages. First, they won't be good for getting search rankings (the content will always be changing as you add new posts), and second, it could be considered duplicate content pages if you have numerous that are nearly identical.

When you combine all of these things together, I simply avoid this system completely because it is just not worth the headache and the lack of control.

5-4 WORDPRESS PAGES

In the previous chapter, I went over the WP Post system. In that chapter, I explained a number of the important areas on the post creation screen. Many of those sames areas exist when you create pages, so I will not revisit those particular points. In that regard, make sure you have read the previous chapter before going through this chapter.

In WordPress, the **Pages** menu can be found in the main sidebar menu on the left:

Unlike Posts, the Pages menu only has two links – one to view/edit existing pages and another to create a new page.

This means that Categories and Tags ARE NOT USED with Pages!

In WordPress, Pages are not grouped together at all – they're just simply website pages.

There are a few reasons why I like using Pages instead of Posts:

1. I get to control all of the content in Pages.

2. Pages are not associated with a specific date. This is definitely better for sites that will not be updated on a regular basis! I also believe date based posts can sometimes lose their ranking power on search engines over time, while pages do not seem to experience it (just my personal opinion here but could be true).

3. I can still manually group pages together and even create my own customized "Category" pages (not WP Categories – WP Pages that essentially act like a Category page by linking to related pages on the site).

I am now going to create a WP Page to show you how this system works and how it compares to the post system.

Start out by clicking on the **Add New** link in the **Pages** menu.

You should notice that everything looks very familiar here because it is extremely similar to the **Add New Post** page.

I'm going to go ahead and set the title and content of this page to be identical to the previous page, so the differences will easily stand out. I went ahead and deleted the previous Post that I created.

The picture below shows that initial content being added to the **Add New Page** screen:

The main differences with the Page editor compared with the Post editor actually involve the various settings boxes that are on the page.

For example, the **Categories** and **Tags** boxes are no longer in the right-hand column.

Another main difference, at least if you are using the Weaver II theme, are the options that are provided by the theme for Pages. There are actually many more options available here than there were for Posts, yet another reason why I like to use Pages over Posts.

Here is the top section of options available through Weaver II on the Page Editor:

Weaver II Options For This Page   ▼

Page Templates ⑦   (This Page's ID: 13)
Please click the (?) for more information about all the Weaver II Page Templates.

Per Page Options ⑦
These settings let you hide various elements on a per page basis.
☐ Hide Page Title   ☐ Hide Site Title/Tagline   ☐ Hide Menus   ☐ Hide Standard Header Image
☐ Hide Entire Header   ☐ Hide Info Bar on this page   ☐ Hide Entire Footer
Note: the following hide "Page on Primary Menu" options work with the default menu - not custom menus.
☐ Hide Page on the default Primary Menu   ☐ Hide Page on mobile devices (default menu only)
☐ Hide Page on the default Primary Menu if logged in   ☐ Hide Page on the default Primary Menu if NOT logged in
☐ Menu "Placeholder" page. Useful for top-level menu item - don't go anywhere when menu item is clicked.
☐ Disable Visual Editor for this page. Useful if you enter simple HTML or other code.
☐ Allow Raw HTML and scripts. Disables auto paragraph, texturize, and other processing.
                        ▾   Select *Sidebar Layout* for this page - overrides default Page layout.
              Per Page body Class - CSS class name to add to HTML <body> block. Allows Per Page custom styling.

At the top are a number of checkboxes that control the display of various parts of the website, so you can easily disable page titles, menus, headers, footers, and more.

The drop-down box towards the bottom of this picture is something I commonly find myself using. You can easily disable the sidebar entirely on a specific page using this drop-down box (other options are also available, but this is the most common reason I use it).

Even more options, that are not pictured above, can be used to hide or show specific widget areas on a specific page (without affecting other pages on the site).

I'm going to go ahead and publish this page so you can see what it will look like live:

At the top, there is still the breadcrumb link that goes back to the home page (this can be disabled in the Weaver II options – it is the **Info Bar**).

Beyond the breadcrumb link, the only other content that gets displayed on this page is content that I have complete control over! This is why I like to use Pages – because they are not filled up with junk content that I can't control and may not even be that helpful for the visitors of my site (at least with the way I build sites).

This allows me to make each page into whatever I need it to be. If I want to make a page that has some content and then links out to other pages on my site (ie, a custom-made category page), then I can simply build the page that way.

Obviously, the idea of doing something like that may be a bit daunting for a first-time user.

You may actually be thinking that the Post system looks easy to use, while my method looks more complicated. Honestly, that is entirely true.

The point of using the Page system is not to make it easier on the site builder but to make the site better and easier to use for your website visitors.

I believe it makes more sense to take the hard part so I can make it easier for my site visitors. After all, isn't that who the site is really being made to cater to?

5-5 WORDPRESS CORE, PLUGINS & THEME UPDATES

Although there are plenty of other minor things about WordPress and/or special ways that you could use the system, I have at least explained all of the basic concepts needed to build a site so far.

The last thing that I need to talk to you about before I conclude this lesson involves maintaining your site by keeping your software up-to-date.

WordPress is obviously updated on a regular basis, as are many plugins and themes used with WordPress. To take advantage of these new versions that could have bug fixes or even new features, you simply have to perform the updates.

To start, click on the **Updates** link in the **Dashboard** menu:

On this page, you'll be able to perform updates (when available) for everything.

Here is a look at my page at the moment:

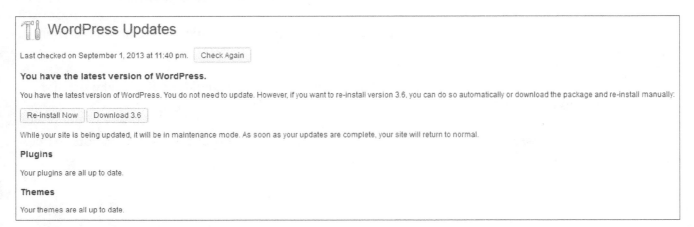

There are actually not any updates available right now because this is a fresh installation using the latest version of WordPress. Any software I have installed (plugins/themes) was done directly through WordPress, so that also obtained the most recent versions for me.

However, this page can easily change at any time. When Updates are available, you'll actually see a black circle with a number in it next to Updates in the Dashboard menu. That number indicates how many updates are available for your site.

Here's what that black circle with a number will look like:

Whenever you see a number show up there, just visit this page to perform the update.

Here is another site of mine that has updates available:

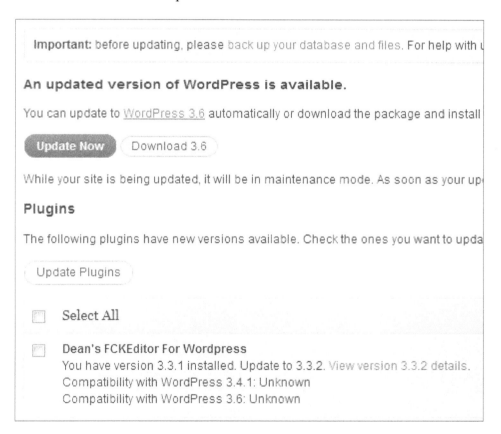

All you have to do to perform a WordPress update is simply click the **Update Now** button.

To update plugins/themes, just click on the checkbox next to what you want to update and click the **Update Plugins** or **Update Themes** button.

WordPress Backups

Note the message in the yellow box at the top that says you should back up your database and files before performing an update. This allows you a way to undo the changes if it causes problems with your live site. For most of you, it is probably a good idea to do this to ensure you don't run into any problems. Make sure you backup both the files in the public_html folder of your site and the entire WordPress database – both will be needed to restore the site.

I've covered backups previously in my cPanel training class for Techie Master Class. I thought I would just share that particular class with you here to be sure that you have that information. I could have simply added that information to this ebook, but there are other things in this cPanel class that you will likely find useful, if you haven't already seen this.

Get my cPanel training ebook and video here, along with four more Techie Master Class ebooks and videos (nothing to buy here): http://ryanstevensonplugins.com/tmc/

6 SITE CONSTRUCTION 1/2

In the sixth class, we finally begin to build the actual website. The website construction has been broken down into two classes, so this class is the first part. We'll get started with a tutorial on writing content and also writing to get good search engine rankings. After that, we will move on to create the home page of the site and three category pages. Finally, we will learn how to create a custom HTML menu to use on the home page to link to the category pages.

Primary Lesson Objective

☐ Create your Home Page, 3 Category Pages & an HTML Menu

Lesson Steps Checklist

☐ Learn How to Write Useful, Creative Content for Affiliate Sites

☐ Learn How to Write for Great Search Engine Rankings

☐ Build the Home Page of your Website

☐ Build Three Category Pages for your Website

☐ Create a Custom HTML & CSS Menu for the Home Page

Chapter Notes

Chapter Notes

6-1 CONTENT & SEO WRITING

Before you write a single word of your site, it is important to understand the ultimate goals of your writing. Obviously, you are building the site to try to refer sales on Amazon products to earn commissions, but you don't just want to build a complete site full of blatant product sales.

The entire concept behind my site building strategy is to build a useful and helpful website for consumers of a specific niche. The foremost goal is to educate the consumer to help to select the best product for their needs.

Think about this logically. There are a number of reasons why this approach works:

1. By helping and educating your site visitors, you are building trust with them in the only way that a simple website really can accomplish this goal. When you build that trust and help them out without asking for anything in return, people will buy. Obviously, not everyone is going to buy, but enough will to make it worth your while.

2. When you help your site visitors buy a product that is best of their particular needs, especially when they are educated about all of the important topics relating to the product, then those consumers are much more likely to be happy with their purchase. When they're happy, they don't return the product to Amazon, which means you don't lose your commissions to refunds. When Amazon refunds a consumer, they take back the commission paid on that sale too, so it can help a lot to avoid this problem.

3. When you accomplish #1, you will get good search engine rankings and be able to maintain them long-term. Ultimately, trying to trick search engines is a fruitless labor because they will figure it out sooner or later – especially since they actually use real people to rate their live results to weed out sites that are using spamming or other devious tactics to gain their rankings. Google wants websites that are useful for a specific topic, so why try to fight it? Just embrace this one simple fact and everything else follows in due time.

Try to always keep this in the back of your mind while you work on your site, especially when you are writing.

Writing Basics
Writing in general is something that actually scares a lot of people. The truth is that everyone can

write – all you have to do is translate your spoken words into text.

Yes, you do want to try your best to avoid spelling and grammar errors, but you also don't have to obsess about it being perfect. As long as the information being your writing is sound and that information is easy to pick up from your writing, then everything will be fine.

One of the biggest writing mistakes is actually trying to get too fancy or complicated. Just take the facts and put them in your own words. You don't have to be an Amazon Shakespeare.

If you aren't comfortable with writing and don't have a lot of knowledge on a subject, you can actually just collect information from a wide variety of sources online and essentially rehash that information on your own site in a useful way that uses your own words.

Think of this like natural, manual article spinning. If you don't already know, article spinning is typically an automated method that takes writing and rewrites it (but usually does a really poor job rehashing it in a way that makes sense).

Here is a good practice example for you to try...

First, start with this sentence:

Down comforters keep you warm.

Now, try rewriting that sentence without reusing all of the same primary words: down, comforters, and warm. As long as the meaning is still basically the same but the words are different, you could reuse that sentence and still be unique.

Here are just a few quick examples I was able to come up with:

-Feather blankets are a great heat insulator.

-Bed covers with fuzzy, soft filling are perfect for use in the winter.

All these sentences use completely different primary words but still basically mean the same thing.

If you can get comfortable with simply rewriting sentences, you can easily create entire websites about any topic in the world by simply researching the information and putting it into your own words.

The other key to writing is trying to convey the information to your reader in a way that makes sense. If there is any way to organize the information, start there. I often start with a broad topic, and then proceed to get more specific as I write.

Writing Structure

Think of writing a website page like presenting a case in a court of law. Start by summarizing your topic and objective of your writing, then proceed to provide points to prove your objective and elaborate on your summary in more detail, and finally provide a conclusion.

You don't necessarily have to maintain a structure like this for everything that you write, but you may find it helpful to get started writing this way if you are not very comfortable with it or completely new to it.

Think back to grade school when you learned how to write essays or do a science experiment. Everything had a very methodical approach that often started with brainstorming. You can take this same tactic and apply it to help you with your writing too.

When you start to write on a particular topic, just begin by brainstorming all of the main points you want to talk about. Then, make a list of these points and try to organize them – much like I did when I was coming up with a list of topics to use for the pages of my website.

Once you have a list of organized points that you want to talk about for a particular topic, try to arrange them in an order that makes sense. If one point depends on the information for another point, be sure to present the dependent information first and follow up with the rest. This helps to ensure that people don't have to jump around in your writing to actually learn what you are trying to teach.

With your list of points arranged, you can simply elaborate on each point to create the body of your article. Then provide a summary / introduction before the body along with a conclusion after it.

One more thing worth mentioning is that you don't have to stick to plain sentence and paragraph writing. Think about the information you want to get across to your site visitors.

If you need to list a number of things, use an HTML list instead of trying to put that information into a series of sentences and/or paragraphs. There are tons of instances like this when simplicity really makes more sense. It is easier on you, it will look better on your live website to break up large areas of text, your site visitors will find it more engaging, and search engines will even love it.

Also try to think about instances where other types of content may work for a topic in addition to writing. You should always provide some writing along with each of the pages of your site, but you may also want to include pictures, audio, and/or video when it fits to do so. These types of content are definitely more engaging for your site visitors.

As long as you are writing some unique content of your own for each of your site pages, it is OK to go out on the internet to try to find additional content that you could use. A YouTube video is a great example of something like this – just embed an existing video along with your own unique content and perhaps an advertisement.

SEO Writing

There are tons of strategies out there on SEO writing and methods that people will recommend to use on your site to get better search rankings. However, I truly do not follow a specific format for my writing.

With each page that you build on your site, you'll obviously have a particular keyword phrase in mind that you want to target. The worst thing you can do is to overuse that keyword phrase on that page.

First, make sure you have researched your topic that you are writing about. With general knowledge and keyword phrases, most people could probably write an article about a topic while knowing nearly nothing about it. However, you'll find writing easier to do when you actually have decent knowledge on your subject matter.

When it comes to your content, Google doesn't want to see a particular keyword phrase repeated over and over again. They want to see a page that is ABOUT a particular keyword phrase.

Since I'm writing about down comforters, I will want to be sure to use relational keyword phrases without overusing those two words. This could be a long list of potential words like bedding, fill power, thread count, feathers, stitching, pillows, sleep, etc.

Beyond using plenty of relational words of your target keyword phrase, you want to be sure to write naturally. That means using plenty of general words that could be found in any given article. This basically just means that if you are simply listing keyword phrases and relational words, you're doing it wrong – they must be used within natural writing (how it would sound if you were talking about those keywords and relational words).

Keyword Density

Many first-time writers and even seasoned experts can find themselves using their target keywords too frequently in their writing.

If you're using your entire phrase in more than 3-5% of your content, you're easily treading into dangerous waters with keyword spam. However, these limits may not apply to individual words. For example, my target phrase is down comforter guide.

I definitely don't want to overuse that phrase, but if the word "down" is used a bit heavily in my content, that will be OK (and likely expected unless there are other words that could be used and mean the exact same thing).

If you find that you are using your target words too often, try to imply those words in your writing or simply replace them with synonyms (other words that mean the same thing).

For example, instead of saying "down comforter this..." and "down comforter that...". I could use it at the beginning of a paragraph in the first sentence, and them simply refer to the "down comforter" as "it" in other sentences in the paragraph.

You really do not want to obsess with your keyword density as your are writing your content, but your definitely want to be confident that you aren't overdoing it before you publish your writing on your website.

WordPress users can use one of a variety of free plugins to help them check their keyword density.

One that I often use is called Keyword Statistics. Just search for it through **Plugins → Add New** in the WordPress admin menu.

After you install the plugin, just look for it in the admin menu on the left, as seen in the picture on the next page.

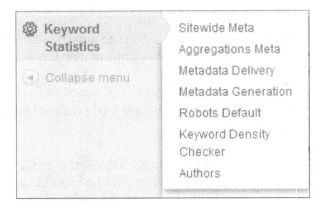

First, visit the **Metadata Delivery** page. If you use SEO Ultimate, that plugin already handles a number of the things that Keyword Statistics will try to do, so we need to disable these things.

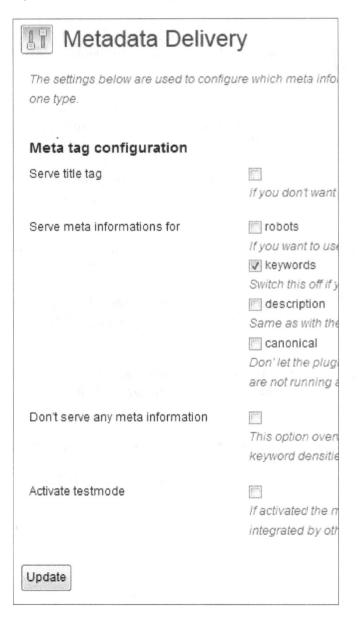

Under **Serve meta informations for**, deselect the check next to **robots, description**, and **canonical** – just leave **keywords** checked. Then click the **Update** button to save your changes.

Next, go to the **Keyword Density Checker** link in the admin menu for **Keyword Statistics**.

On this page, you can set the default language to use (if you are not building an English site).

Beyond the language selection, there are two other things that I want to do on this page:

1. In the **Items in keyword lists** drop-down box, select **10** instead of 5. This provides us with more keyword densities for our content.

2. Deselect the checkbox for **Automatic Update**. Without this, the editor page can lag if you have a decent amount of content on a single page. We'll simply update keyword densities manually from that page when we want to check them.

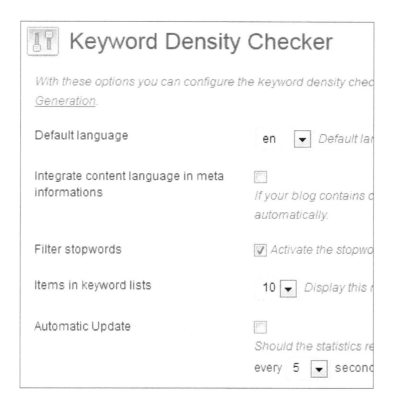

I didn't include **Keyword Statistics** in the initial plugin setup because I don't consider it to be an essential plugin for all of your sites. Once you've been writing content for a while, you may find that you don't need it anymore, but it can be very handy for beginners.

For this particular site, it isn't entirely useful because it actually strips out the word "down" as a stop word, and the plugin doesn't offer an easy way to edit those. You can still view keyword densities with stop words included, but most of them end up being real stop words like "the".

To actually use this plugin, just look for the **Keyword Statistics** box in the WordPress page editor.

Use the Update button to refresh the information. One word, two word and three word phrases, their counts and percentages are shown.

The main idea here is to simply ensure that you are not overusing your keywords, so make sure you have a variety of words showing up here, although your main words should still have a presence in these lists.

The **Keywords** text box will be automatically filled with your top used single word keywords, but I recommend unchecking the "use generated keywords" box and proving your own. You can use single words or multi word phrases. Split each phrase with a comma and do not provide too many (5-8 words/phrases total is a good max level).

The **Title, Robots,** and **Description** settings here will not actually do anything since we have disabled them in the plugin settings. With that said, don't bother spending time on them here (all of these things are controlled through SEO Ultimate instead).

6-2 HOME PAGE CREATION

To start creating the home page of your site, click on **Add New** in the **Pages** menu:

Next, provide a title for your page at the top of the page editor. For my home page, I usually just title it after my primary keyword phrase.

After you enter the title, a URL will automatically be designated for the page based on your title (highlighted in yellow below):

Notice how it used the words **comforter** and **guide** in the URL but not **down**. WordPress is actually recognizing down as a stop word, so it doesn't use it in the URL. A stop word is a word that typically does not have any specific meaning in a sentence. **Down** used as a directional indicator would be a stop word but this usage of **down** is not.

If this was a normal page on my site, I might want to manually edit this URL to add the word down back on the beginning of it (be sure to split words with hyphens if you edit the URL). However, since this is going to be the home page of my site, I don't need to worry about the URL.

Next, I simply need to add the content of my page into the large editor window below the title.

For this tutorial, I have obviously had to go ahead and write my content ahead of time. Instead of writing it in the live class, I can actually talk to you about it here to explain it in more detail.

At least for the home page of the site, I wanted to actually show you the content here so I can explain why I did what I did.

To start, I have a brief introduction:

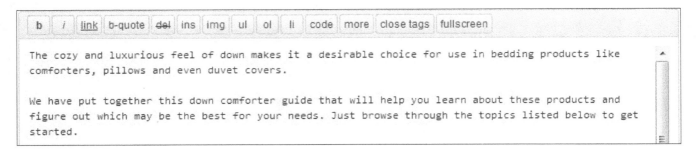

```
b  i  link  b-quote  del  ins  img  ul  ol  li  code  more  close tags  fullscreen

The cozy and luxurious feel of down makes it a desirable choice for use in bedding products like
comforters, pillows and even duvet covers.

We have put together this down comforter guide that will help you learn about these products and
figure out which may be the best for your needs. Just browse through the topics listed below to get
started.
```

Note the use of a number of relational words and then the use of my primary keyword phrase, down comforter guide, in the second paragraph. I try to include my target phrase in the first two paragraphs. This content is just meant as a brief introduction for the site visitors and also to satisfy search engines a bit.

Next, I want to introduce the main category pages of the site and possibly sub-category pages too. For this tutorial, I have three main category pages and have listed five of their sub-pages. You don't have to list the sub-pages here, especially if you have a lot of them. However, it can be good to provide some easy navigation to the important pages of your site on the home page on way or another.

I will actually be creating some custom HTML to use here to draw attention to this portion of my page, but for now, I just need to worry about getting the text in place that I want to use.

```
Buying Guide
Learn about the important features to truly understand these products so you can select one that is
right for you.
--Comforter Sizes
--Fill Power
--Thread Count
--Color Selection
--Down Alternative

Consumer Concerns
Find out about the most common points of concern for users, and how to avoid these problems when
selecting your own.
--Shifting Feathers
--Leaking Feathers
--Washing Down Comforters
--Lightweight Down for Summer
--Hypoallergenic Down

Brands
Read our brand reviews on a few of the most popular companies, and browse some of our top product
picks.
--Pinzon
---Primaloft
---Pyrenees
--Ikea
--Pacific Coast
```

Next, I continue with more content. For now, this will just be basic text, but that will change as this page progresses.

The content that you use here could really be anything, as long as it is highly relational to your target keyword phrase and niche.

Since down and specifically down comforters are my main topics on this site, I want to talk about them more. This gives me a chance to provide the user with some useful information so they can quickly identify this as a useful website, and it also allows me to earn some brownie points with search engines.

To start, I talked about the down filler of these comforters, especially since this isn't really a main topic of any of the pages of my site.

```
What is Down?
The down that is used in bedding sets is actually the feathers of birds - but not just any feather.

There are actually many different types, but the kind that we sleep on at night is called body down.
It is a fluffy feather that is found under the flight feathers of a bird.

We use it for the same reason birds do - it is a great thermal insulator because of the loose and
airy structure. The specific type that we use is ideal because it also happens to be extremely soft
and fuzzy.

This isn't something that humans started doing recently either. Bird down has been used by humans
for many centuries for a variety of purposes including religious ceremonies!

Most down used in comforters and other bedding materials these days comes from domesticated geese.

However, some of it comes from wild Eider ducks in the mountains of northern Europe. Eider down is
considered to be the most luxurious in the entire world with a fill power of up to 1200 - twice that
of average goose down.

While higher fill power is great for comfort, the average consumer will find goose to offer plenty
of insulation, while Eider is often only recommended for the coldest regions. A fill rating of 550
offers great insulation and comfort but not too much heat, especially in the summer months.
```

Next, I provide a bit of information that gets more specific towards the products I am targeting. This is very helpful information for consumers and geared towards earning their trust.

```
Product Labeling
One of the most confusing things about products made with this material is how companies actually
label them. Not all down comforters are made entirely of real feathers - some of them use a mixture
of real and synthetic fibers.

In the USA, there are regulations that require companies to maintain certain levels of down feathers
depending on how they label their products. The most common labeling has been listed below to help
you understand how this works.

100% Down - Must contain nothing but real down feathers.
Goose Down - Must contain a minimum of 90% goose feathers.
Down - This vague labeling can actually be used for products that are simply a mixture of synthetic
fibers and real down feathers, although there is not a required feather percentage.
```

Most industries have something about them that companies will often try to use to confuse or possibly deceive consumers, so this makes a great opportunity to bust through that confusion and gain the trust of your site visitors in the process.

All of this additional content is a bit boring for now, but this is something I can change as the site progresses. It is really easy to simply go back through the site to add images, style text in various areas, or make other changes to the content to break up the large paragraphs of text.

In general, you want to avoid large paragraphs – no more than a couple of lines of text all together. This helps with readability of your content, which is a lot more important than you might think.

I can highlight portions of text in my content and use the WordPress toolbar buttons at the top of the editor to easily add some basic styling to my text.

For example, if I highlight "What is Down?" and click on the "b" button in the toolbar, it will wrap that text in HTML strong tags (which will cause the text to show in bold text).

```
<strong>What is Down?</strong>
```

I am also going to do the same for other text at the bottom of the page: **Product Labeling, 100% Down, Goose Down,** and **Down**. This is what that part of the content looks like after I am done:

```
<strong>Product Labeling</strong>
One of the most confusing things a
label them. Not all down comforter
of real and synthetic fibers.

In the USA, there are regulations
depending on how they label their
you understand how this works.

<strong>100% Down</strong> - Must
<strong>Goose Down</strong> - Must
<strong>Down</strong> - This vague
```

The three down phrases that I changed at the bottom aren't really sentences – they're content that I wrote to be used in an HTML list. This can be easily done with WordPress buttons in the editor toolbar.

First, I want to select all of my list content:

```
<strong>100% Down</strong> - Must contain nothing but real down feathers.
<strong>Goose Down</strong> - Must contain a minimum of 90% goose feathers.
<strong>Down</strong> - This vague labeling can actually be used for products that are simply a
mixture of synthetic fibers and real down feathers, although there is not a required feather
percentage.
```

Next, I want to click on the "ul" button in the editor toolbar:

```
ul
```

This wraps my highlighted text in "ul" HTML tags, which designates this as a list. Now I need to select each row in the list to designate it as a list item. You can see the first row selected below:

```
<ul>
<strong>100% Down</strong> - Must contain nothing but real down feathers.
<strong>Goose Down</strong> - Must contain a minimum of 90% goose feathers.
<strong>Down</strong> - This vague labeling can actually be used for products that are simply a
mixture of synthetic fibers and real down feathers, although there is not a required feather
percentage.
</ul>
```

Now if I click on the "li" button, it will wrap "li" HTML tabs around the highlighted text. Continue to do this for each row (the last row of the list actually occupies three lines of text). Here is what this content looks like after I am done:

```
<ul>
        <li><strong>100% Down</strong> - Must contain nothing but real down feathers.</li>

        <li><strong>Goose Down</strong> - Must contain a minimum of 90% goose feathers.</li>

        <li><strong>Down</strong> - This vague labeling can actually be used for products that are
simply a mixture of synthetic fibers and real down feathers, although there is not a required
feather percentage.</li>

</ul>
```

Notice the three <li> tags at the beginning of each row in the list. I now want to add some custom CSS code to two of these three tags (the first two). At the end of the top two opening "li" tags (right before the closing greater than symbol), I want to add a blank space and then this HTML/CSS code:

style="margin-bottom:6px;"

This is how my code looks now:

```
<ul>
        <li style="margin-bottom:6px;"><strong>100% Down</strong> - Must contain nothing but real
down feathers.</li>

        <li style="margin-bottom:6px;"><strong>Goose Down</strong> - Must contain a minimum of 90%
goose feathers.</li>

        <li><strong>Down</strong> - This vague labeling can actually be used for products that are
simply a mixture of synthetic fibers and real down feathers, although there is not a required
feather percentage.</li>

</ul>
```

Here is what that looks like on the live site:

- **100% Down** – Must contain nothing but real down feathers.
- **Goose Down** – Must contain a minimum of 90% goose feathers.
- **Down** – This vague labeling can actually be used for products that are simply a mixture of synthetic fibers and real down feathers, although there is not a required feather percentage.

As you can see, this is much clearer, easier to understand and more visually appealing than it would have been if I just wrote another paragraph here.

SEO Settings

Below the page editor window, you'll find the **SEO Settings** box. For now, I am going to go ahead and set a description for my home page.

This description can potentially be used by search engines to show up in their search results, so we want this to quickly summarize the site in an appealing way that will help to increase the click through rate on our search result (which can also help to improve your rankings over time because Google considers results that get clicked on more often to be more relevant).

Here is what I have come up with for my home page meta description:

SEO Settings

Search Engine Listing   Social Networks Listing   Links   Miscellaneous

Title Tag:

You've entered 0 characters. Most search engines use up to 70.

Meta Description: Interested in down comforters? Learn about common consumer complaints and how to pick the best one for your needs in our extensive guide.

You've entered **137** characters. Most search engines use up to 140.

Read through that description a few times and really think about it for a minute.

Can you see what I am doing here?

I'm accomplishing a few goals with this short bit of text:

1. I'm screening my potential leads immediately to target the right people browsing through the search results. I want visitors on my site that are considering buying down comforters, especially those that might have some questions or concerns before they purchase.

2. I'm already trying to build trust with my potential site visitor. A site that just exists for sales wouldn't blatantly invite you in to talk about consumer complaints, so the entire second sentence is also designed towards gaining their trust and changing their preconceived notions about your site before they even visit your site.

3. I'm offering up some keywords that are either the same or highly relational to my target phrase. Down, comforters, and guide can all be found in that description (but not necessarily all together). This makes the keyword placement much more natural and keeps the focus on the message you really want to get across with your description.

Weaver II Options

Below the SEO Settings, you will find the **Weaver II Options**.

Here I want to select the checkboxes for **Hide Page Title** and **Hide Info Bar**.

I also want to select the **No** sidebars options from the drop-down for **Select Sidebar Layout**.

The picture below shows what these settings look like when I am done:

Weaver II Options For This Page

Page Templates (?)
Please click the (?) for more information a|

Per Page Options (?)
These settings let you hide various eleme|
☑ Hide Page Title ☐ Hide Site Title/Tagli
☐ Hide Entire Header ☑ Hide Info Bar o|
Note: the following hide "Page on Primary|
☐ Hide Page on the default Primary Menu
☐ Hide Page on the default Primary Menu
☐ Menu "Placeholder" page. Useful for to|
☐ Disable Visual Editor for this page. Use
☐ Allow Raw HTML and scripts. Disables
No sidebars, one column content ▼ S|
Per Page body Class

Set Home Page

I have more to do on this page, but for now, I am going to go ahead and publish it (blue button in the upper-right corner of the page editor).

I will be revisiting this page to do more work later in this class and again before site construction is complete.

The last thing that I need to do before I proceed is to actually set this page as the home page for my site.

First, click on **Reading** in the **Settings** admin menu:

Settings   General
SEO 23   Writing
                     Reading
ExtendAzon   Discussion
Keyword   Media
Statistics   Permalinks
                     SEO Ultimate
Collapse menu   WP Super Cache

At the top of the **Reading Settings** page, you'll see a setting called **Front page displays**.

On the right, you'll see two circles, with the top one selected. Click on the second circle (**A static page**) to select it and deselect the first.

Now the drop-down boxes below the second circle are available to be used. The first drop-down box, for **Front page**, is the one you want. Just select the page you created.

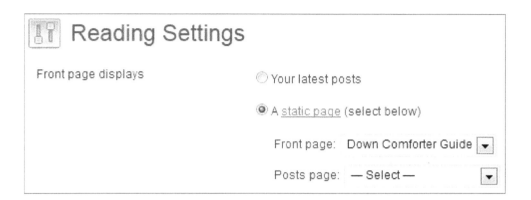

This designates the custom page we created as the home page of the site instead of using the standard blog-style listing of recent posts on the site.

6-3 CATEGORY PAGES CREATION

Now I am going to proceed with creating my category pages. These will basically act just like the home page of the site and link up to other pages, except they are going to be more specialized.

If you remember from previous classes, I mentioned that I don't actually use the WordPress Category and Post system. I create WordPress pages, just like I did for the home page.

Since these pages will be created in a very similar manner to the home page, I won't go through every single detail about them. After the live class for this session, you can actually visit the home page of DownComforterGuide.com to see these pages in complete detail.

Depending on how you have decided to organize your site, it may make sense to build your category pages in a particular way. They could be done just like the home page, but they could also be done somewhat differently.

To show you at least one other possible way you can change up the way you present other pages on your site, I have decided to make my category pages a bit different from the home page.

Now I am going to create my first category page: **Buying Guide**. This page will have five other pages that it links to – all of which are buying guide related topics.

This gets created just like the home page. Go to **Pages → Add New.** Then provide a title and the page content.

For this page, I am going to title it: **The Essential Down Comforter Buying Guide**

Take a look at the URL that was automatically generated for this page:

The Essential Down Comforter Buying Guide

Permalink: http://downcomforterguide.com/ essential-comforter-buying-guide / | OK | Cancel

---

This URL uses 4 of the 6 words from my title. I could simply leave it like it is, or I could change it. How do I decide which? If I change it, what do I change it to?

Think about all of your planned page titles and imagine them getting transformed in URL form like this. Do you foresee many of the pages containing the same word(s) in the URL? If the answer is yes, then I recommend trying to strip those words out of the URL in many situations.

This is even more true if those words are part of the primary keyword phrase for your entire site. You simply don't want to get into keyword spam territory, and page URLs is another area where this can easily happen.

For my site, "down" and "comforter"/"comforters" will be very common words (and are also part of my primary keyword phrase), so I want to strip these out from many of my pages.

For this page, I am simply going to change the URL to "buying-guide".

When you think about it, this really makes perfect sense. It is simple, and it is really the base keyword phrase that I am trying to target (minus the main part of my primary keyword phrase, which is implied on my site – down comforter).

As a result, this page should have decent potential to rank for the phrase "down comforter buying guide".

Now on to the actual content of the page.

```
Before you can actually buy a down comforter, there are really a number of things that you need to
learn about so you can make an educated decision when it comes to selecting the right product for
your needs.

This buying guide has been put together to help you with that decision making process by providing
you with reliable information in one location.

Most people research products before they purchase them, but this process is more important with
down comforters than it is with many other goods. Browse through our topics below to get started.

Comforter Sizes
Just like beds, comforters are sold in different sizes. If you already own a bed, you likely know
what size you need to buy. However, if you have not yet bought a bed or need to figure out what size
you already own, this guide is the first step in the decision making process.

It is important not to go by dimensions alone. Different bed sizes require accessories of various
sizes, so we have provided you with a size chart to help you figure out what you need.

Fill Power
Down feathers are rated based on their fill power, which is a number presented to the consumer. This
number represents how much space an ounce of down occupies. Higher fill numbers results in better
thermal insulation and comfort.

Use our fill power chart as a guide to figure out what these numbers really mean so you can figure
out what comforter is best for you. Most people assume that a higher number is best, but this is
definitely not always true. Different people have different needs, so be sure to make this your
second stop to learn.
```

I start with a summary, just like I did with the home page. I then follow it up with a heading and a decent description for each of the pages that I will link to from this category page.

```
Thread Count
Another important but often confusing aspect about comforters or other bedding products like sheets
is the thread count. This is actually the number of threads of material in a square inch of the
product, both horizontally and vertically.

This count is intended to measure fabric quality, with higher numbers being higher quality material
and often more comfortable. However, some companies have been able to artificially inflate their
numbers, so it is important to learn more about this before you buy.

Color Selection
Most people like to decorate their homes and will often give each room a particular theme. When they
are shopping for bedding goods like down comforters, they may be searching for a specific color.

White is the most common color to find, although a wide variety of other colors are actually
available. In general, if you are searching for something besides white, you may need to be willing
to sacrifice a brand preference to get your desired color.

Down Alternative
In recent years, a new type of down comforter has been made available to consumers - alternative
down. What exactly is the filling for these products, and when might you need to consider one of
them instead of traditional down?

Whether you end up getting a down alternative or the real thing, it is important to have knowledge
on this subject before you make a final choice. There are a number of reasons why someone might want
this type of product, despite the fact that it can often be cheaper than real down.
```

The rest of this category page should be set up and published just like the home page, with one exception – the Weaver II options.

Weaver II Options For This Page

Page Templates ⑦
Please click the (?) for more information about all the

Per Page Options ⑦
These settings let you hide various elements on a pe
☐ Hide Page Title ☐ Hide Site Title/Tagline ☐ Hide
☐ Hide Entire Header ☑ Hide Info Bar on this page
Note: the following hide "Page on Primary Menu" optio
☐ Hide Page on the default Primary Menu ☐ Hide P
☐ Hide Page on the default Primary Menu if logged in
☐ Menu "Placeholder" page. Useful for top-level men
☐ Disable Visual Editor for this page. Useful if you en
☐ Allow Raw HTML and scripts. Disables auto parag
    ▼ Select *Sideba*
Per Page body Class - CSS class

This time around, we want to show the page title, so don't check that box, but still check the box to hide the info bar. Also, do not select any Sidebar Layout this time because we want to use the standard sidebar on the right-hand side of the public website.

I will now proceed with creating the two additional category pages for the site: **Consumer Concerns** and **Brands**. These will be done in the exact same manner as the **Buying Guide** category page, so I will not get repetitive and show that here. However, the content from these pages can always be viewed on the live site.

6-4 CUSTOM HTML MENU CREATION

The last thing that I will be doing for this part of the site construction process is creating a custom HTML menu to use on my home page. This menu is going to link out to the category pages of my site as well as a number of the other secondary pages of the site.

Remember the section of my home page that I said I would be turning into custom HTML to make it more appealing and eye-catching? Now is the time to make that happen. That section of my home page content has three different parts – one for each of my site categories. For each of those three parts, I need to add some HTML code. Here is the base HTML code that I will be using for each part (so I will use this code a total of three times on this home page):

```
<div class="dcg-box dcg-box-margin">
<div class="dcg-box-title">
LINKED CATEGORY PAGE TITLE
</div>
<div class="dcg-box-description">
BRIEF CATEGORY DESCRIPTION
<div class="dcg-box-image">
THUMBNAIL IMAGE (150x150) - LINKED TO CATEGORY PAGE
</div>
<ul class="dcg-box-list">
<li>
LINKED PAGE TITLE
</li>
<li>
LINKED PAGE TITLE
</li>
<li>
LINKED PAGE TITLE
</li>
<li>
LINKED PAGE TITLE
</li>
<li>
LINKED PAGE TITLE
</li>
</ul></div><div style="clear:both;"></div></div>
```

Notice the text portions of that code that are in all caps – these are the portions of the code that should be changed each time it is used. There is a category title, description, and image location, as well as 5 locations for linked page titles.

It may actually be easier to take the content from your page and paste it into the base code (overwriting the capital letters).

Replace the category title, description and page titles. Leave the image text in place for now – we will change this is just a moment.

Depending on the HTML being used in WordPress, you may need to remove all of the line breaks from the code to prevent WordPress from automatically adding paragraph HTML tags (which can mess up the intended look/spacing of your content). I'll show you how this is done quickly in the live class.

Add Images

With the edited code in place on your site, we need to add our images. Find some type of relational image that is legal to use (I discussed things like this in previous classes). We can then upload the image as a category image to use here.

To start, I want to select the image text that I will be replacing in my HTML code. Here is the first part of my HTML code, for the **Buying Guide** category:

```
<div class="dcg-box dcg-box-margin"><div class="dcg-box-title"><a href="">Buying Guide</a></div><div
class="dcg-box-description">Learn about the important features to truly understand these products so
you can select one that is right for you.<div class="dcg-box-image">THUMBNAIL IMAGE (150x150) -
LINKED TO CATEGORY PAGE</div><ul class="dcg-box-list"><li><a href="">Comforter Sizes</a></li><li><a
href="">Fill Power</a></li><li><a href="">Thread Count</a></li><li><a href="">Color Selection</a>
</li><li><a href="">Down Alternative</a></li></ul></div><div style="clear:both;"></div></div>
```

Now, click on the **Add Media** button towards the top of the page:

Click on the **Upload Files** link at the top:

Then click on the **Select Files** button in the middle of the screen:

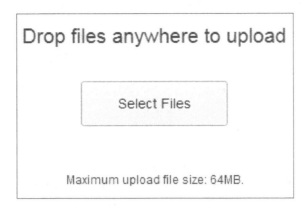

Find and select the image file on your computer that you want to use. Once you do that and the image finishes uploading, look in the bottom-right of the screen for the **Attachment Display Settings**.

Select **None** from the **Link To** drop-down box, and then select **Thumbnail** from the **Size** drop-down box.

Above that group of settings, you could also set **Alt** Text for the image. This is text that will show up if in place of the image if it is unable to display for some reason (like if it doesn't load or if the user simply has images disabled in their browser).

This **Alt Text** rarely gets seen by public site visitors, but search engines will pick it up, so it is often used by marketers for keyword targeting. Personally, I like to set something here, especially for important images on my site, but I also try to be very careful with keyword spam. Be specific with your **Alt Text** and briefly describe your image without going overboard or using too many keywords.

Once you're done, just click the blue **Insert into page** button in the bottom-right. This adds the image in place of the selected text in your HTML code. Just repeat this process for the other categories to complete the images and the HTML code.

Now we need to link up the category title and the image to the corresponding category page.

Here is my current HTML code for the first box, which is for the Buying Guide category:

```
<div class="dcg-box dcg-box-margin"><div class="dcg-box-title">Buying Guide</div><div class="dcg-
box-description">Learn about the important features to truly understand these products so you can
select one that is right for you.<div class="dcg-box-image"><img src="http://downcomforterguide.com
/wp-content/uploads/2013/09/white-down-closeup-150x150.jpg" alt="white-down-closeup" width="150"
height="150" class="alignnone size-thumbnail wp-image-29" /></div><ul class="dcg-box-list"><li><a
href="">Comforter Sizes</a></li><li><a href="">Fill Power</a></li><li><a href="">Thread Count</a>
</li><li><a href="">Color Selection</a></li><li><a href="">Down Alternative</a></li></ul></div><div
style="clear:both;"></div></div>
```

I have selected Buying Guide towards the beginning of this code – this is the page title. Now I want to click on the "link" button in the editor toolbar:

link

This opens the Insert/edit link window. At the bottom of this window, look for the downward pointing arrow with the text **Or link to existing content** next to it.

Click on that arrow/text to get a list of the existing pages on the site. Simply find the page that corresponds to the link you want to create, click on it in the list, and then click the blue Add Link button in the bottom-right.

This adds the link HTML around the text you had selected.

Now you want to repeat that same process with the image HTML code (select everything from the less than symbol through the greater than symbol). You can see the previous link that was created and this selected HTML for the image below:

```
<div class="dcg-box dcg-box-margin"><div class="dcg-box-title"><a href="http://downcomforterguide.com
/buying-guide/" title="The Essential Down Comforter Buying Guide">Buying Guide</a></div><div
class="dcg-box-description">Learn about the important features to truly understand these products so
you can select one that is right for you.<div class="dcg-box-image"><img
src="http://downcomforterguide.com/wp-content/uploads/2013/09/white-down-closeup-150x150.jpg"
alt="white-down-closeup" width="150" height="150" class="alignnone size-thumbnail wp-image-29"
/></div><ul class="dcg-box-list"><li><a href="">Comforter Sizes</a></li><li><a href="">Fill Power</a>
</li><li><a href="">Thread Count</a></li><li><a href="">Color Selection</a></li><li><a href="">Down
Alternative</a></li></ul></div><div style="clear:both;"></div></div>
```

The addition of these two links now means that the header category title and the category image will link up to the category page

You may also notice that I actually have blank links set up for the remaining page titles in each of the boxes. These will eventually link up to those pages on my site, but they do not currently exist (will be creating them in the next class). I put the blank links there so the text would display correctly on the site according to the rules I have set in the CSS code (which I will cover in just a moment).

At the very end of the three parts of HTML code, add this one line of HTML code:

** **

This prevents content after this point from wrapping up into space that should be reserved for those three category sections in our HTML code (it clears the float CSS we used on those HTML boxes to get them to sit next to each other).

Theme CSS Code for Home Page

The last thing we need to do is to set the CSS code that controls how this custom HTML code gets displayed on the public website.

I have already created this code for you, and you can simply copy and paste it into your site without making any modifications.

If you are using a theme other than Weaver II or find yourself needing to arrange things a bit different from the way I have, you may be able to make minor changes to your CSS (like adjusting the width of various elements) to get this code to work for your site too.

Here is the CSS code for my custom HTML on the home page:

```
.dcg-box
{
    width: 285px;
    float: left;
}
.dcg-box-margin
{
    margin-right: 15px;
}
.dcg-box-title
{
    text-align: center;
    padding: 5px 0px;
    border-bottom: 2px solid #B3B3B3;
}
.dcg-box-title a
{
    font-weight: bold;
    font-size: 24px;
    font-variant: small-caps;
}
```

```css
.dcg-box-description
{
    width: 100%;
    font-weight: normal;
    font-size: 15px;
    text-align: left;
    border-top: 1px solid #B3E0FF;
    padding: 10px 0;
}
.dcg-box-image
{
    width: 165px;
    float: left;
    padding-top: 10px;
}
.dcg-box-list
{
    width: 120px;
    float: left;
    padding-top: 10px;
    margin: 0;
}
.dcg-box-list
{
    list-style-type: none;
}
.dcg-box-list li, .dcg-box-list2 li
{
    margin-bottom: 6px;
}
.dcg-box-list li a, .dcg-box-list2 li a
{
    font-size: 12px;
    text-decoration: none;
}
```

All of this CSS code will need to be entered into your site to make these custom HTML menu boxes display correctly on your live site. Go to your WordPress site. Click on **Weaver II Admin** in the **Appearance** menu.

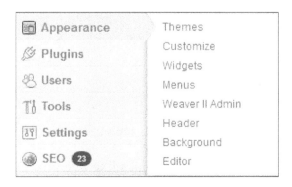

Now select **Advanced Options → <HEAD> Section** from the Weaver II menu at the top of the page:

Scroll down to the Custom CSS Rules section and paste the CSS code into the large text box:

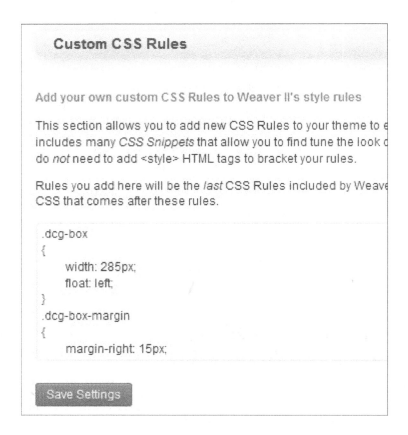

Click on **Save Settings** when you are done.

Now we can visit the live home page of our site to see our work.

Here is what the custom HTML we just created looks like live

The actual text sizes and design may be slightly different depending on your theme settings.

I am using 13px Helvetica fonts in Weaver II, as seen below (note the navigation at the top to get to this page):

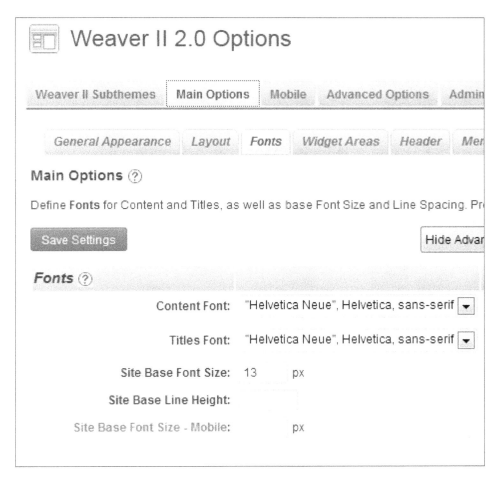

7 SITE CONSTRUCTION 2/2

We will now complete the construction of our site, with the exception of our Amazon advertising. We first need to create the remain content pages for the site. We can then build HTML menus for the Category Pages to link to all of the site content. We will then learn some additional tactics you can use to make your site more user-friendly and also help it rank better with search engines like interlinking your content, finalizing your site menus, and creating custom page widgets.

Primary Lesson Objective

☐ Complete Website Minus Amazon Advertising

Lesson Steps Checklist

☐ Build Additional Content Pages for the Site

☐ Create Custom HTML & CSS Menus for Category Pages

☐ Interlink Content on Your Site

☐ Finish Top Menu & Build Sidebar Menus

☐ Add Sidebar Menus as Custom WP Page Widgets

Chapter Notes

Chapter Notes

7-1 CREATION OF ADDITIONAL SITE PAGES & CONTENT

Now that we have the basic structure of the site set up and the category pages created, we can continue with creating the additional content pages for the site.

Your writing for these subjects should be very focused to ensure that you can pick up search traffic from some of your targeted secondary phrases, but still be sure to maintain an informative and helpful position throughout your writing.

When you can accomplish your goal of helping your site visitors, you'll be able to funnel them through links on your site to get to the right pages where they can complete a purchase.

In general, I have four different types of pages that I'll create on the site in addition to the home page and main category pages.

I have actually created an additional 16 pages on my site for this stage of the tutorial. However, I will just be discussing the four main types of pages here to avoid repetition.

All of the site content can simply be viewed on the live website at DownComforterGuide.com after the live class for this lesson has been held.

I've discussed the four main types of pages that I am building below.

About Page

The first page type that I create is actually just a personal preference of mine. I create an About Us page for my sites. I use this page to summarize the site and basically provide a mission statement.

In addition to that information, I will also use this page to add some generic legal disclaimers for the site – as long as those disclaimers do not need to be seen on specific pages (ie, on pages with Amazon ads).

This is at least one page of the site that can be left untargeted to any specific keyword phrase, and I actually believe it to be beneficial to have at least of couple of pages on the site that aren't heavily targeted to a keyword.

Sub-category Page

Some of my sites will have sub-category pages in addition to the main category pages – it really just depends on the content that I have planned for a given site.

For this tutorial, I actually have one sub-category page on the site – Pinzon. This page is being used as a sub-category for the PrimaLoft and Pyrenees pages, which will promote actual Amazon products. I could technically add some Amazon product ads to this main category page as well, although I would want to ensure that it did not take over the links to the other pages.

Feel free to change up the way you design your category and sub-category pages, if you are comfortable with doing so. This particular sub-category is actually going to be designed just like the main category pages of the site. I will be getting back to this during the next chapter of this guide when I create the HTML menus for the category pages and also for this one sub-category page.

Informational Page

A large majority of the pages on my site are going to be informational pages. Each of these pages should exist to educate the website visitors on a specific subject matter that is highly relational to my niche and the products I want to promote on Amazon.

The ultimate goal of these pages is to bring in search traffic, help them out with a problem to gain their trust, and then direct them along to another page of your site to complete a sale. This process actually allows you to screen your website visitors and pass them along to the page where they are most likely to buy something, which is much better than simply leaving them to blindly navigate your site in hopes that they stumble upon the right information.

Product Page

The last type of page that I build is a product page. These pages can exist solely to review and promote specific Amazon products or even highly relational groups of Amazon products. However, they could also be a combination of a product review page and an informational page.

The actual direction you take with your own sites is really up to you. I highly recommend that you do some experimenting of your own with your product pages to try a few different approaches to find out what works best for a particular niche or product type. What works the best for one niche may simply not work at all for another.

For this particular niche, I feel like maintaining the informational and helpful approach that I have started on the rest of the site is the best approach to try to sell these down comforters. I will be trying to direct people from their research or a consumer problem along to a relational product that should be appealing to them, so I want to try to solidify that approach on this last step by providing them with more helpful information about the products and/or brands.

All of the product pages on this site are going to be found in the brands category with the exception of the colors page in the buying guide. Some of those pages will just promote a single product, while others may promote bedding set packages or simply multiple comforters. I reached a decision on each of these pages individually based on the topic of the page and the products available on Amazon. Ads will be set up for these in the next class, number 8.

7-2 CUSTOM HTML MENUS FOR CATEGORY PAGES

Once all of my site pages are built and my content is in place, I can begin to link everything together. Just like I had previously done with the home page of my site to link up to the category pages, I can now do the same to my category pages to link them up to the new pages I've created on the site.

I could use a custom HTML menu for these category pages that is basically identical to the one I used on the home page of the site. However, I thought I would actually use a slightly different design for these pages just to give you some variety that you can use for your own sites. There really isn't a right or wrong way to do this for your own home page and category pages – whatever works best for your content, your niche, and the variety of pages you'll be building on the site.

I have three category pages: buying guide, consumer concerns, and brands. I also have a sub-category page for Pinzon. All four of these pages will be receiving this new custom HTML menu.

At the bottom of each of those four pages, I have headers and some text that go along with each of the sub-pages that I will be linking to from these category pages. This is the portion of my content that will be getting turned into a custom HTML menu.

Create Custom Menu HTML

To start, I have my basic format that I am using for each of these menu items:

```
<div class="dcg-box2">
<div class="dcg-box2-title">
LINKED PAGE TITLE
</div>
<div class="dcg-box2-description">
<div class="dcg-box2-image">
THUMBNAIL IMAGE (150x150) - LINKED TO PAGE
</div>
LONG PAGE DESCRIPTION
<a href="LINK TO YOUR PAGE">Read More&raquo;</a></div>
<div style="clear:both;"></div></div>
```

This HTML code works just like it did for the home page. The portions in capital letters will get replaced with your own content. Simply re-use this same base code for each menu item on each of the category pages.

I have taken this code and applied it to the first menu item on the brands page. I have uploaded an image to be used along with this menu item. That image, the page title, and also the Read More text at the end of the page description all get linked to the page.

At this point, you should be familiar with performing these tasks. However, if you find you need a refresher, just refer back to the previous class for more detailed info on creating links or uploading images.

You can see my final HTML code for this particular example below:

```
<div class="dcg-box2"><div class="dcg-box2-title"><a href="http://downcomforterguide.com/pinzon/"
title="Pinzon - An Amazon.com Exclusive Brand">Pinzon</a></div><div class="dcg-
box2-description"><div class="dcg-box2-image"><a href="http://downcomforterguide.com/pinzon/"
title="Pinzon - An Amazon.com Exclusive Brand"><img src="http://downcomforterguide.com/wp-content
/uploads/2013/09/pinzon-down-comforter-150x150.jpg" alt="Down comforter from Pinzon by Amazon"
width="150" height="150" class="alignnone size-thumbnail wp-image-101" /></a></div>Amazon.com has
their own private label brand called Pinzon. Their product line includes mostly household, personal
care and beauty products.

Pinzon products are only available by purchasing them online through Amazon, which gives them a
unique competitive advantage in this market. Since they do not run brick-and-mortar retail stores,
their overhead costs are significantly lower than other brands, which translates into lower prices
for consumers.

Even though Pinzon prices are very affordable, do not be deceived and instantly think that their
product quality is poor. In fact, they offer excellent products that are manufactured by the same
companies that make products for other quality brands.

Pinzon features two different types of down comforters called <a href="http://downcomforterguide.com
/pinzon-primaloft/" title="Pinzon PrimaLoft - Hypoallergenic, Alternative Down
Comforter">PrimaLoft</a> and <a href="http://downcomforterguide.com/pinzon-pyrenees/" title="Pinzon
Pyrenees - Real, White Goose Down Comforter">Pyrenees</a>. A page is available here to discuss each
of these and direct you to Amazon to purchase them, if you decide that one is right for you. <a
href="http://downcomforterguide.com/pinzon/" title="Pinzon - An Amazon.com Exclusive Brand">Read
More&raquo;</a></div><div style="clear:both;"></div></div>
```

There are a total of three menu items like this on this particular page for my site. Unlike the home page, I do not need to add any additional HTML code after all of the menu items.

I will then repeat this same process for all of my category and sub-category pages throughout the site.

Next, I need to add CSS code for this new menu design.

Start by going to the **Weaver II Admin** in the **Appearance** menu.

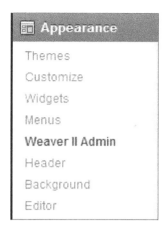

Now, navigate to the **Advanced Options** tab and then the **<HEAD> Section** tab.

This is the same page we visited in the last class to add CSS code for the home page menu.

Look for the **Custom CSS Rules** header.

The large text box there should already contain your CSS code for the home page menu.

DO NOT erase the home page menu CSS that we previously saved there.

We want to add new CSS code to the bottom of that existing code without messing up anything that is already there.

Just scroll down to the very bottom of the existing code. Create a blank line after all existing code and curly brackets.

I've already created the CSS code for you that you will need to use for this particular menu, just like I did for the home page menu.

You should not need to make any alterations to this code, although you are more than welcome to do so and adopt it for your own use if you are comfortable doing so.

Now, copy all of this CSS code and paste it into that blank line.

```css
.dcg-box2
{
    margin-top:20px;
}
.dcg-box2-title
{
    text-align: left;
    padding: 5px 0px;
    border-bottom: 2px solid #B3B3B3;
}
.dcg-box2-title a
{
    font-weight: bold;
    font-size: 32px;
    font-variant: small-caps;
}
.dcg-box2-description
{

    width: 100%;
    font-weight: normal;
    font-size: 16px;
    text-align: left;
    border-top: 1px solid #B3E0FF;
    padding: 10px 0;
}
.dcg-box2-image
{

    width: 165px;
    float: right;
    padding-top: 10px;
    padding-bottom: 10px;
    padding-left: 10px;
    text-align:center;
}
```

On the following page, you can see the Custom CSS Rules section.

The line that starts with **.dcg-box2** marks the beginning of this new code, while the previous code was the home page menu CSS.

Custom CSS Rules

Add your own custom CSS Rules to Weaver II's style rules

This section allows you to add new CSS Rules to your theme
includes many *CSS Snippets* that allow you to find tune the loc
do *not* need to add <style> HTML tags to bracket your rules.

Rules you add here will be the *last* CSS Rules included by We
CSS that comes after these rules.

```
.dcg-box-list li a, .dcg-box-list2 li a
{
    font-size: 12px;
    text-decoration: none;
}
.dcg-box2
{
    margin-top:20px;
```

Save Settings

After you add the new CSS to the existing code, click the **Save Settings** button. You can now look at the live site to see your menus in action.

I've shown a menu item here from the brands page I have created, so you can see how this looks on my site:

IKEA

The Sweedish company Ikea is a major producer of household products and among the leading furniture retailers in the entire world. Their products are sold through their catalogue, online, and in Ikea retail stores and are often assembled at home by the consumer.

They are known for selling discount products. The quality of their goods obviously suffers from their lower prices, but for those on a very tight budget, Ikea can offer one of the cheapest down comforters on the market. Read More»

I like this setup because it puts links at the top, bottom and right-hand side of each menu item. Since it is a larger menu item because of the description, I like having the better link coverage and also believe it makes it more clear to site visitors that these sections are linking up to additional content on the site.

If you have not done so already, be sure to revisit the home page as well to complete menu links to the various pages of your site. For my site, I had a number of blank page links that needed to be completed once those pages were actually created.

7-3 INTERLINKING CONTENT

The next step to building our site is to interlink content of our pages to other pages on the site.

I recommend to try to get your informational pages to link up to your product pages to try to funnel traffic through your site to your money pages.

This step accomplishes a few purposes:

1. **SEO** – By linking particular words and/or phrases in your site content to other pages of your site, you can boost the relevance of keywords on your pages. Just like all keyword related SEO, be sure to use this in moderation so you do not get flagged for keyword spam.

2. **Navigation** – Visitors on your site can easily tell when you have content relating to a particular word and can simply click on it to view that page. Major websites like Wikipedia use this same tactic. For these Amazon affiliate sites, this can also help us funnel our traffic to specific pages on the site.

You can actually accomplish this step in one of two ways or even use a combination of both: manual or automatic.

Manual interlinking is pretty straightforward. Just browse through your site and pick out specific places or words that you want to link to other pages on the site. This is definitely more time consuming. However, if you have very specific places that you want your content to link up to other pages of your site, this may be necessary to do manually.

This same tactic can also be done automatically, although with much less control. Depending on your plans for interlinking site content and the number of pages on your site, this auto solution may be a better choice. Extremely large sites would be very time consuming to set up interlinking manually, for example. Addition of new pages on a site can also require revisions on many other pages, while the automatic solution avoids this problem.

The SEO Ultimate plugin that we installed on the site actually offers a module called Deeplink Juggernaut that allows us to automatically interlink content.

I'm going to walk you through the setup of this particular feature, and show you how it works.

To get started, look for the **SEO** menu in the WordPress admin sidebar.

Hover over **SEO**, and then click on **Deeplink Juggernaut**.

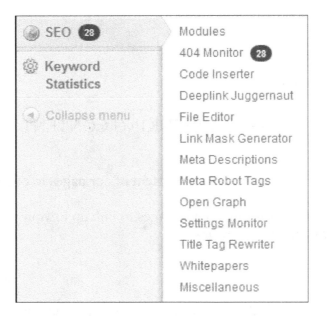

On the Deeplink Juggernaut admin page, click on the **Content Link Settings** tab.

On this tab page, look for **Quantity Restrictions** on the left, which can be seen towards the bottom of the picture above.

Click on the three checkboxes here to select them. This prevents the plugin from creating too many links on each page and too many links to the same page from each page.

I also want to change the numbers here. For my site, I'm just going to set the first number at 3 and the second number at 1 (they were 5 and 2 at their default settings).

These number adjustments simply limit the amount of interlinking that can take place on my site, which will help to reduce chances of keyword spam.

The next step is to visit the WordPress page editor. We'll start out by just clicking on the **Pages** admin menu link.

Looking through your site pages, identify the pages that you actually want visitors to end up on because they are your money pages that are promoting Amazon products.

For my site, this is going to be the brand pages: Pinzon, Pyrenees, PrimaLoft, Ikea and Pacific Coast.

I now want to edit each of these pages.

Below the WordPress editor, you'll find the **SEO Settings** box that is created by the SEO Ultimate plugin.

I want to click on the **Links** tab.

In this tab, I want to add text that should get automatically linked to this particular page from other pages on my site.

For this example, I have edited my PrimaLoft page. When I was writing, I had a number of pages where I made a specific reference to PrimaLoft, so I know there is content on my site containing this word in relevant places that I would want linked to this page.

PrimaLoft is also the base of the keyword phrase I'm targeting on this product page, so this makes this particular word a good word to pick for my autolinks. I'll just add the word PrimaLoft to the large text box in this tab, as seen in the picture below.

SEO Settings

Search Engine Listing   Social Networks Listing   Links   Miscellaneous

Inbound Autolink Anchors: PrimaLoft
(one per line)

Autolink Exclusion: ☑ Don't add autolinks to anchor texts found in this post.

SEO Ultimate 7.6.1 by SEO Design Solutions

I also want to be sure to click on the checkbox for the Autolink Exclusion to ensure that these links aren't created on this same page.

Although I'm only using one autolink word for this example, you could choose to enter multiple words/phrases here – just add each one on a blank line in the large text box.

You can choose to try to target your full keyword phrases with these autolinks, but this can easily become keyword spam. You may also not have used the full, exact phrase throughout the site in many places. I prefer to use shorter phrases and maybe even single words when possible for my autolink text.

Try picking the most relevant word to target to the page if you are just using a single word. For this example, I could have easily used "Pinzon PrimaLoft" or even just "Pinzon", but "PrimaLoft" is really the most relevant single word to target for this page (and I know I have referenced this word in my content a few times).

Once you have made changes to that tab and set up the autolink(s) for that page, be sure to click on the blue **Update** button on that page to save the changes. When this is done, the links are automatically created on the other pages throughout the site where your word/phrase is found. This is also done according to the settings we initially set in the SEO Ultimate plugin.

If I visit a page on my live site, you can see the word PrimaLoft in the third paragraph has turned into a link because of this autolink I have created.

What Other Alternatives Do I Have?

In addition to real down that has been sterilized to be hypoallergenic, you also have the option of using a down alternative filled comforter. These alternative materials are actually synthetic fibers that are designed to have the same properties as real down.

For severe allergy sufferers, the synthetic alternatives may be the best way to go because these materials will be completely sterile since they are manufactured in a lab.

Besides being a hypoallergenic down alternative, synthetic fill materials like PrimaLoft actually offer the same advantages as real down but without many of the downsides.

You can find more information about this synthetic fiber on our PrimaLoft page.

Notice how the second occurrence of PrimaLoft in the last sentence doesn't get converted into a link. This is because of the settings I created previously.

If I wanted both instances to be linked, I would have to manually link the last one or set the last two numbers on the settings page to 2 instead of 1.

If I only wanted the last occurrence of the word PrimaLoft to get linked, I would have to remove the autolink for this page and manually create the link on this page and other pages myself.

7-4 FINALIZATION OF SITE MENUS

Beyond the custom HTML menus that I have created on some of my pages and the interlinking content, there is no additional navigation for the site.

Websites should always be sure to be easy to navigate, so you never want to rely on a single link location to ensure someone can find the content they want.

Personally, I like to use primary menus at the top of my site and in the sidebar. I then like to use menus/links within my page content, which I have already done.

Now all I need to do is create the primary menus.

To start, I'm going to work with the main menu at the top of all pages of my site. I had created a custom menu called Top Menu for this particular menu. I am now going to revisit this menu and complete it.

Go to **Appearance → Menus** in the WP admin sidebar.

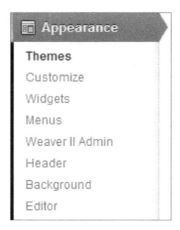

Since this is the only menu I have created on this site, it should already be open on this page and ready for me to edit.

On the left side, there is a box called Pages that should now be loaded with all of the pages that exist on the site.

I simply want to find my three category pages here and add them to this menu. Just click on the checkbox next to those pages and click on the **Add to Menu** button.

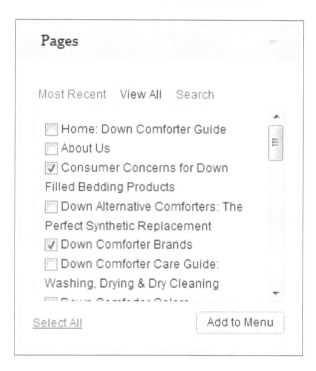

On the right side, you can now see all of the pages in the menu including the home page and the category pages we've just added.

The main problem with how this is automatically created is that the menu links are the same as the page titles. If you have longer page titles like most of mine, you'll find that simply won't work to use the titles as the link text.

The picture below shows the pages set up for my menu and the initial link text for them, which will obviously be too long.

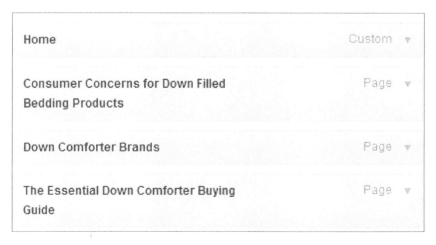

Now I need to edit each of these menu items to change the link text. Just click on the down arrow on the right side of a link box to expand the options to edit that link.

I've expanded the first category link here. This is how it looks right after I have expanded it:

The **Navigation Label** is the long text that I want to replace for the link text. The **Title Attribute** is blank, so I also want to set that while I am here.

An easy way to make these link text changes is to simply move the existing page title into the **Title Attribute** box, and then add a short version to the **Navigation Label** to be the anchor text for the menu link.

I've done this below with the Consumer Concerns link:

After I have done this with all of the menu links, I can then drag and drop specific links to change their order (if desired).

I'm also going to add one more link to this menu – for the **About Us** page on the site.

The picture below shows what my Top Menu now looks like in the menu editor:

Once I'm done, I'll click the **Save Menu** button to ensure my changes are saved and live on the site.

You can see the menu at the bottom of the picture below:

I am now going to proceed to create three new menus – one for each of my main categories.

At the top of the menu page look for the **create a new menu** link and click it.

Next, name your menu after your category so you can easily identify it in the future. After you have given it a name, click on the blue **Create Menu** button.

I will then add pages to this menu in the exact same way that I did for the home page. On the left, simply select the sub-pages that go with this particular category and add them to the menu.

Be sure to edit the link text and title attribute, then arrange your menu items in the proper order you want them to display.

Here is my Buying Guide menu completed:

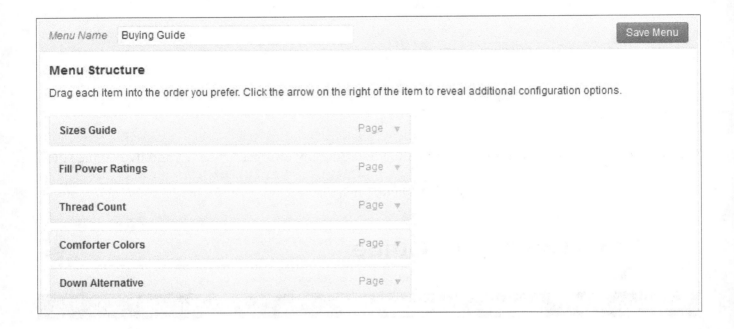

When you're finished, click the **Save Menu** button. Then proceed with creating additional menus for each of the categories on the site.

7-5 CUSTOM WP PAGE WIDGETS

My next step is to add my custom category menus to my site as custom widgets.

Depending on the theme you use on your WordPress site, this particular step may actually not be possible. I am using the Weaver II theme that offers this particular feature. There are other ways this could be done (with free plugins, for example – search "per page widget"), if you are not using this theme.

The idea here is to have a custom menu in the sidebar of the pages of my site. However, I want to use a total of three different menus, and only one of those should show up at a time depending on what page they are viewing.

To start, I need a new plugin on the site to help me do something that Weaver II actually doesn't allow me to do.

First, click on **Plugins → Add New**.

Then search for and install a plugin called **Shortcode Menu**.

When this plugin is installed, you'll have a new menu link:

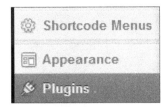

Now click on **Shortcode Menus** in the sidebar to get to the admin page for this plugin.

At the top, look for the **Select Menu** drop-down box. Then, just pick one of the menus you've created.

At the bottom, notice the text show up in the green box. This is called a shortcode – everything from the opening bracket [through the closing bracket].

Simply copy the shortcode provided and paste it into a Notepad file to use later. Now, repeat this process for all of your menus so you have shortcodes for each one.

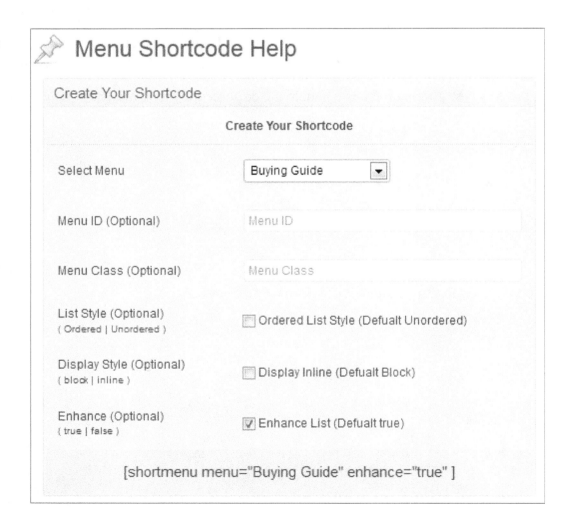

Next, I need to create a widget that can be used on select pages to show a specific menu.

I'll begin by clicking on the **Widgets** link in the **Appearance** menu:

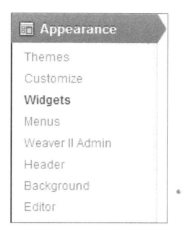

On this page, look for the Weaver II Per Page Text widget. Click on and drag it into the primary sidebar under the search bar widget that is already in place.

The widget is shown above. You may notice the instructions that come along with it. It says we need to create Custom Fields to specify this widget on each page.

Now we will go back through each page of the site, except for the home page, and edit it.

On each page, scroll down towards the bottom and look for the box titled **Custom Fields.**

The bottom part of this box allows you to add a new custom field. We need to create two here.

If the names of the fields are not already in the drop-down box provided, click on the Enter New link to get a blank text box that allows you to specify your own field name.

The first field we want to create needs this name: **wvr_pp_title**

The value of the field will be the title used on the public site for this particular menu. I'll just use the words "Buying Guide" for this because the page I am editing is one of the buying guide pages.

The next field should be named this: **wvr_pp_text**

The value of this field should be one of the shortcodes from the **Shortcode Menu** plugin. Just pick the appropriate shortcode from your Notepad file and paste it in here.

You can see what I have input below for this particular page. All I need to do now is click the **Add Custom Field** button to save this last field, and then click on the **Update** button to save the changes to the page.

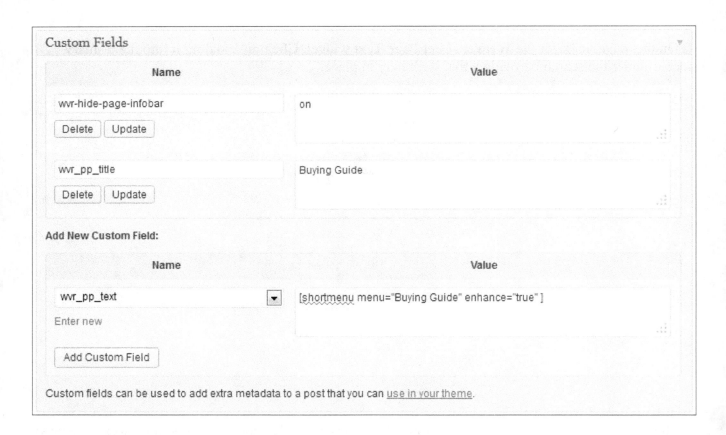

If I visit this page on the live site, I can now see my custom menu show up in the sidebar.

```
Search Site

Buying Guide

Sizes Guide
Fill Power Ratings
Thread Count
Comforter Colors
Down Alternative
```

Simply repeat this process on all of the pages, except the home page, to have a custom menu in the sidebar of every page that will link to the other relational pages in the same category on your site.

8 AMAZON ADVERTISING

We will now add our Amazon affiliate advertisements to the site and learn how to get signed up with the Amazon Associates Program and obtain API keys. The ads are created with my five Amazon affiliate WordPress plugins. These five plugins were ONLY included in this course for my live coaching students and NOT customers of this book. If you wish to obtain these five plugins and videos of the live training, pick up option #3 on the page below:
http://ryanstevensonplugins.com/azon-coaching/

Primary Lesson Objective

☐   Add Amazon Affiliate Advertisements to the Site

Lesson Steps Checklist

☐   Sign up for Amazon Associates Program & Obtain API Keys

☐   Build Product Advertisements with Product Style

☐   Include UpsellAzon & ExtendAzon for Automated Features

☐   Build Amazon Gold Box Ads with Daily Deal Azon

☐   Build Product Bundle Ads with ComboZon

Chapter Notes

Chapter Notes

8-1 JOIN AMAZON ASSOCIATES PROGRAM

If you have not done so already, now is the time to join Amazon as an affiliate because we will need information from that account to be able to create our advertising for the site.

Start by visiting https://affiliate-program.amazon.com

In the top-right of that site, you can see where you enter your login information after you have created an account – this is where you can go to manage your account, view your earnings, or look at reports. Affiliate links can also be generated through here, but we will be using my WordPress plugins to accomplish this for us instead.

Note the USA flag in the corner. You can simply hover over that flag to get a list of all of the Amazon locales. If you want to create an account for other locales or simply view other accounts, just select the appropriate country.

If you only intend on promoting Amazon.com products on your site, you will not need to worry about creating an account for the other locales.

Below the login boxes, you will see a large button that says **Join Now for Free**. Simply click on it to start creating a new affiliate account.

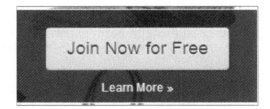

Next, provide your email address, select the bubble next to I am a new customer, and then click the Sign in button to proceed.

If you already have an Amazon.com account, even one that you have previously created to use as a customer on Amazon, you can actually use the same info here to create your affiliate account instead of creating a completely new account.

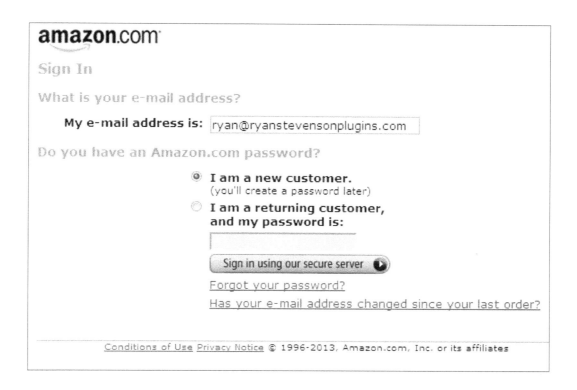

The first step of the account creation process is pretty simple – just provide your name, email and password.

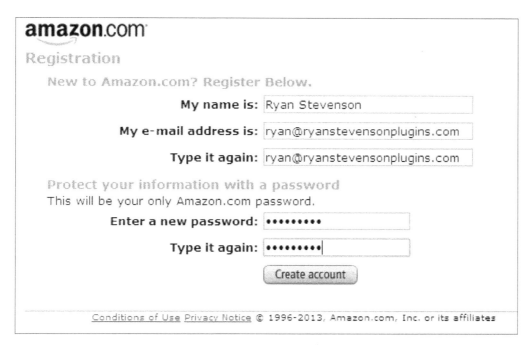

Once you click on **Create account**, you'll get to a 4 step process that you'll need to complete to be able to use your account.

I have shown the top portion of the first step below. This step should be pretty self explanatory because it just asks you for your personal information, which is necessary so you can get paid.

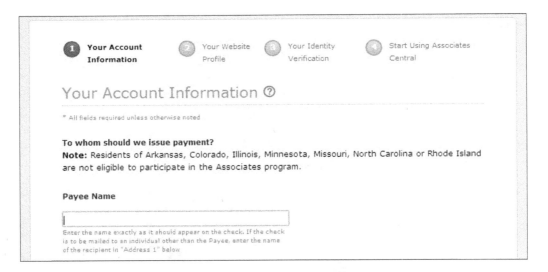

Click the **Next: Your Website Profile** button when you are done filling out your account information.

The second step requires you to create a website profile. This is for the website that you'll be putting Amazon ads on. The next three images I have provided cover this step in detail since this is the most confusing part about joining Amazon as an affiliate.

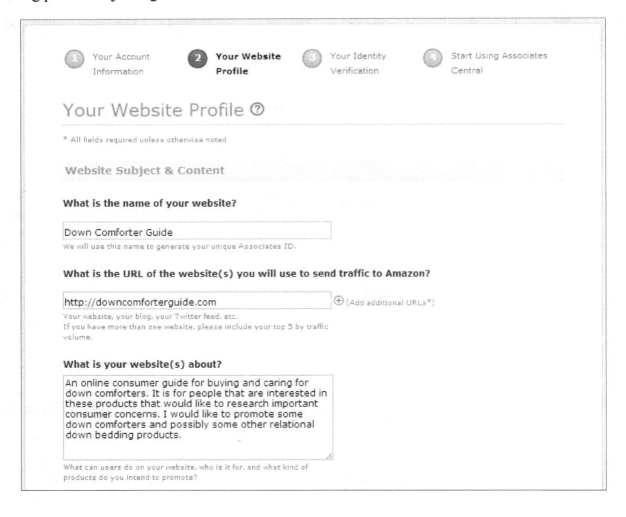

First, just provide your website name, URL and a brief description about the site.

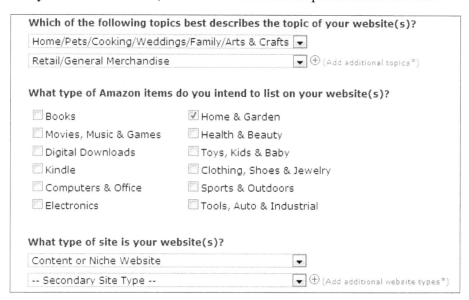

Next, select general categories that relate to your website niche. My site is for down comforters, which is within the **Home** niche. I selected a second category, but this is really optional if something else fits. Then I select the types of Amazon items I intend to promote, which will just be **Home & Garden** products on this site. Last, I need to pick a website type. If you are building a site based on my recommendations, you're building a **Content or Niche Website**.

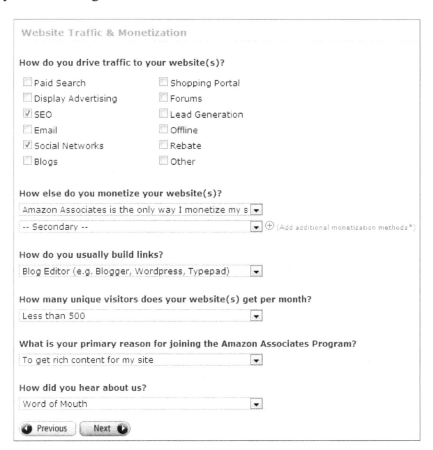

First, pick how you drive traffic to your sites. I teach SEO and Social Networks, so this is all I select here.

Then I pick how I will monetize the site. I just recommend using Amazon, so this is an easy choice.

I'm building my links through WordPress, and the site is new, so the traffic selection is easy. Do not worry about whether you have any traffic yet or not – Amazon will take all traffic levels.

Finally, I always recommend picking that you want to join Amazon to get rich content for the site. Obviously you are doing it to monetize, but rich content is a big reason why Amazon is the affiliate network of choice.

Click the Next button to proceed. The remaining steps are straightforward, so I have left those out here.

Amazon Affiliate ID

Once you are all signed up, you'll have to wait for approval to be able to get paid, but Amazon will go ahead and let you begin promoting (typically because they will approve most that apply).

When you are logged into your Amazon affiliate account, look in the top-left for your associate id:

This shows my affiliate id, but yours will be different. You can also create tracking ids for each of your sites, which act like an affiliate id. This helps you to track the results from each of your individual sites so you can figure out which ads perform good/bad and make changes to your site accordingly.

To view stats for your ads, just click on one of the **View full report** text links in the summary box in the top-right of the page.

Amazon API Keys

The next thing we need is to create API keys to use with the WordPress plugins. Start from your Amazon affiliate account and click on the **Product Advertising API** button at the top.

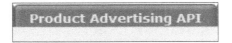

On that page, scroll down and look for the **Resources** header. Click the **Manage Your Account** link here.

Resources

- Manage Your Account
- WSDL

Next, click on the **click here** link next to **Access Identifiers**.

On the next page, you will be promoted to login to your Amazon AWS account. Just provide the same information here to login.

Important Note: If your Amazon affiliate and AWS information do not match, the API keys you generate will not work correctly, so make sure you're using the same account here.

Amazon is changing the way this system works. As of this moment, both the old and new system are available to use to create/manage API keys. However, I will just be going over the new system here to ensure this guide will apply in the future as well.

Currently, you can access this new system through a **Your Security Credentials** text link found in a yellow message box towards the top of the screen on the main AWS account page.

Look for the Access Keys section on this page and click on it to expand.

Your Security Credentials

Use this page to manage the credentials for your AWS account. To manage credentia

To learn more about the types of AWS credentials and how they're used, see AWS Se

+ Password

+ Multi-Factor Authentication (MFA)

+ Access Keys (Access Key ID and Secret Access Key)

Then just look for the **Create New Access Key** button.

Create New Access Key

Once you've done this, DO NOT close the window that opens – you need to do something first or you will have to delete the key and create it again to be able to use it.

Look for the text link that says **Show Access Key** and click on it. This will expand the page to show your **Access Key ID** and **Secret Access Key**. Record BOTH keys for future use. I recommend just saving them into a Notepad file.

You can retrieve the Access Key ID at a later time, if needed. However, the secret key cannot be retrieved EVER once this window is closed!

Here is my screen, so you can see the keys you are looking for. Obviously, I will be deleting this key after I am done with this tutorial.

Joining Foreign Amazon Locales

If you want to join the affiliate program for other Amazon locales, especially those that are not in a language that you can read, I highly recommend using Google Chrome to do so.

At the top of the page, it will ask you if you want to translate a site you are browsing if it is in a language that is not standard for where you live.

This feature makes it much easier to apply for all of the Amazon locales – the application procedure is basically identical on all of their sites but can still be confusing and time consuming if you can't understand the language.

Amazon Affiliate Site Requirement

Amazon specifically requires you to have this statement on your site, modified slightly:

[Insert your website name] is a participant in the Amazon Services LLC Associates Program, an affiliate advertising program designed to provide a means for sites to earn advertising fees by advertising and linking to [insert the applicable site name (amazon.com, amazonsupply.com, or myhabit.com)].

For my site, this is how I will modify that statement:

DownComforterGuide.com is a participant in the Amazon Services LLC Associates Program, an affiliate advertising program designed to provide a means for sites to earn advertising fees by advertising and linking to amazon.com.

Where you place this statement on your site is up to you. It could go in the sidebar or footer of each page of the site, or you could also simply hide it on the About Us page of the site. Amazon's agreement isn't specifically clear about whether that statement should be on every single page that has an Amazon ad or whether it simply should be on the site. However, I have made a lot of sites that simply use that statement on the About page and have never had issues by doing so.

8-2 PRODUCT STYLE

The first plugin of mine that I am going to talk about is Product Style. This plugin can be used to make standalone ads and/or comparison charts.

First, I need to install it on the site.

Go to **Plugins → Add New** in the WordPress admin menu. This is where we went to search for plugins. However, this time we want to upload the plugin that was downloaded from my website, so click the **Upload** link at the top.

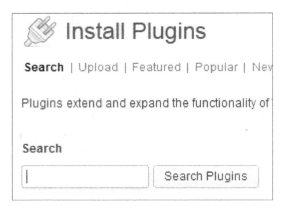

Click the **Browse** button and select the amzps file that you downloaded.

Once you have that selected, just click **Install Now**. Then click on the **Activate** text link on the following page.

You should now be able to find Product Style in the sidebar menu. Click on it to start the plugin setup process.

This setup process exists to ensure that the plugin has the information that it needs to be able to work and so you can earn commissions from the ads it creates.

The first part of the setup process involves selecting an affiliate network. This really just controls what type of settings it will ask you for next to ensure that it has everything it needs to run. Just select Amazon here and click Continue.

This takes us to the Amazon setup.

First, specify whether you will use one or multiple Amazon affiliate locales on this site.

I will just be using Amazon.com on this particular site. However, the plugin can be used with more Amazon locales to automatically attempt to change ads depending on where a visitor lives. Specific information on using the plugin in that manner can be found in the plugin guidebook, linked from the download page.

Next, just select the Amazon site to use:

Now provide your Amazon.com affiliate id:

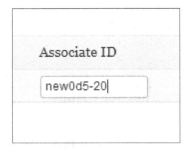

Enter your Access Key and Secret Access Key from AWS API:

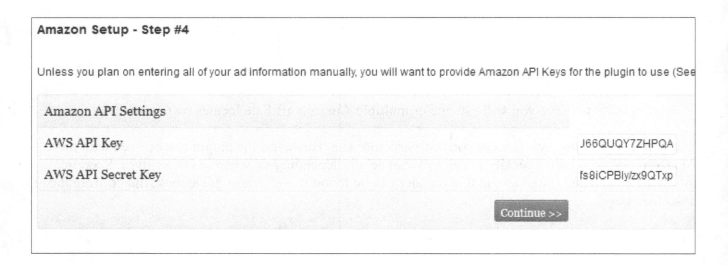

Now select a link type to use. I will just be using the Direct (Standard) Affiliate Links.

The other two options are for use with the Amazon API shopping cart system. I will actually be using that system in this tutorial, but I am going to be doing it with ExtendAzon and not Product Style (I'll get to more on that in the ExtendAzon chapter).

After this step, the plugin is ready to use. A variety of tutorial video links are available there, but extended information on everything the plugin can do can be found in the plugin guidebook.

I am now going to go to the **Auto Amazon** page of the plugin to start creating ads to use on this site.

To start, I just provide a keyword phrase to search for products. I'll be using **pinzon down comforter** for this search to pull up the two products I want to promote for that brand.

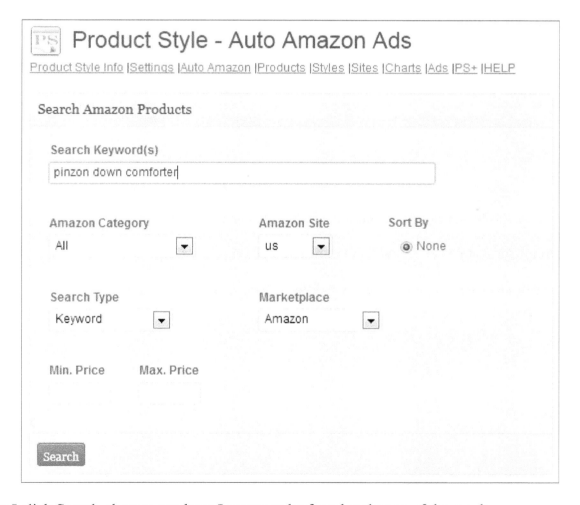

After I click Search, the two products I want can be found at the top of the results:

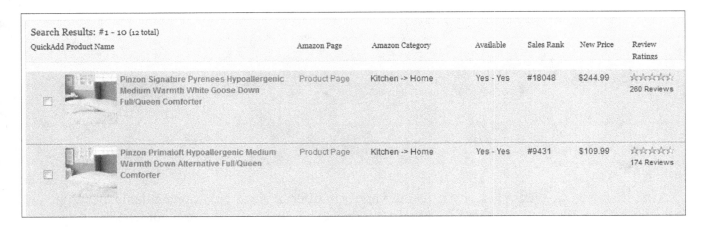

To start, I am going to click on the Pyrenees product at the top (either the Image or the Title of the product).

Clicking on the product opens a very long window. At the top, you'll find a product summary and additional product info.

Scroll down and look for the section with the header **Plugin Category Selection**.

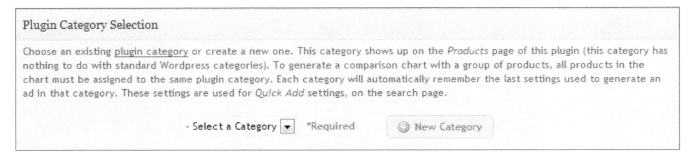

Now, click on the **New Category** button here. Provide a name for the category that you will use for this product. Nobody will see this name but you. It is used to group together products and also controls memory settings for Auto Amazon (will get to memory settings in a few).

I will just call this category Comforters. Click **Save New Category** when done.

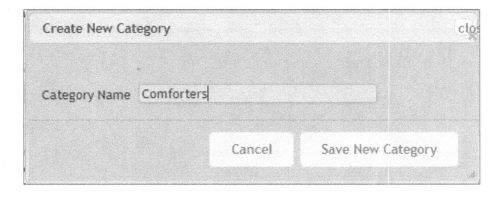

After the category is created, you can see it automatically selected in the drop-down box:

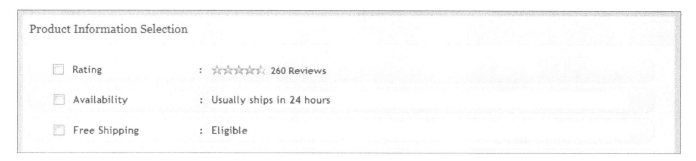

Now, scroll down to the next section called Product Information Selection:

In this section, there are many different items listed. All of this is the product information available through Amazon API. Product Style allows you to pick and choose what information you want to display with your products.

Just click on the checkbox next to one or more items in the list to add the information to the ad for this product. You can drag and drop items to rearrange the order they will display in the live ad.

I have selected three items to show with this ad:

You can choose to edit the product information provided here, if you want. There are two boxes for each row. The first is the Field Title and the second is the Field Information.

If you select an item, change the order of items, and/or change the Field Title for an item, that also gets stored in the category memory. Future products in the same category will have those selections and customizations automatically done for you (both manually created product ads, like this one, or using

Quick Ads, which I will get to shortly).

Notice my Product Summary item. The information for that is quite long and actually includes HTML code. Anytime I see HTML code here, I want to be sure the ad isn't going to look messed up (since that HTML can potentially break the design of the ad HTML). Just click on **Preview Ad** at the bottom to see what it will look like.

For this ad, I need to remove that HTML because it is an image file that has a specific size and will force my ad size to change beyond the size that will fit on my site. The Product Summary section is typically the only place you will find really long text and/or HTML like this that could break the ads.

At the bottom of the window, you have some Ad Creation Options.

Style controls the design of the ad (preview to see how these look). I will use Grey for this ad.

For the image, I will select the Medium size.

The only other changes I have made here involve shortening the Link Anchor Text and Header Title. This text will be shown in the actual advertisement and sometimes Amazon can provide too much text here, so I often find myself shortening it.

Ad Creation Options	
Ad Name (Not Publicly Displayed)	Pinzon Signature Pyrenees Hypoallergenic Medium Warmth White Goose Down Full/Queen Comforter
Style	Grey ▼
Ad Type	Image & Text ▼
Image Size (Image / Image & Text Ads Only)	Medium (160 x 160) ▼
Link Anchor Text (Text Ads Only)	Pinzon Signature Pyrenees Hypoallergenic White Goose Down Comforter
Amazon Preview (Not for Enhanced Ads)	Off ▼
Header Title	Pinzon Signature Pyrenees Hypoallergenic White Goose Down Comforter
Open Links In New Window	Yes ▼
Show Special Button	No ▼

| Cancel | Preview Ad | Create Product Ad |

Once I am satisfied with the ad, I click on **Create Product Ad**.

Proceed with creating additional ads to use on the site, depending on your plans.

If you find yourself wanting to edit text or make changes to each ad, just proceed with creating your ads in the same manner. If you select an existing category, it will recall your information fields and ad creation options from the first ad, which helps to save time.

If you find that you want a few different variations of product information for different kinds of product ads, just create new categories to use for each variation.

The other option is to create Quick Ads, as long as you have created one ad using the method I just described. To do this, first select one or more products in the search results. I've selected the other Pinzon comforter here:

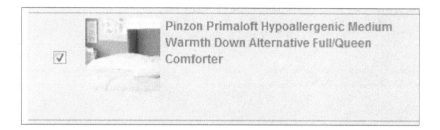

Now scroll to the bottom of the page and look for the drop-down and Quick Add button.

Just select a category here and click the button. The ad(s) will be automatically created for you based on the memory settings from that category!

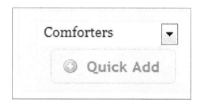

The automatically created product information can later be manually edited through the Products admin page, if you later find that you need to make some changes to the ads you didn't create yourself.

If I need to arrange some of the ads together into a comparison chart, I can do that from the Charts page of the plugin.

Ads and comparison charts can then be inserted into the live site through the page editor.

Just look for the blue PS icon above the post editor window:

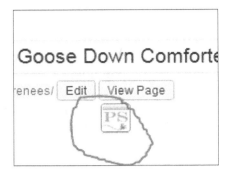

That will open a window where I can add saved ads or comparison charts to the page. Just click the **Saved Ads** button, select the ad, and click the **Insert Ad** button.

Product Style Plugin - Insert Ads & Charts

Saved Ads   Saved Charts   Fast Ads

Category Filter: All

Insert Ad

#1-Pinzon Signature Pyrenees Hypoallergenic Medium Warmth White Goose Down Full/Que...

select a styled ad to insert

Special Ad Type

--None

optional - special, partial ad types

Insert Ad

This inserts the ad shortcode into the page content where I had the text cursor:

[amzps id="1"]

On the live site, the ad will show up where this shortcode is placed.

Here is this ad on the live site:

8-3 UPSELLAZON

The next plugin I want to install is UpsellAzon, which will create Amazon accessory ads for me automatically.

Install this plugin in the same manner as Product Style. When it is active, click on UpsellAzon in the admin menu to start the setup process.

This setup process works just like the one for Product Style – it collects needed settings to be able to run.

For step #1, just provide your Amazon API Keys. You only need one set of keys to use for all of the plugins.

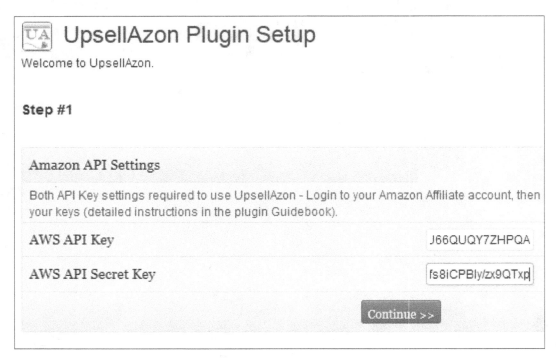

For step #2, I select the Ad Placement. I want to use Widgets for this site, which allows me to control where the ads are displayed.

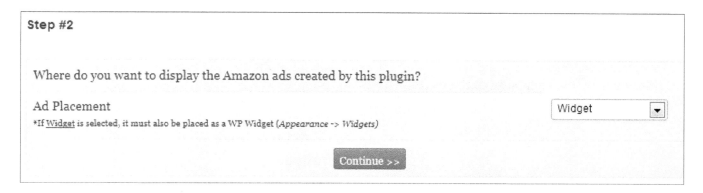

At this point, the plugin is ready to run! To actually get it working on my live site, I just need to setup the widget. Click on **Appearance → Widgets**.

On that page, look for UpsellAzon in the list of Available Widgets:

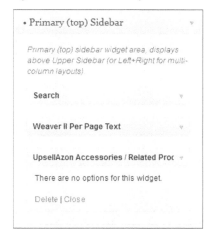

Now simply drag and drop that widget into the Primary Sidebar:

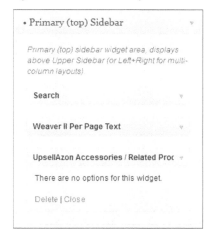

When I visit the live site, UpsellAzon will automatically display accessory ads in the sidebar on any pages where I have an Amazon ad!

I've visited the Pinzon Pyrenees page where I just created the Product Style ad. You can see the accessory ads on the right side of the page:

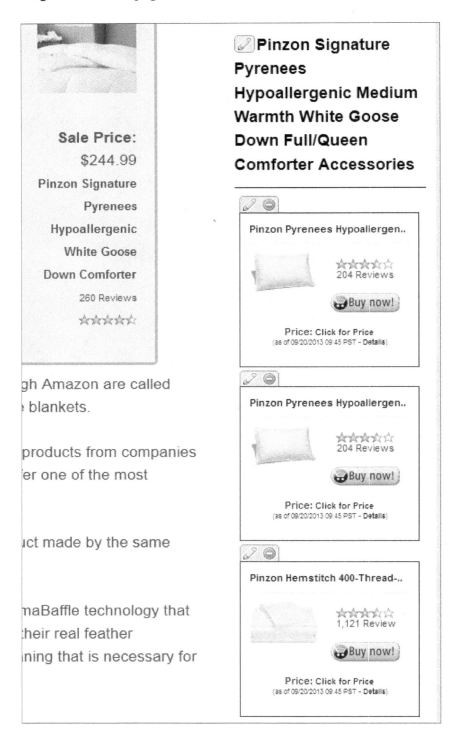

Note the pencil icon next to the widget title and in the tab above each product. This allows you to edit the title text of these areas.

Also note the red circle icon with a white line inside of it, next to the pencil icons. This removes this accessory ad from being displayed on the page. For example, two pillows are shown above. They are definitely separate products, but they appear identical in this advertisement, so it may be worthwhile to remove one of them by clicking this icon.

These icons are only available when you are logged into your admin account and viewing the public website. Any changes you make will reflect on the live site, so this gives you some level of control over these automatic ads.

8-4 EXTENDAZON

Next up is ExtendAzon. This is the shopping cart plugin. ExtendAzon ties together links into a single shopping cart from Product Style, UpsellAzon, certain product links from Daily Deal Azon, and many other HTML based Amazon affiliate links to direct product pages.

Install this plugin just like the others. Once is is active, click on ExtendAzon in the sidebar menu to start setup.

Step #1 requires your API keys again:

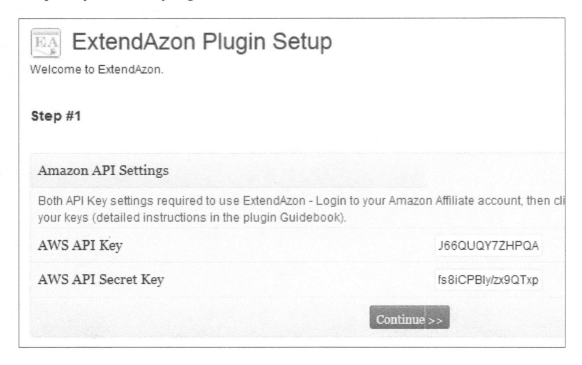

Step #2 asks what kind of shopping cart links to use – on-site or direct.

On-site links utilize an on-site shopping cart as a sidebar widget, so multiple products and different quantities of those products can be added to the cart by the site visitor before proceeding to checkout on Amazon. I'll be using these on this site.

Direct links go straight to Amazon but to the add to cart confirmation page instead of the product page.

Either link type offers the 90 day cookie lifespan (visitors have to confirm the add to cart operation on Amazon for that cookie to be set).

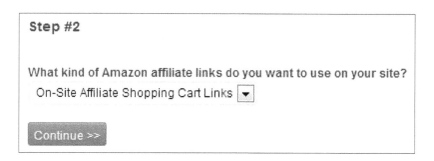

This completes setup for ExtendAzon. All that is left to do now is set a sidebar widget for the on-site shopping cart (this is not needed if direct shopping cart links are used).

Go to **Appearance → Widgets**, just like we did with UpsellAzon.

Add the ExtendAzon widget to the sidebar:

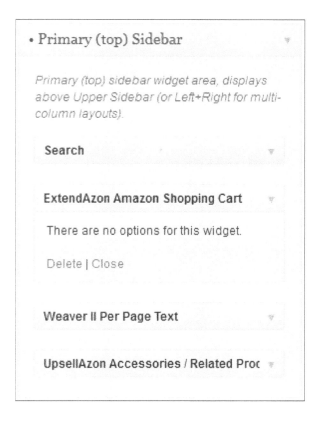

This adds the shopping cart to the live site:

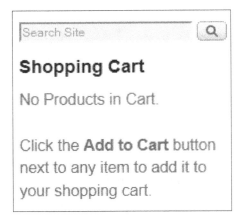

Now when someone clicks an Amazon link on the site, it adds that product to the shopping cart.

More products can be added and/or quantities can be changed in the cart. When finished, the customer can simply click the Checkout button to proceed to Amazon to complete the purchase.

8-5 DAILY DEAL AZON

The next plugin is Daily Deal Azon. This plugin automatically creates Amazon Gold Box ads for you.

Since Gold Box deals may not be available for all types of products, some sites may not be a good fit to use this particular plugin. However, I recommend installing it to see what you can find that will fit your site and keep it if you can find something relational to promote.

Install this plugin just like the others. When it is activated, click on the Daily Deal Azon link in the admin sidebar menu to start the setup process.

For Step #1, provide your affiliate id and API keys, just like we've done with previous plugins.

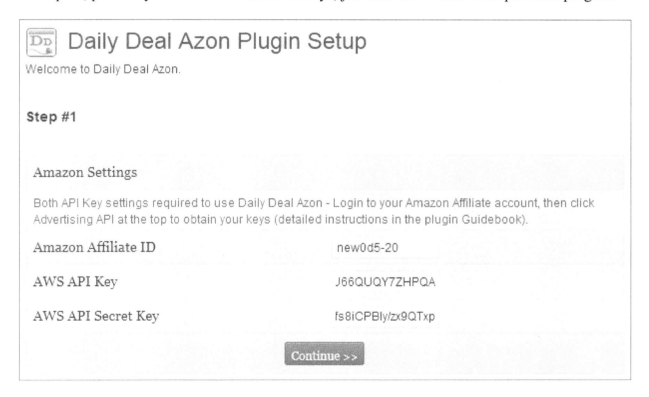

Next, select options for two settings.

Javascript Loading determines whether your content in these ads will get indexed by search engines (Off will get indexed and On will not). This also affects the general appearance of the ads, since a loading box will display with this setting set to **On**. I'll be leaving it off for this site.

Ad Placement determines where the ads generated by this plugin show up on your live site. For most purposes, I recommend using the **Shortcode** option so you can control where the ads are displayed.

Even though **Widget** is available here (which works like UpsellAzon or ExtendAzon widgets), you could use the **Shortcode** in a widget also. This could be used to make the widget show up on specific pages (something I covered in the last class).

Step #3 just requires you to wait for a minute or two. The plugin needs to download the Gold Box deals to be able to work, so this step verifies that your server is set up to work with the plugin and then downloads those deals. If there is a problem, an error message will be shown telling you what to do to fix it.

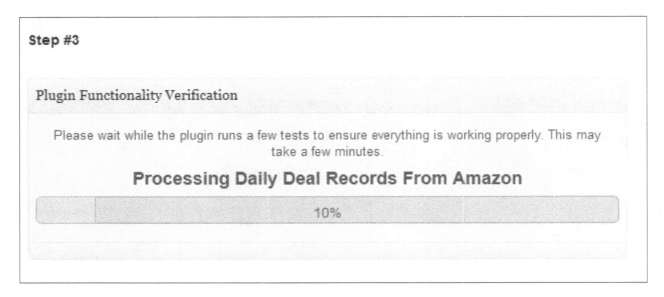

Once the progress bar has filled to 100%, a **Continue** button is provided. Clicking it will complete the setup process and allow the plugin to be used.

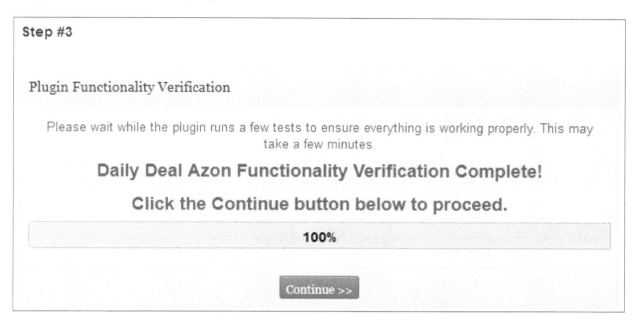

I am going to visit the **Filter Options** admin page for Daily Deal Azon now.

At the top of that page, you'll find four checkboxes for the four possible ad types this plugin can generate. Select one or more ad types to consider them for inclusion.

Next, the filter keywords section can be used to provide one or more keywords and/or category titles that will be used to try to find results relevant to your site.

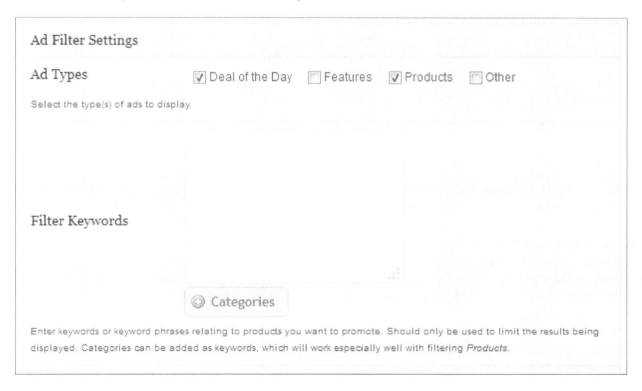

Since I picked Shortcode insertion, I need to visit the WordPress Page editor. I will simply create a new page for this shortcode. If I can find ads, I may just make a standalone page for relational deals.

Click on the **DD** icon at the top of the editor:

Select **Auto Deal Ads** and click **Insert Deal Box**.

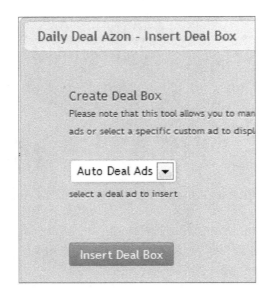

This adds the shortcode to the content:

Now, just view the page on the live site to see the current ads. You can rotate through a few different ads using the arrow buttons (if more than one is found).

If the plugin does not return relational product ads, then it they simply don't exist at the moment (the plugin will try to display something instead of nothing if the filters do not return results). It is possible that some could show up in the future, since these Gold Box deals are updated on a regular basis. However, it may not be worth having a page on your site for these deals if there are not any available that relate to your site.

For this site, I don't believe it is going to be a good fit because I cannot find bedding products to promote here.

Here is the Deal of the Day ad (the default ad) that was shown on my site:

8-6 COMBOZON

The last plugin is ComboZon, and it is used to create product bundle ads.

A product bundle ad combines multiple products of specific quantities into a single affiliate link and advertisement. It utilizes the 90 day shopping cart feature but does so with direct shopping cart links (this is not compatible with ExtendAzon and UpsellAzon currently but may be in the future – they can still be used on the same site though).

Install and activate the plugin, then click on ComboZon in the sidebar menu to start setup.

For Step #1, just provide your API keys.

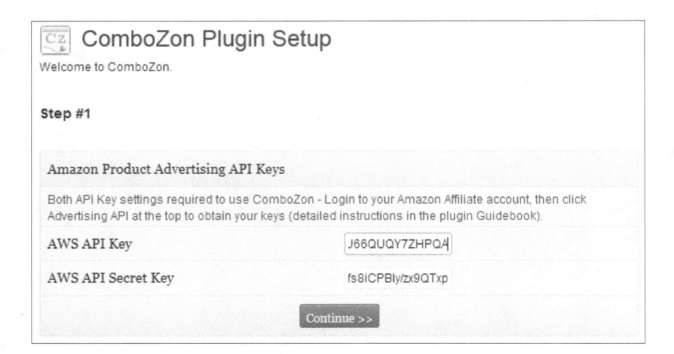

For Step #2, enter your affiliate id and select the Amazon country for that affiliate id.

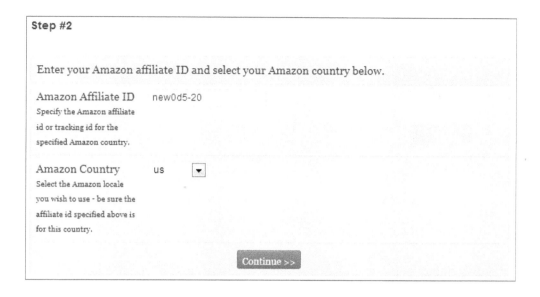

This completes the plugin setup.

Now, click on ComboZon Ads to create an ad. Click on the **Create New Ad** button on that page.

This creates a blank ad. On the left, you can search for products to add to it. On the right, you can see a real-time preview of the ad. Many areas of the ad preview can simply be clicked to edit them in place!

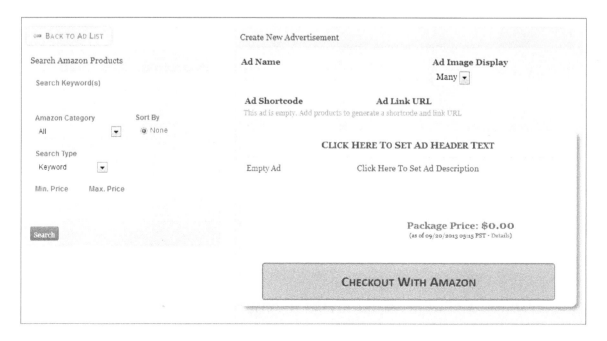

I searched for "pinzon primaloft", which returned these two results:

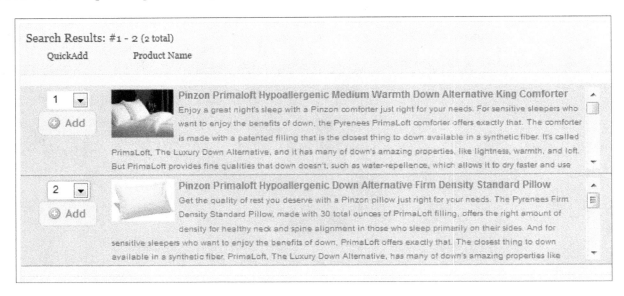

This is the comforter and a matching pillow, an excellent opportunity to make a combo ad (more than two products can be used, if desired).

I'm going to simply click the **Add** button next to each product. For the pillow, I could change the drop-down box to the number 2 to set a different quantity for this item.

Doing this updates the ad preview to reflect my changes:

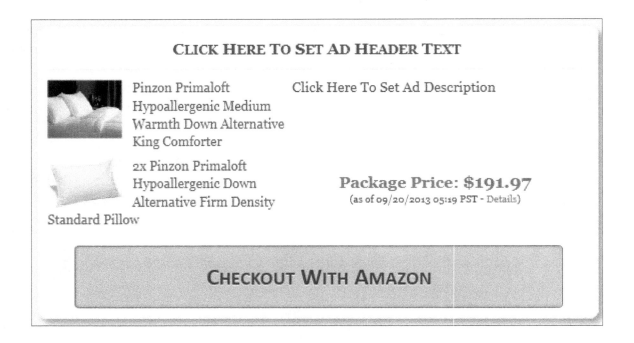

Up above, if I change **Ad Image Display** to **One**, it updates my ad to only use one product image (and a larger image):

Now all I need to do is set the Ad Header Text and Ad Description. Simply click on those text areas in the ad preview to edit them. Here is my ad when I am done:

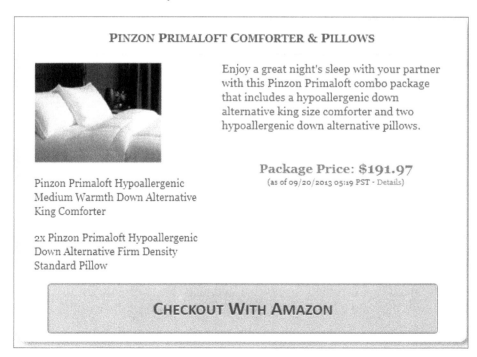

You could also rearrange the products in the ad by simply dragging and dropping them into a new order.

Once the ad is done, be sure to give it a name. You can then leave that page if you are done there – no need to click a Save button (everything updates as you work).

To insert the ad into a live page, just visit the page editor and look for the **Cz** icon (just like the other icons).

Now, just select the ad you want and click **Insert Ad**:

This puts the shortcode for the ad in your content:

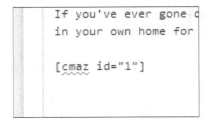

When you view the live page on your site, you will see the combo ad just like on the preview ad screen.

The live ad can vary slightly from the preview ad because they will stretch to fill up the horizontal space in the content where they are placed. However, you should find them to be extremely similar.

Here is the live ad I created:

PINZON PRIMALOFT COMFORTER & PILLOWS

Enjoy a great night's sleep with your partner with this Pinzon Primaloft combo package that includes a hypoallergenic down alternative king size comforter and two hypoallergenic down alternative pillows.

Package Price: $191.97
(as of 09/20/2013 05:19 PST - Details)

Pinzon Primaloft Hypoallergenic Medium Warmth Down Alternative King Comforter

2x Pinzon Primaloft Hypoallergenic Down Alternative Firm Density Standard Pillow

CHECKOUT WITH AMAZON

9 FACEBOOK MARKETING

Any kind of online or even offline business can benefit from having a presence on Facebook. As an affiliate marketer, you can take advantage of targeted leads here – both for free and through paid advertising (which is optional). We will learn how to create a Facebook Fan Page, add our Fan Page news feed to our website, create a Facebook Group and create targeted Facebook advertising campaigns.

Primary Lesson Objective

☐   Build a Facebook Fan Page & Group

Lesson Steps Checklist

☐   Create a Facebook Fan Page for your Niche / Website

☐   Create a Basic Facebook App

☐   Add Facebook News Feed to your Website using the App ID

☐   Create a Facebook Group

☐   Build Custom Audiences & Create Facebook Ads (Optional)

Chapter Notes

Chapter Notes

9-1 FACEBOOK FAN PAGE CREATION

Facebook has become too large to ignore these days. Whether you're building a small Amazon affiliate site or running a large corporation, it can be well worth the effort to establish a presence on Facebook.

The easiest way to begin doing this is to create a Facebook Page. A lot of the other Facebook tactics I'll discuss can actually be done without a Facebook Page, but there are some advantages to having one.

The biggest advantage actually comes with advertising on Facebook, which will be discussed in more detail later in this guide, but it can help you to save money with your advertising and gain more exposure at the same time.

For now, we will go ahead and get started by creating our Facebook Page.

First, I recommend using Google Chrome for this Facebook class. I actually use Firefox as my primary browser, but there are a few particular things that I do on Facebook that are not possible or are much more difficult to do with Firefox than with Chrome. These things are actually just for those that want to advertise on Facebook, which I will cover more in that chapter, so some of you may not need to worry about this particular point.

You will need to login to your personal Facebook account before you can create your page. This brings me to my next point that I need to discuss before I proceed.

Consider who your Facebook friends are. In some situations, you may not want your friends to know about your Facebook Pages that you create while others will want to share those pages with friends. In general, if you have marketing friends that you may not completely know or trust, you may want to consider privacy settings to prevent particular people from seeing posts from that page.

There is a lot to privacy settings, but you should be able to find that information on Facebook if you need more help. To get to Privacy Settings, just look for it in the menu that opens when you hover over the gear icon in the top-right of Facebook:

The reason I recommend this is because there are some marketers out there that will not hesitate to copy unique content and try to reuse or abuse it in some manner.

For me, a lot of my Facebook friends are customers or other marketers, so I am forced to take measures to hide many of my pages from them.

If you feel like this is something that you may need to be concerned about and do not want to both with privacy settings, you can always create a separate Facebook account that you only use for your Amazon affiliate endeavors. This is actually another reason why using Google Chrome could be useful if you use another browser as your default – you can stay signed into two Facebook accounts at once (one on each browser).

I use a separate Facebook account for the Pages and Groups that I do not want to share with other marketers, but you are welcome to choose your own direction based on your situation. You will obviously be able to get a quicker start by using your existing account and sharing your page with friends, if that is something you think you can do without prolems. However, I at least wanted to discuss this point before going on to creating the actual page.

At the top of Facebook, just type **create page** into the search bar. Then click on **Create New Facebook Page**, which will show up below the search bar.

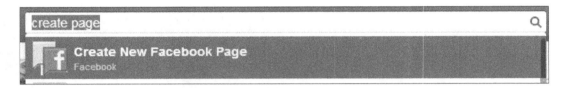

Next, you have to select what type of page you want to create. You could really follow this tutorial loosely to create any kind of Facebook Page, but we will be creating a **Company, Organization or Institution** Page.

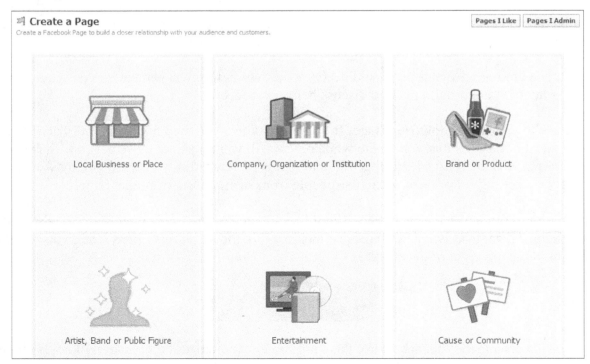

Once you click on **Company, Organization or Institution**, it will change to show a drop-down box, text box and checkmark. You can see the picture below that shows this area and how I have filled it out.

Note the link to the Facebook Pages Terms: https://www.facebook.com/page_guidelines.php

Make sure you are following these policies. You should not be creating a page that makes it confusing or misleading to people so they may think that you represent a company that you do not (ie, don't create pages for Brands).

In general, I usually just go for my website name, especially since it is my primary keyword phrase (makes for good SEO). However, make sure you don't violate those guidelines by doing so – they do not allow the use of only a generic term like "beer" or "pizza". However, something more specific like "Down Comforter Guide" should be fine, especially since it is the name of the website.

When you select a category, try to find something that matches the niche of your website, if you can. If you cannot, you may just want to select Retail and Consumer Merchandise for now. I will be doing this on my site since there is not a Home & Garden category available here.

I will actually be going into the Page Settings once I am done to make some changes to this because it creates this Page as a Community Page. That type of page doesn't allow Insights (demographics stats for your FB Page).

Once you have selected a category, provided your company name, and checked the check box, click on the **Get Started** button to proceed. Now you just need to provide a series of information to create your Page.

First provide a brief description of your site. This can be up to 155 characters in length, so try to pack as much power into this one statement as you can. It can help you get more exposure by including relational keywords here and/or emphasizing your main keywords again.

Next provide your website address. This will show up on the **About** page linked from your FB Page, so people will be able to easily visit your site if they want.

Finally, provide a URL for your Facebook Page. I try to just use the same thing as the name as the site, especially since this contains my keywords. However, you may have to pick an alternate if someone else has already claimed the URL.

Once you set this, you cannot change it without creating the page again and starting over completely, so be sure you have it set to what you want before you proceed by clicking the **Save Info** button.

Next you need to set a profile picture. This can be an image that you upload from your own computer or you can provide your website address to pick from images you have already used there.

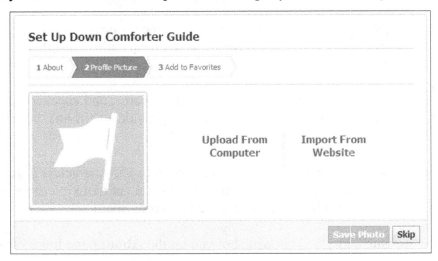

Click on either **Upload From Computer** or **Import From Website**, depending on where you want to retrieve the image from. Then just select your image that you want to use.

I have added in the picture for my profile, which is a picture that I also used on the site.

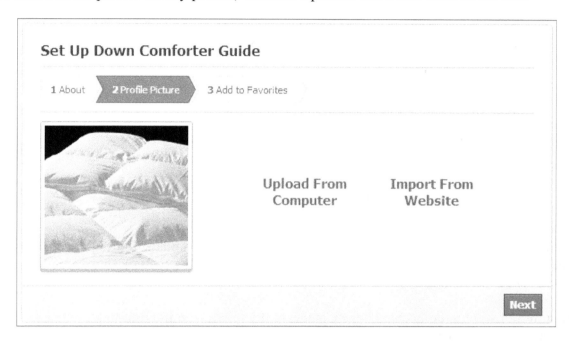

Once you have loaded a picture, click the **Next** button to proceed.

The final step is actually optional. It just recommends adding the Page to your Facebook Favorites menu so you can find it easily. This will show up in the left-hand sidebar menu when logged into your Facebook account.

Just click on **Add to Favorites** and then the **Next** button (or the **Skip** button if you don't want to do this step).

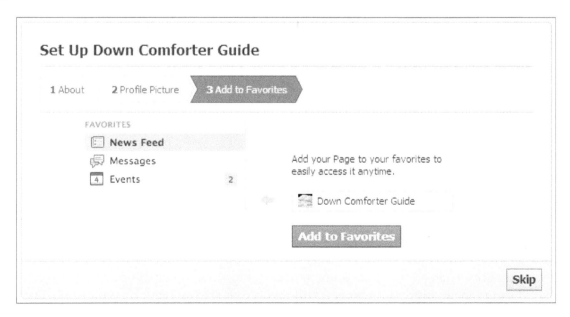

After you proceed past this step, you will be taken to your Facebook Page, which is now live!

The first thing I want to do is edit the settings for my page. Look for **Edit Page** in the top-right. When you hover over that, you will get more options – just click on **Update Page Info**.

On that page, there are a number of settings that we will want to update. During the creation of the page, Facebook just asked us for basic information to get it set up, but there is actually more info we can provide to enhance this page a bit.

The first thing I want to do is change the Category. If you click on the Edit link on the far-right of that row, you can set a new category.

I am changing my site to **Websites & Blogs → Home/Garden Website**. This classifies my Facebook Page as a Home & Garden Website Page and not as a Community Page. The main reason for this change is to get access to Insights – demographics stats for the Page.

Beyond the Category change, there are some other settings here that can be set that were not previously set during the creation of the page. Although these are optional, the more information you can provide about your site and your niche here, the easier it will be for people to find your Facebook Page.

Topics	Choose three words to describe your Page	Edit
Start Info	Joined Facebook	Edit
Release Date	Enter a release date	Edit
Short Description	Learn about down comforters and avoid many of the common problems that consumers of these bedding products experience.	Edit
Long Description	Write a long description for your Page	Edit

The first setting here is **Topics**. This allows us to set some relational keywords for our page, which can also aid with additional exposure within Facebook.

As you start to type a word for this setting, you'll see that various Facebook pages begin to show up below your typing. You can actually choose an existing page or interest on Facebook to use as a Topic to get potential exposure from people that like those pages or search for them.

Beyond **Topics**, the other main setting here that I would recommend that you update is the **Long Description**. Treat this just like the Short Description, except you're allow to provide much more text. All of this text will show up on the About page, which is linked from your Facebook Page and available for the public to see.

There are some other settings that could be provided here, but the ones I've discussed are the most important that will help you attract more visitors to your page from Facebook and/or search engines.

Once you're done editing settings, you can simply leave and return to the main Facebook page.

There are a couple of additional things that I would like to mention here. The first is Facebook Insights. This is the main reason I changed the page category – to get this section. If you don't see this in the center of your page towards the top, change the category to something else until this shows up.

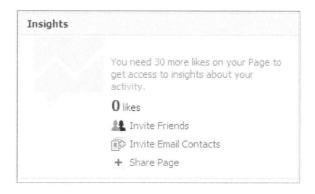

Once you reach 30 likes on your page, you'll receive information about your page likes, engagement with your posts, and even demographics for your fans. This information can be valuable to help you figure out what is working and what isn't for your particular niche and products.

The next thing I want to briefly mention is the status update bar. This should look familiar to you if you're familiar with Facebook. Just go here on your Facebook page to make posts. Posts can be made on a regular basis, if you would like, or they can simply be done sporadically. However, more frequent posting (especially non-promotional posts) will help you to build a following faster.

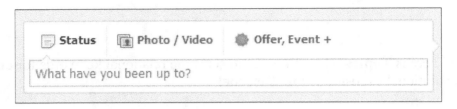

9-2 FACEBOOK APP CREATION

Beyond the basics of making posts on a Facebook Page, there are more things that you can do with it that the average user never figures out how to do.

To begin to utilize this power, you will need to create a Facebook App to get an App ID.

Click on the gear icon in the top-right of your Facebook page. Then click on **Manage Apps**.

On the Apps page, click the **Create New App** button towards the top-right of the page. This will open a window that asks for some basic information – an App name, a namespace (URL) for the App, and then a category.

Just provide the information you see below but replace with the name of your own site. Select **Apps for Pages** as your **App Category**.

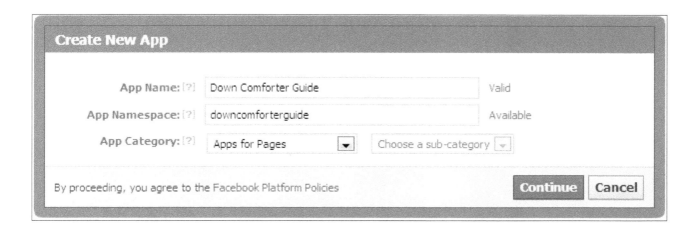

Now, look for the App ID at the top of the page – you'll need this ID for your page App in the next chapter.

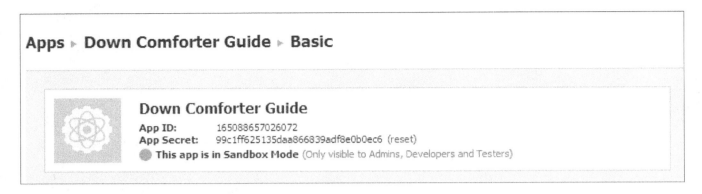

Below that you will see the Basic Info section. Here, you will simply need to change the Sandbox Mode from Enabled to Disabled so this App ID can be used.

9-3 ADD FACEBOOK TO YOUR WEBSITE

Now that we have a Facebook page setup, the next thing to do is connect it with our website. This allows us to build some of our fan page following directly from the site, which also gives you a shot at repeat business.

Since we're using WordPress, we could take advantage of plugins that already exist to help us integrate Facebook into the website easily. However, Facebook has made a number of changes or additions over the past year that have actually caused many of the WP plugins to break.

Here are the available things that you can integrate with your website:
https://developers.facebook.com/docs/plugins/

You may be able to search for a particular social plugin listed above to see if there is a WordPress plugin for it, in case you do not want to try to install one of these manually. However, I thought it would be best to show you how to do this straight from the source so you will be able to accomplish any of these tasks.

I'm going to walk you through a practical example of using one of these so you could repeat the process for others, if desired.

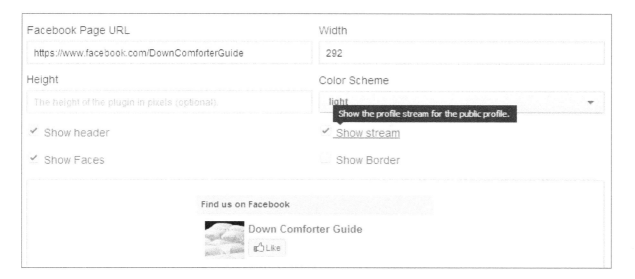

First, click on **Like Box** – this will be the Facebook social plugin that I will setup on the site.

On that page, simply specify your **Facebook Page URL** and choose other options.

The only other change I made was to uncheck **Show Border**.

Once you're done with the settings, scroll down and click on the **Get Code** button.

A window will open to provide you with code to install on your site and instructions on where to place that code.

Before you copy the code to use, be sure the right app ID is selected at the top.

Simply copy both pieces of code and paste them into the sidebar of your website (as a text widget).

The Facebook instructions say that the first piece of code should go right after the opening <body> HTML tag on your site, but this is not easily done with WordPress themes in general. However, using the code together still works just fine.

If you visit the live site, you can now see it working:

You may notice a couple of things about this.

First, it has a large blank space. This happens because I have not made any posts on my Facebook Page yet.

I could choose to simply not show the stream or set a height in the settings on Facebook before generating the code to change this (or just start making posts).

The second thing is that the right-hand side of it is cut off on my site using the Weaver II theme. This is because the Facebook social plugin has a minimum width of 292 pixels.

To make this all display on the site correctly in the sidebar, I need to change the width of the sidebar. To do this, go to **Appearance → Weaver II Admin**.

Now go to **Main Options → Layout** in the Weaver II menu:

About halfway down that page, look for the **Sidebar Wrappers Properties** setting:

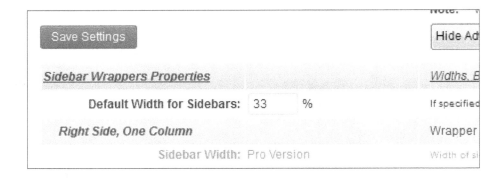

This box will be blank by default – just enter the number **33** here to change the sidebar width to fit our Facebook widget.

Now when I view the live page again, the full widget shows.

This will allow the full new feed stories to show up properly.

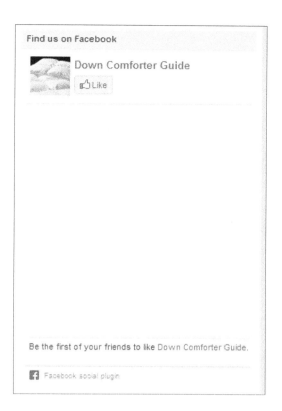

This allows me to build Facebook likes direct from my website and also share my posts with the website visitors. By building likes here, you will also get future exposure to those visitors through your posts on Facebook since those can show up in their personal news feed on their Facebook account.

9-4 FACEBOOK GROUP CREATION

Another great way to build a following is with the use of Facebook groups.

You can actually visit existing groups for a relational subject and make useful posts to try to attract users to your own page/group. However, the main purpose of this chapter is to teach you how to get started with creating your own group.

The main point of a group is to allow your followers a way to interact with you on a more personal level and even interact with other fans of yours.

A group will require personal work from you to get it started and popular, but it can actually become fairly self-maintaining once it reaches a tipping point (the member count can vary depending on their activity and sharing level).

From your Facebook Home page, look for **Groups** in the left-hand menu. Then click on **Create Group**.

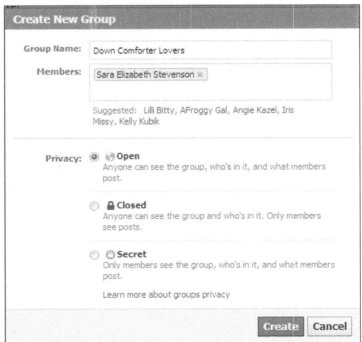

This opens up a window for you to name your group, add members, and set its **Privacy**.

You can name your group after your website or go for a more general name to target your niche/keywords.

I try to keep it relevant to my niche but will often change up the name slightly.

I've gone with **Down Comforter Lovers** for this group to make it more inviting to those looking to chat instead of coming across as a business.

You will need to add at least one member to a group to create it.

This is where it can be handy to have friends on your Facebook account already.

I always change the group **Privacy** to **Open** for these groups because I want them to be easy to find and enticing to join to get in on the conversation.

When you are finished, just click the **Create** button to proceed.

Next, choose an icon for your group. This is used when people see a link to your group in the left-hand menu in Facebook, among other places.

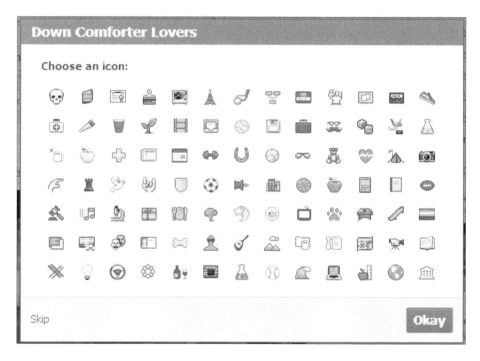

If you can find an icon that somewhat relates to your niche/products, go for that. Otherwise, just choose something you like but try not to make the icon misleading for your niche just so it isn't confusing to others. I've decided to pick the moon and star for my icon (since people sleep with down comforters at night and there isn't a bed or home icon).

Once this step is done, the group is created!

Although you could just go from here and start making posts in the group, there are some additional settings that you will want to take care of first.

Click **Edit Group Settings** under the gear icon in the top-right of the group page:

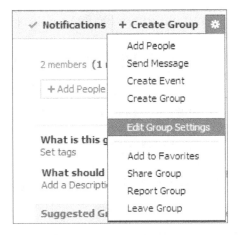

A number of settings on this page need to be setup initially and others may be settings that some of you may be wondering about.

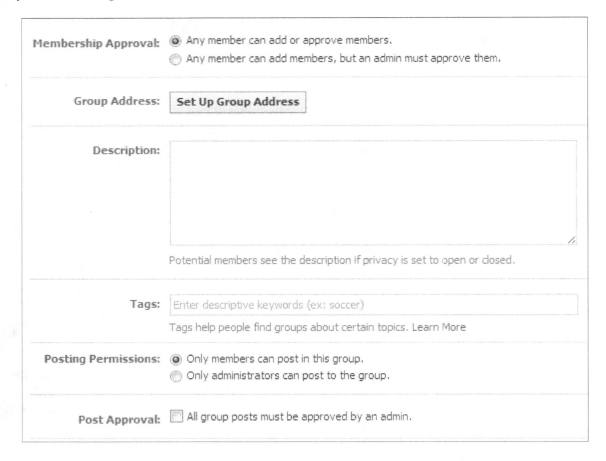

First, the **Membership Approval**. You can leave this set as the default, as you see above, or change it to force admin approval by you to join the group. The first can help newcomers engage in your group faster but may need to be disabled if you encounter spam problems frequently.

Next, set a **Group Address**. This is the URL people will use to get to your group. It is just a number by default, so setting it to real words can help people find it on Facebook and search engines easier. This can just be set to the name of the group as long as it contains the keywords you want to target.

The **Description** is shown on the group page, so this is a good place to briefly talk about the group or introduce people to it (don't give rules here).

Next, enter keywords for **Tags**. These will be for Facebook Interests, so target anything that may be of interest to people that you would want to join your group.

The last two settings here can be used for additional control, although I just leave these set to their default values.

Save your changes when you are finished with your settings.

If you would like, you can add a group photo at the top by hovering over the top-right corner. Click on the icon that appears and then click on **Upload Photo**. You can then reposition the picture you upload, if it isn't the right size.

When you are done with the Group Photo, it will show up at the top of the group, like this:

Beyond that, the rest is just about bringing in new group members and interacting with them by making posts using this post bar (you can also post videos, pictures, ask questions, or add files to download here as well).

To bring in new members, simply promote the group URL provided on the settings page (after you provide the Group Address). You can easily create a link to it from your website or your Facebook Page. Facebook will also attract new members for you based on the name, interests you selected as tags, and what people search for on Facebook.

9-5 FACEBOOK ADVERTISING

For those of you that are interested in speeding up the process of bringing people to your website, FB group or FB page, advertising on Facebook is actually an affordable option.

This guide is not intended to give you a complete overview of Facebook advertising because there is a lot you can really learn about it. However, I did want to show you one of the easiest ways that you can target specific groups of people with your Facebook ads and get cheap prices too.

My best recommendations for building ads:

- Target a Facebook Page/Group instead of your website
- Keep it simple and appealing – ie, "Like" us if you love down comforters
- Build custom targeting audiences

Facebook ads are all about targeting. You are better off targeting a small group of people that should be very likely to be interested in your ad compared with a large amount of people with less interest.

Facebook offers a ton of targeting options. You can easily enter specific interests, age groups, and/or countries to refine your targeting.

The real reason I wanted to create this chapter was to talk about building custom targeting audiences. You must use Google Chrome to do this because it is only offered in that browser on Facebook.

Before you can actually proceed with creating that audience for Facebook ads, you need to have a text file that contains a list of the people in that audience.

I have a special technique that I use for this purpose that I want to show you.

There are a ton of ways that you can find people on Facebook that are interested in the things that you want to target – it could be fans of other Facebook pages, people in other Facebook groups, or possibly just people that are actively commenting on a subject elsewhere on Facebook.

Simply put – just find people on Facebook that you would want to target with an advertisement. When you find them, just visit their Facebook page by clicking on their name.

I will use my page as an example:
https://www.facebook.com/ryanstevensonmarketing

From their page, edit the "www" from the URL and change it to "graph", as seen below:

This takes you to a page with text information:

This tells you the ID of the person right at the top – that long number is what you are after. Just copy that number and paste it into a Notepad file. You can also see information here, like the locale, which can help you if you want to avoid collecting Ids for people from certain countries (they could still be targeted by country in your ad targeting later though).

Continue collecting Ids for people that you want to target – just put one new id on each blank line of the Notepad file. You can actually collect hundreds of Ids using this technique in just 15-20 minutes once you get used to doing it.

Save the notepad file – we will need it in just a minute. We are now going to create a custom audience with that file.

From your Home page, click on **Manage Ads** from the menu under the gear icon in the top-right of the page.

Next, click on **Power Editor** in the left-hand menu.

This **Power Editor** is the feature that is only available in Google Chrome.

Now click on **Audiences** in the left-hand menu.

Then click on **Create Audience → Custom Audience** in that page towards the top.

Finally, just provide a name for your Audience, upload the file, and select the type of information that is contained in that file.

Once the Audience is approved by Facebook, you can simply create a Facebook ad as normal but choose from these Audiences to use as your targeting instead of using normal controls.

10 GOOGLE AND YOUTUBE MARKETING

Google is a major source of traffic for my Amazon sites, so I focus a lot on them and a number of their services. I always add Google Analytics and Google Webmaster Tools to my sites. Google Plus is also useful to make your site more attractive in the search results, increasing the chances of obtaining traffic. I also utilize YouTube, a Google property, for many of my sites because unique, targeted videos can bring in a lot of traffic.

Primary Lesson Objective

☐ Add Analytics, Webmaster Tools & Google Plus to your Site

Lesson Steps Checklist

☐ Add Website to Google Analytics

☐ Build Sitemap & Add Website to Google Webmaster Tools

☐ Create Google Plus Account to Socialize your Search Listings

☐ Create a YouTube Channel for your Niche

☐ Create & Publish Custom Videos on YouTube

Chapter Notes

Chapter Notes

10-1 GOOGLE ANALYTICS

Google has a number of different services that I like to utilize for my Amazon sites. The first of these is Google Analytics, which allows us to track the traffic on our site.

To get started, visit http://www.google.com/analytics/

You will then need to sign into an existing Google account or create a new account. Look for the **Sign in** or **create an account** links in the top-right. Proceed through logging into your account or click Sign Up in the top-right to create a new Google account.

Sign in or create an account

Once you are logged into a Google account, you can then proceed with creating your Google Analytics account.

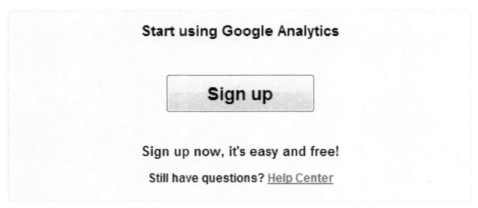

They are currently allowing sign ups for two kinds of Analytics accounts. I would recommend going with Universal Analytics, since this seems to be the new system that will likely eventually replace Classic Analytics.

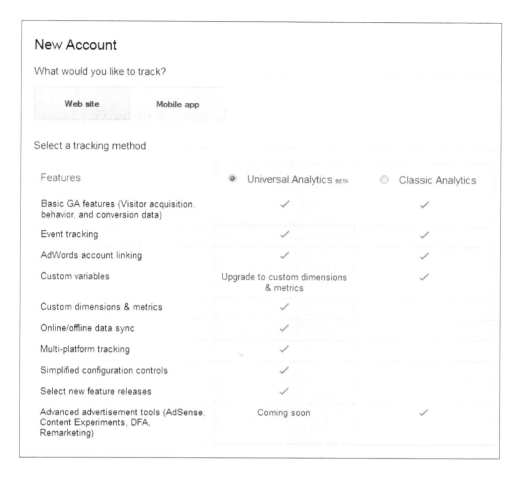

Next, provide information for your account including the account name, website name, website URL, category, and time zone. You can see the information I have provided to create my account below.

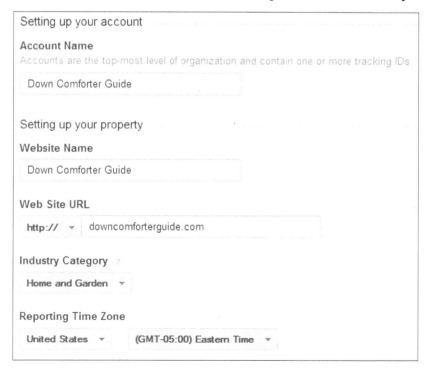

The last part of the account creation process involves data sharing. I would recommend to deselect the last check box for **Account specialists** – this is really only useful for those using Google Adwords/Adsense and want Google to get involved to try to help improve your campaigns (likely by selling you services).

Once you are done providing the necessary information, just click on the **Get Tracking ID** button.

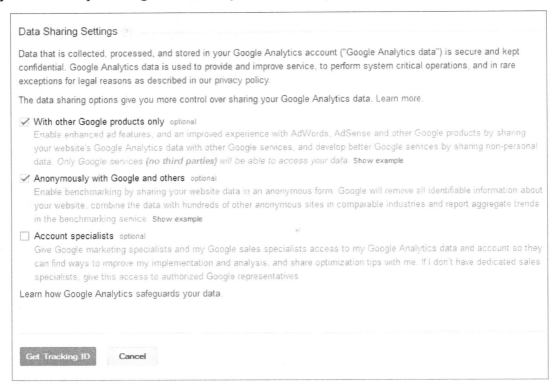

You will then be shown a Terms of Service Agreement. Click on the **I Accept** button to complete the creation of your Google Analytics account.

Once your account is created, you will be shown the tracking code that needs to be put on your site.

Just select all of the code and copy it.

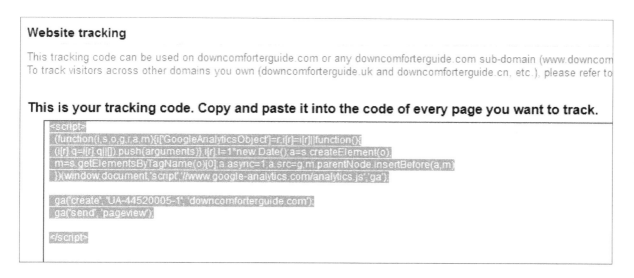

Now go to your WordPress site. Click on **Appearance → Weaver II Admin**.

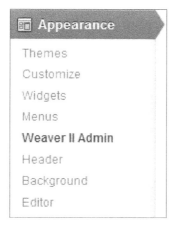

Navigate to **Advanced Options → HTML Insertion** in the Weaver admin tabs at the top of the page.

On this page, look for the **Footer Code** section. Paste the Google Analytics code into the text box here, and then save the changes. You can now track your site traffic through Google Analytics.

Footer Code

This code will be inserted into the site footer area, just before

```
ga('create', 'UA-44520005-1', 'downcomforterguide.com');
ga('send', 'pageview');

</script>
```

10-2 GOOGLE WEBMASTER TOOLS

The next Google service that I use is Google Webmaster Tools. This service helps to ensure that Google indexes all of the pages of our site. It is also useful to let us know if there are problems with the site and where the site stands in search rankings.

Visit https://www.google.com/webmasters/tools/

As long as you are still signed into your Google account, you can proceed with adding a site to Google Webmaster Tools (use the same Google account).

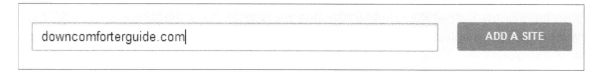

At the bottom-center of the page, look for the text box and the **ADD A SITE** button. Just enter your domain name here and click the button to get started.

Next, you will need to verify ownership of your site. I use the HTML file upload method, which is also Google's recommended method because it doesn't add any extra code to your live site.

Just download the file using the text link for #1. Then upload that file to the base directory of your public site. This can be done in your cPanel using the File Manager, or it can also be done through FTP.

Once you have uploaded the file, click on the link for step #3. You should see a message like this in your browser if you have uploaded the file correctly (letters/numbers at the end will be different in your message).

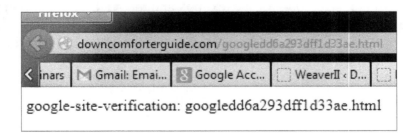

Now that you know the file was uploaded to the right place, just click on the red **Verify** button at the bottom of the Google Webmaster Tools page.

Google will then verify the site, and show you a message like this – just click on the **Continue** link to proceed.

Once you are in your Google Webmaster Tools account, navigate to **Crawl → Sitemaps** in the left-hand menu.

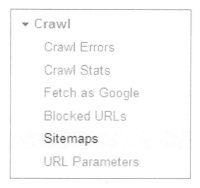

In a different browser tab/window, go to your WordPress admin. Install a new plugin called **Google XML Sitemaps (Plugins → Add New**, then search for it). Click on **Install Now**, and then the **Activate** link.

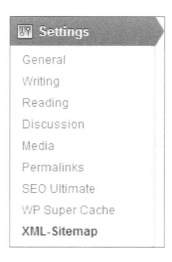

Once that plugin is installed, you can find the settings page for it under **Settings → XML-Sitemap** in the WP admin menu.

Now, click on the **Click here** text link at the top of that page to generate the sitemap for your site.

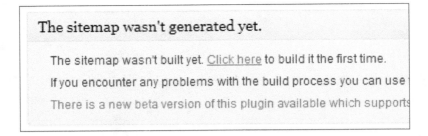

Now go back to Google Webmaster Tools. Click on the **Add/Test Sitemap** button.

This opens up a text box – just type in **sitemap.xml** and then click on the **Submit Sitemap** button.

You will then see the number of pages submitted in your sitemap. Check back in a day or two to see if there are any problems detected with your site. Google Webmaster Tools can provide a variety of useful information, so be sure to browse through the available pages to see what can be done here.

10-3 GOOGLE PLUS

Google has their own social network, Google Plus. Although it can be a good way to connect with others and build a network of friends and even site visitors, just like Facebook, I actually use it primarily for the search ranking benefits that it can offer.

In particular, I want to be able to get my search results to show up with a picture of me next to them, which can drastically help to increase click through rates.

While signed into your Google account from other steps, visit http://plus.google.com/

Proceed through the creation of your account. In the first step, you just need to provide your name, gender and birthday.

The second step involves adding people to your account. You do not necessarily have to do this step though. Instead of adding people you know in the first part of this step, you can actually skip it and then add people/companies that you don't know that are relational to your niche to get in their circles.

I added the family category to my circle, since this looks to be the most relational and would also likely have my target consumer in it already.

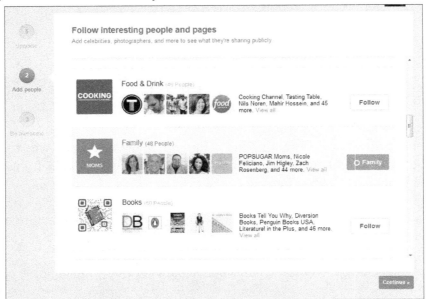

In the third step, you need to upload a picture of yourself.

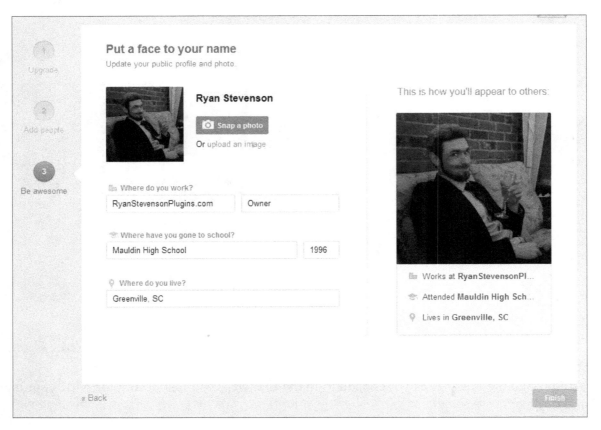

I know some people may be paranoid about doing this, but it really isn't that big of a deal – create a fake name and profile, if you must. However, it can be good to use your real name/picture to set up a real profile that you could actually use for all of your Amazon sites.

Once you are finished with creating your profile, click on the **Finish** button in the bottom-right.

Now that you are in Google+, visit the **About** link at the top of the page.

You should do your best to provide as much information here as possible – Google likes completed profiles.

One particular thing that you must do is scroll down and look for the **Links** section on the page. Click the Edit link at the bottom.

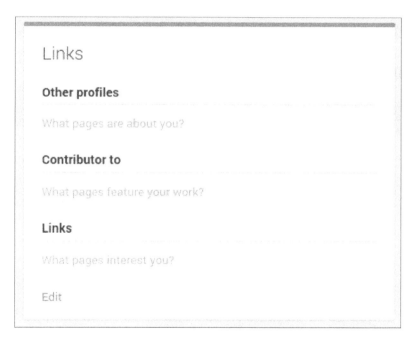

Here, you can connect other accounts like Facebook or YouTube to your Google+ account. Assuming you have relevant accounts with these other services, add them here (or come back and add them when you do).

Also add your website to the contributor list, as seen below:

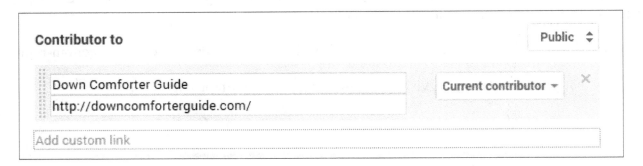

Now, take note of the URL of this page – everything up through the word **about**. Select and copy it.

Now that we're done with Google Plus, we need to integrate this into our WordPress site. In particular, we want to set up Google Authorship so that our Google Plus profile is associated with the content we have created on our site. This is what allows that information to be shown in search results, although doing this does not guarantee that will happen (but it is required to make it possible).

On the WordPress site, search for, install and activate a plugin called **Google Author Link**.

Now go to **Users → Your Profile**.

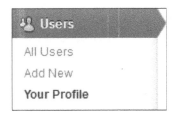

On the profile page, provide the your **Google Profile URL** and **Google+ Profile URL** (both the same – the URL you just copied) and save the changes.

Contact Info	
E-mail *(required)*	ryan@ryanstevensonplugins.com
Website	http://downcomforterguide.com/
Google Profile URL	ıs://plus.google.com/111336807012583649985/about
Google+ Profile URL	https://plus.google.com/111336807012583649985/ab

Now go to **Settings** → **Google Author Link**.

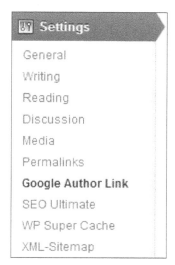

On this page, select your user profile in the drop-down box under **Home page user profile**, and then save the changes.

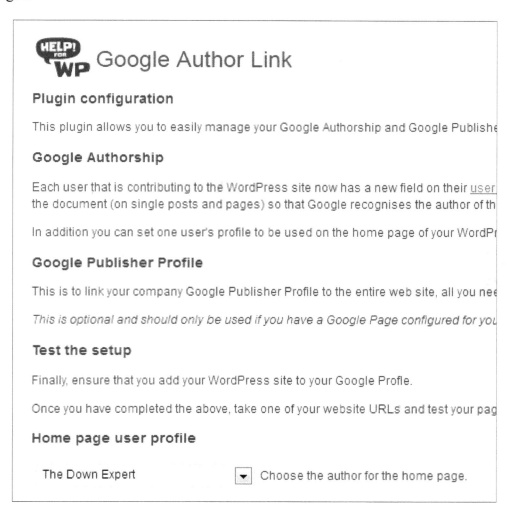

Once this is done, we need to run a test to ensure this is setup properly. Under **Test the setup**, look for the text link that says **Rich Snippets Testing Tool**. Click it.

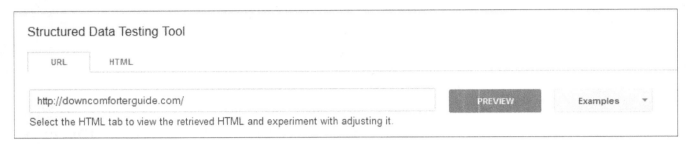

This actually takes us to Google Webmaster Tools. Just enter your home page URL in the text box at the top, and click the **Preview** button.

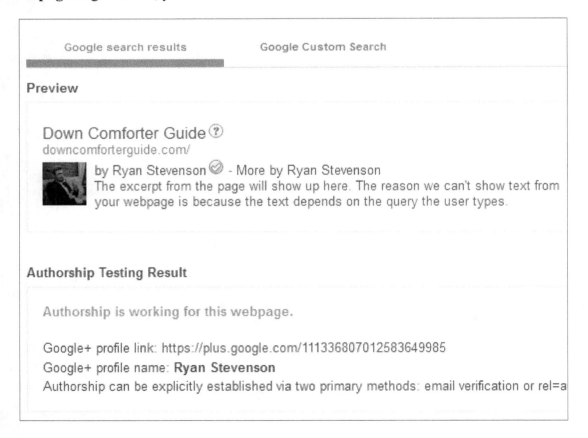

You should now see your website search result preview with your name and profile picture, like it might show up in the search results.

Look for the part that says **Authorship Testing Result** – as long as it says **Authorship is working for this webpage** in green text, you are all set.

10-4 YOUTUBE CHANNEL CREATION

The other Google services I have covered in this guide so far should be considered mandatory for each of your sites. With that said, there is one more Google service, YouTube, that can be very helpful for your site, although it is something that you can consider optional.

To create a YouTube account, you have to create your own videos. This can be done in a variety of ways, but all of the video creation options will require you to record your voice (which some people object to doing).

It really doesn't matter if you have a great speaking voice or not, and even the worst speaking voices will improve with practice. If you don't believe me, search out some of my plugin tutorial videos from 2010 or 2011 on YouTube – just a couple of years ago – and compare them to the videos from this training course.

To get started, just visit: http://www.youtube.com/

Since YouTube is Google owned now, you don't need a separate account. Once you visit the site while logged into your Google account still, you should see the window below show up over the YouTube website:

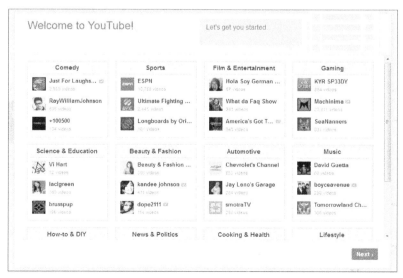

This window is to add subscriptions, which you don't have to do. However, if you don't plan on creating many videos, you can actually subscribe to some highly relational channels to boost the relevancy of your own channel.

For now, you can just click on the **Next** button because you can always search for channels to subscribe to later. Then, click the **Cancel** button on the next screen.

If you click on your name in the top-right of YouTube, it will open a menu for you:

Click on the **My channel** link to create your channel. You can do this using your name or you can also do it under a business/other name. You can actually have multiple channels on a single account, if you want, so you could use a single Google account to run many Amazon sites.

I'm going to click on the text link in the bottom-left: **To use a business or other name, click here.**

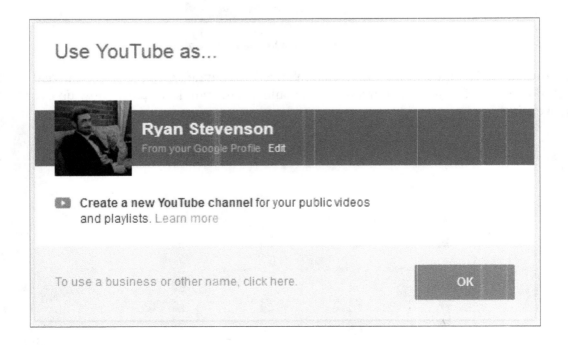

This allows me to name my YouTube channel, which I will call Down Comforter Guide. Just provide a name for your channel, and select the other options, as seen below (make sure your content selection for the last drop-down box is accurate). Click the **Done** button when you are finished.

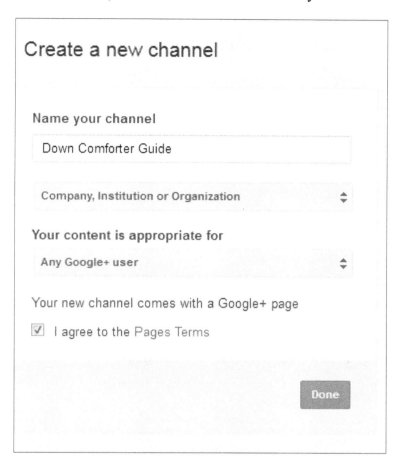

YouTube will then walk you through a brief tour of your channel. The **Channel Setup Checklist** is the last part of this, which shows up in the top-right of the page.

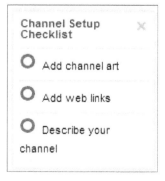

The channel art is optional but feel free to add a relational picture if you have something large enough.

I'm mainly interested in the web links and channel description here. Click on the **About** tab in the middle of the page to set these.

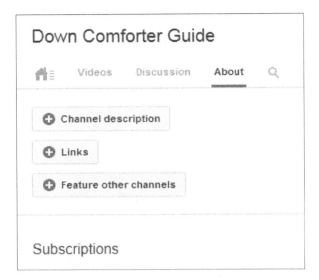

Now just click on **Channel description** and then **Links** to provide relevant information.

The **Channel description** is a great place to describe your niche, your products and ultimately the purpose of your channel (good place for search keyword usage).

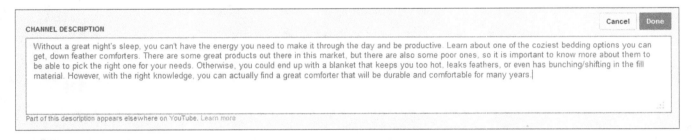

For **Links**, you should obviously be providing a link to your site, although multiple links can be provided. You can also set it to show social links here. Social links, like to your Facebook page, can be set in the **YouTube Settings** (through the top-right menu when you click on your name).

10-5 VIDEO RECORDING

One option with Amazon product videos is to simply use a webcam to record a video. If you have one on your computer and are comfortable doing this, it is a simple option (there should be software on your computer for your webcam that can be used to record audio/video).

You could simply talk about a product or your target subject. Targeting product names is definitely one approach, but you will find yourself able to gain more followers by providing useful videos relating to your niche – think about the content I recommend to build. There isn't anything wrong with offering a combination of both types of videos though.

You could also choose to buy products to unbox and review them in person on camera. However, if this is of interest to you, I strongly suggest you try it out with cheap products first to get a reliable method worked out that will be profitable for you to cover the cost the products you review.

A lot of people won't want to do webcam videos, which is quite alright. There is another option.

For video recording of your screen, I recommend using HyperCam – free software (see the bold note below – very important to avoid the adware in this software). This allows you to simply show people what you are doing on the computer while you talk about it.

Visit this site to download a copy: http://www.hyperionics.com/hc/

Now, just click the download link:

What is HyperCam™?
New! Ver. 2.28.01 is now available for download

HyperCam version 2, a product of Hyperionics, is now offered free for world-wide usage, both for private use and commercially.

Download HyperCam™ v2 For Free

281

The one downside to HyperCam is that it actually has "adware" included. However, it can be installed without that adware.

During the installation, look for the screen below. Select the bubble next to Custom Installation, and then deselect both of the check boxes. You can then click Next to install HyperCam without the adware!

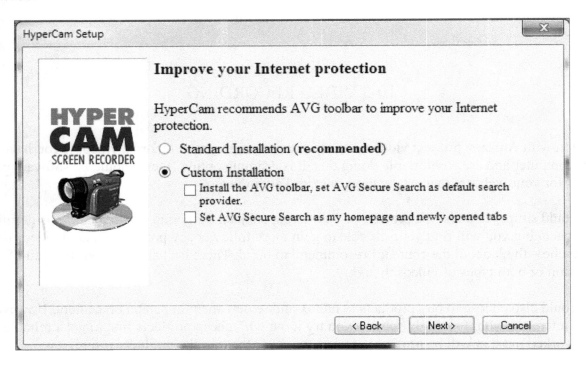

Once you have this running, you'll see this page (but likely with different settings):

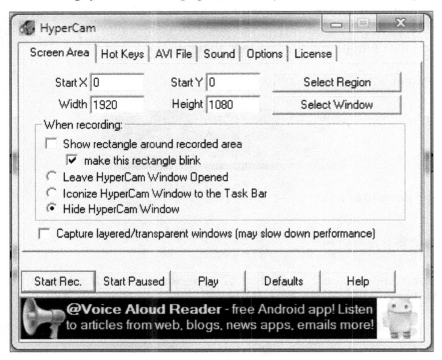

The area of settings that says **When recording**, make sure these are copied based on this picture.

The Width and Height settings above are set to 1920 and 1080 for mine – this is 1080p HD. You could also use 1280 and 720 for those settings for 720p HD. The lower HD can help to reduce file size for your videos and also give you an area of your screen that isn't being recorded if you have a 1080p HD resolution screen (laptops may need to use the lower setting anyways).

Now, go to the **AVI File** tab.

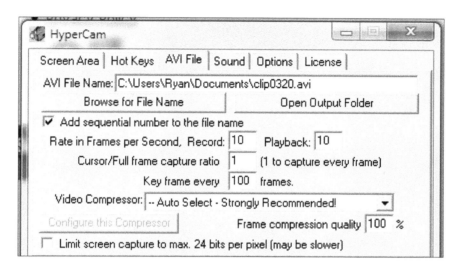

Check the settings here and match them up to my picture (except for the AVI File Name at the top). The most important thing here is to set Frame compression quality to 100%. If this is not done, the video can end up distorted and may make text unreadable.

Click on **Open Output Folder** to find your video recordings, once you have created one.

Before you start recording, check the Sound tab to ensure that your microphone is selected.

I strongly suggest that you practice a few times before your first attempt, and try to record your entire video in one take to eliminate the need for editing (this saves TONS of time).

I like to simply use a browser page and show things to people while I talk about them. You could simply browse an Amazon product listing for what you are reviewing, and maybe even browse some other important sites relating to the product (like a manufacturer page for it).

Another option is to create slideshow presentations about products that use a combination of text and pictures. If you want to try this, check out http://openoffice.org/

Open Office is an open-source (free) software that is designed to be very similar to (and compatible with) Microsoft Office. It has a Presentation/Slideshow creation software like PowerPoint that can be used for this purpose.

There is plenty of documentation out there if you want to learn how to create a slideshow – just start with Open Office help files. You don't have to do anything fancy really – just add an image to each slide and put in some text (possibly with some effects to make it a bit flashy without much effort).

Set up your screen with your browser window or presentation.

You can then press the F2 button on your keyword to begin recording (as long as HyperCam is running). Pressing it again will stop the recording. F3 can be used to pause/resume.

10-6 VIDEO EDITING & PUBLISHING

I strongly urge you to avoid video editing, if at all possible. It will save you an enormous amount of time and work. It is much quicker to simply practice your video a few times until you get it right than it is to do a bunch of takes and edit them together. It also produces a higher quality video in the end.

Video Editing
If you need a video editor and use Windows, you can use Windows Movie Maker to edit the videos that come from HyperCam.

Other software should also be available for Mac, and there are even better titles available for Windows as well.

Whatever software you end up using for video editing should have a fairly extensive help/tutorial system.

With Windows Movie Maker, you simply load up a video. Then you place the cursor (or stop the video) at a point. You can then right-click the video to split it. Then, you can simply delete split off portions of the video that you do not want anymore.

You can find an older video of mine on YouTube that shows you how to do video editing here: http://www.youtube.com/watch?v=xq6mCkpeobc

Video Publishing
The real purpose of this particular chapter is to actually teach you about publishing your video on YouTube.

To start, just click on the **Upload** button in the top-center of the YouTube site:

Next, just click on the large up arrow in the center of the screen and select the video from your computer that you want to upload to YouTube:

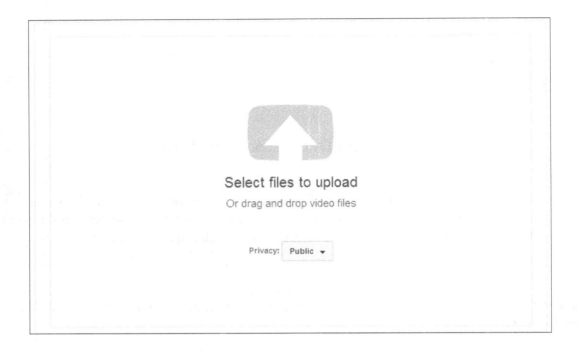

This will begin the video upload. While it is uploading and processing, you can set information for the video.

First, provide a **Title**. Don't be afraid to target a specific keyword phrase here because it can definitely help you bring in traffic from that phrase to your video (just make sure the phrase is very relevant to your video).

Next, provide a **Description**. This can contain a lot of text, which can be beneficial for getting better search rankings on this video – describe your video and what it is about as much as possible. I also take the chance to place a link here to my own site. It can be to the home page or to a relational page of your site. This helps to bring in traffic from the video to your site and also helps to boost the search rankings of your site.

The **Tags** are basically keywords for your video. Target your main keywords for the video here but also target other relational words that people might search for to find your video. As you type, YouTube will make suggestions. Go for these suggestions when they are available but also don't be afraid to make your own keywords when they fit (you can split them with a comma manually).

Next, write out a message to **Post to your subscribers**. This message will be sent out to subscribers of your social media accounts, like Google+ and Facebook, so this message can have a link in it to your own website to help drive traffic to an offer there.

The last thing you need to do here is change the **Category** to something relational. If you can't find a good **Category** to pick, you can just choose **People & Blogs**.

When the video is done uploading and processing, take a look at the **Video thumbnails** section. You can select one of a few choices of thumbnails pulled from the video to make it more appealing to click, but you can also choose to upload your own thumbnail, if you wish.

Also be sure to visit the **Advanced settings** tab for the video:

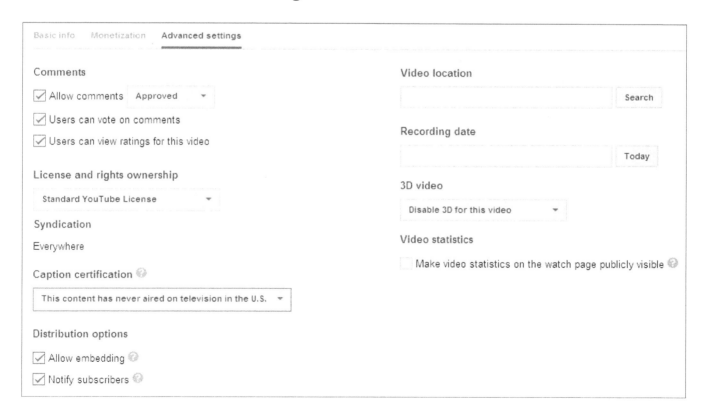

You can do a few things here, like make Comments be set to Approval by you only, set the recording date, etc. I've shown my most common settings above, minus a recording date.

If you wanted to put the video on your own website as well, start by visit the video page on YouTube after it is done uploading and processing.

Click on the **Share** and then **Embed** tabs below the video:

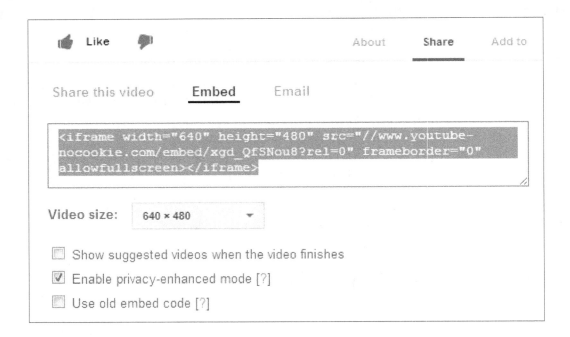

Select and copy the iframe HTML code provided in the box (you can see my normal settings above).

You can then simply paste this code into the HTML content of a page on your WordPress site to show the video there and make it playable directly on your site for your visitors.

11 SQUIDOO MARKETING

The eleventh class is the final marketing class of this series. We will learn how to use Squidoo to generate additional revenue and also to drive more targeted traffic to our site. This lesson will teach you how to create your first Squidoo lens. You will also learn how to get great search rankings with your lenses and even how to avoid problems with Squidoo.

Primary Lesson Objective

☐ Create a Squidoo Lens

Lesson Steps Checklist

☐ Create a Squidoo Account

☐ Research Relational Squidoo Lenses for Targeting & Tags

☐ Build Your Squidoo Lens

☐ Link Your Lens to Your Website

☐ Promote Relational Amazon Products on Your Lens (Optional)

Chapter Notes

Chapter Notes

11-1 GETTING STARTED WITH SQUIDOO

The last marketing site that I will be showing you is Squidoo. This site has always been a long-time favorite of mine and many other marketers because it can be used to promote your own websites in your own way.

The basic concept behind Squidoo is that you build content pages on their site, called a "lens". You can put Amazon ads direct on the lens or even link back to your own website. On top of that, Squidoo lenses are often well respected by Google and can easily get great search engine rankings when done correctly.

I also like that lenses can teach marketers about building content. As you proceed through this Squidoo class, pay special attention to the way others have build their lenses and the variety of options that Squidoo offers to build your own.

You may notice that many lenses are actually quite extensive – a lot of content on a single web page. This is actually a primary reason why Google respects lens content. Google loves to see long, in-depth pages that offer a variety of information. In this same regard, try creating a page like this on your own site and see what it can do for your search rankings.

Creating a Squidoo Account

Before you can use Squidoo to create a lens, you will need an account. Don't worry – it is free.

In fact, there is one more thing that I didn't mention about Squidoo before – they actually pay you!

They have a variety of advertising choices that you can use in a lens, which shares revenue with Squidoo. Amazon ads are available there, but you don't actually have to use those ads. If you promote your own site and refer the sales yourself, you'll get the full commission.

Even if you don't use any of the Squidoo advertising options, you STILL get paid by them! Just the traffic you receive on each of your lenses will each you a paycheck – the more lenses and the more traffic you have, the more you make (even if that traffic just leaves the lens and visits your site).

Unless, you have a decent number of lenses with decent traffic, you won't make a ton of money from Squidoo. However, I look at this as extra earnings. This is essentially freebie money because I would still build these lenses without it.

To get started, just click on the JOIN US link at the top of Squidoo
http://www.squidoo.com/lensmaster/referral/fluffydown

Next, just provide some basic information to sign up. If you want, you can even connect this Squidoo account with your Facebook account that you are using for your fan page and group.

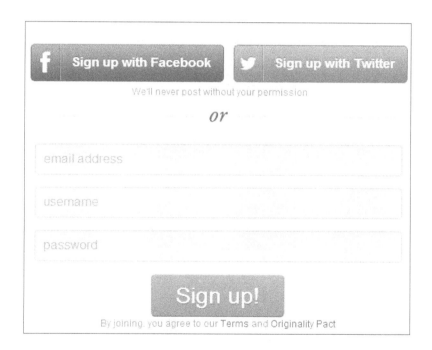

After you enter your information, you will see a notice that you have to agree to if you want to proceed. Read the entire notice because it is very important.

Does the Squidoo approach sound familiar?

Since March 2013, they have started enforcing what I have been teaching affiliates for years – focus on quality, unique content and stop with the automated, cookie-cutter sites with countless affiliate links.

Just in case Squidoo happens to remove this notice in the future, I included it in this book because this really summarizes everything that I have been trying to teach you. Maintain this type of focus throughout all of your online marketing work, and you will find yourself gaining success faster than you ever imagined possible.

An important note from Squidoo to all of our members!

(You'll need to read this and hit the big button at the bottom, and then we'll get out of your way). We have a challenge and we need your help...

Thanks to you and the millions of Squids who have embraced The Scroll of Originality, Squidoo has reached records amount of traffic, charitable donations and user revenue. We stand (we always have) for passionate, original content. Squidoo is about storytelling, first hand reviews and recommendations.

Our site is only as good as the pages our users build, and lately, too many people are taking a short-term view and building pages that don't work, pages the search engines don't like, and pages that are cookie-cutter instead of personal.

We need all of our users to reconfirm that they're committed to our approach to content.

The important rules are still the same: share your passions, tell stories and be personal.

Starting in March, 2013, we'll be running scans on all of our featured lenses to more aggressively detect spun content, junk and keyword stuffing. If your lens gets flagged it will get locked (and eventually deleted without notice) but you have the opportunity to fix these lenses and make them better. And you can start right now.

Check out this lens which explains how you can fix some of the widespread problems we're seeing before you get flagged. It's entirely possible that your lenses need no improvement at all, but if you've actively swapped ratings, added countless affiliate links and focused on the short-term, we need you to take action now.

It's simple: go through your lenses, make them personal, delete extraneous affiliate links and ugly buttons. Make them the sort of thing you'd like to see, not the product of gaming the system and industrialized linkbaiting.

98.4% of Squidoo is amazing. If we work together, we take all of our pages where they need to go.

> **YES! I agree, let's improve the magic.**

Please lock all of my lenses now, I'd rather not use Squidoo as intended.

Once you are in your account, look at the activity stream in the center of the page. The first thing listed there will ask you to fill out your profile – just click on the **fill out your profile** link.

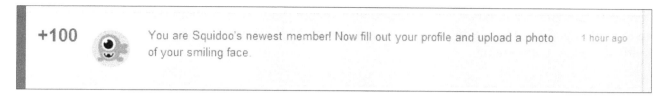

The main reason you want to visit this page is to complete your account profile, but there is also one more thing worth pointing out here. You can connect various accounts to your Squidoo account. At the bottom of the Account tab, you can find a button that allows you to add Google Analytics to your account to allow you to track your lens traffic.

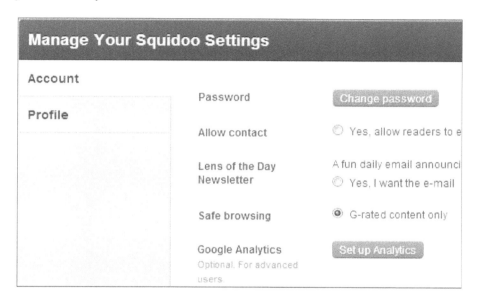

Click on the Profile tab on the left. Then profile your name, a biography for your public profile, and finally upload a picture. When you are done, be sure to save your changes.

The last thing you need to do is verify your payment settings here:
http://www.squidoo.com/lensmaster/payment_settings

You can set a minimum payout amount and also specify your paypal email address, if it is different from the email you used to create your Squidoo account. This information can also be set for each individual lens that you create.

11-2 LENS RESEARCH & TARGETING

Before you build a lens, I recommend doing some research on Squidoo to see what others are doing and to find out what is working.

Look for the search bar in the top-right:

To start, just search for a phrase relating to your niche. I'll search for **down comforters**.

I'm looking to find other related lenses to find what is working the best.

Look right below the title of a lens:

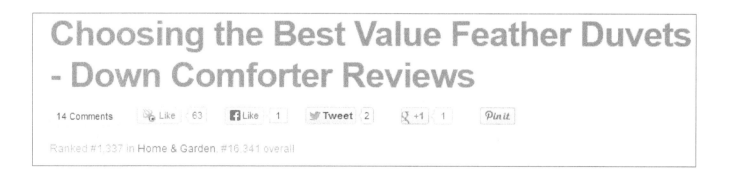

You can see how many comments it has received, as well as likes on Squidoo, Facebook and more.

Some lenses will also show you a ranking. If they do not have a ranking, they may be in the Cozy magazine, so just gauge popularity based on the other information there.

Try to pick out six relating lenses that are also popular. However, go for relational pages over popular ones if there is a limited selection in your niche.

Open a notepad file and record the URLs for these six pages.

Examine those six pages closer to see what type of content they have provided.

When you find one that is popular and also has advertisements on it or links out to other pages, take note of how they did that because it was obviously done in a way that didn't offend the visitors of the lens.

This research may also help to give you some ideas for creating your own lens.

One particular thing to look at on each of those pages are the **Related Tags**. This can be found on the right-hand sidebar of a lens, although it is possible that a lenses has not provided tags.

Copy and paste the tags into a Notepad file to use for reference later.

Some lenses may contain a "More" link in the bottom-right of the Related Tags section. Be sure to click on that to expand the entire list of tags.

Here is the list from one lens I have viewed:

Pretty much anything listed here would also make a good tag to use for my own lens.

On top of that, Squidoo may sometimes display your lens on other lenses under the **Explore related pages** section:

Explore related pages

Finding Cozy Plush Electric Blankets on Sale

Using Alternative Down Comforter Reviews to Buy Great Comforters

California King Comforter

Tangerine Bedding

Queen Size Bed Comforter Sets

King Size Duvet Covers

I will talk more about this during the lens creation tutorial, but for now, I can tell you that using the same tags as popular lenses can help to get your lens to show up on some of those lenses in this section. Beyond that, it can also help with your search engine rankings and even obtaining search traffic from Squidoo.

11-3 LENS CREATION TUTORIAL

We can now begin creating a lens! To get started, just click on the **START A LENS!** Link in the top-left of the page.

First, you have to proceed through a four-step process before you can actually begin to create the lens itself.

Start by telling Squidoo what your lens is about – this ends up being used as the lens title in the next step, although you are given another opportunity to change it.

Click the **Continue** button when you are ready to go to the next step.

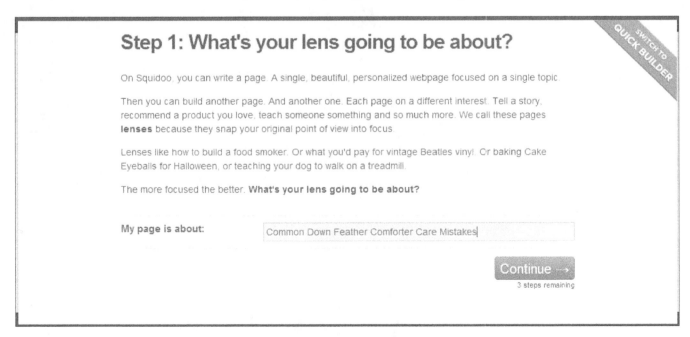

For step 2, you start by providing a title for your lens. If you already did this for step 1, you may not need to do anything with it here.

Take note of the tip from Squidoo – clever lens titles get more attention. Don't be afraid to use more than just a target keyword phrase in your title because it can help you get more traffic to your lens.

Next, look at the lens URL. You can leave this as it is, which will be based on your title. However, you may also want to shorten it or change it to make it more relevant/meaningful. I want a couple of meaningful keywords in my URL, but I also don't want to overdo it, so I will often shorten my URL.

The last thing you really need to worry about here is selecting your lens topic. Just look through the options in the drop-down list and pick the most relevant one. You will then be provided a choice of subtopics. You must also set the appropriate rating for your content, but this will most likely be able to be left unchanged.

Here are the settings I have provided for this step:

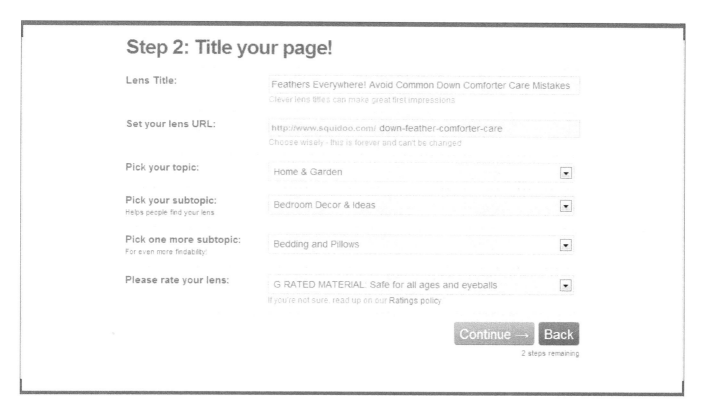

For step 3, we need to provide tags for our lens. Pick four relevant tags to use here. These are keywords or keyword phrases.

I often just pick from tags that I have from my research list, but you can also type in words to get Squidoo to offer you some common choices.

Try to just select four of the most relevant tags you could use for your lens. However, don't stress over this too much because you will able to return to these tags later to edit them and even add more of them.

Once you are done with your tags, just enter the captcha word and then click the Continue button to proceed to the final step.

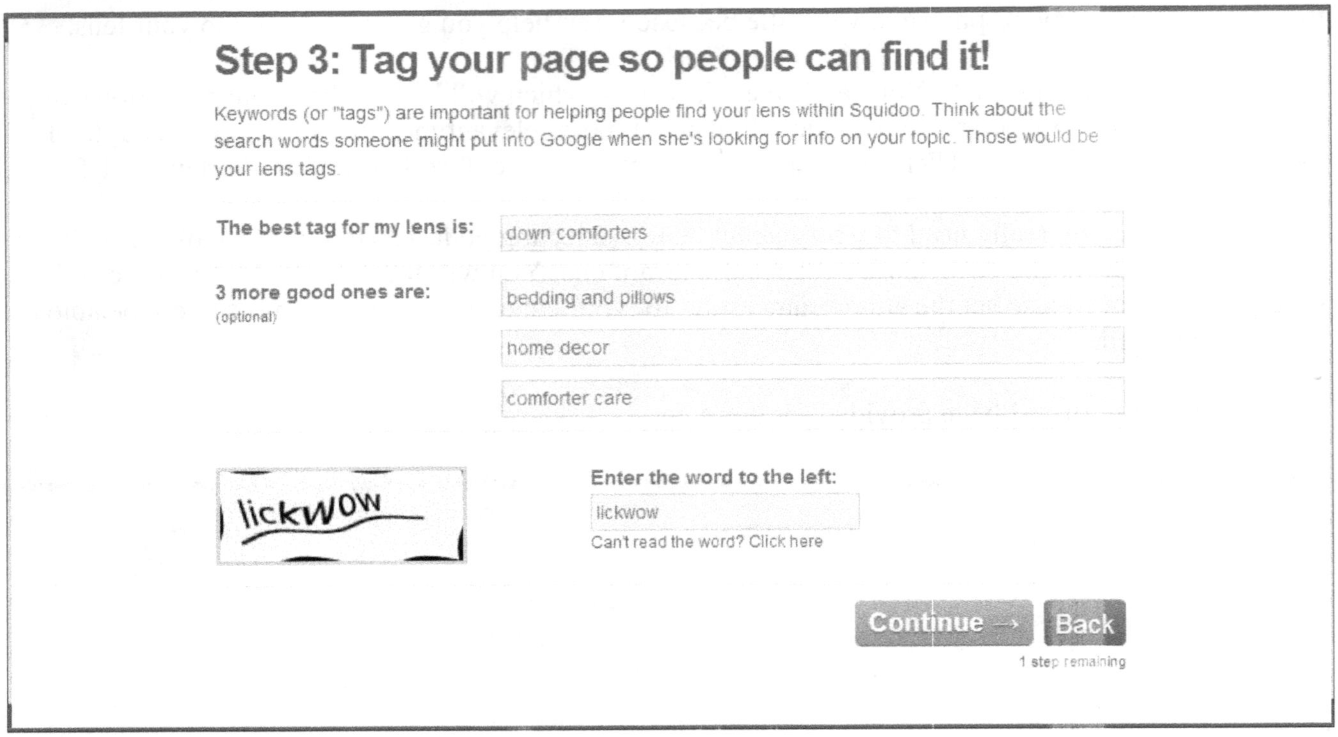

Step 3: Tag your page so people can find it!

Keywords (or "tags") are important for helping people find your lens within Squidoo. Think about the search words someone might put into Google when she's looking for info on your topic. Those would be your lens tags.

The best tag for my lens is:

down comforters

3 more good ones are:
(optional)

bedding and pillows

home decor

comforter care

lickWOW

Enter the word to the left:

lickwow

Can't read the word? Click here

Continue →   Back

1 step remaining

For the final step (not pictured here), you just have to choose how you want to get paid. You can select the cash option at the bottom and provide a Paypal email address where you want to receive your payments. This will be payments for visitors to your lenses as well as any Squidoo powered advertising commissions from sites like Amazon, eBay, etc (just the ads you create with their system).

You can choose to donate your earnings from Squidoo to a charity also, something that can actually help to boost the popularity of your lens. If you aren't focusing on earning money from advertising on the lens, you can select a charity option to try to bring more traffic to your lens and eventually to your own website.

The actual earnings from a single lens without advertising will not be very significant unless you have a lot of regular visitors to it. If you end up creating a number of lenses, try one of them as a charity lens just to see what happens so you can compare it to a cash lens to figure out which is more worthwhile for you.

After you have made your selection, just click on the **Continue** button to proceed to the actual lens creation page.

On this page, you have three main sections.

On the left is the toolbar, which is pictured below. This allows you to add new content to your lens, edit lens settings, check your building progress, and finally publish the lens.

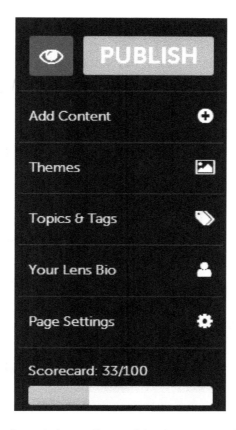

On the far right is the widget and module toolbar. This shows you the pieces to your lens and also allows you to change the order they are displayed on the lens. Simply drag and drop to change the order, and then click the **Apply** button to make the changes save.

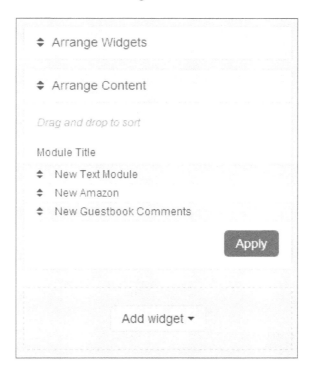

You actually build the lens itself in the middle of the page. A lens is made up of different sections of content, also called modules (seen in the above list).

You're started out with some default modules, but you can also add more using the toolbar on the left-hand side of the page.

Here is the middle section of my page before I've done anything to it. You can also see that my lens qualifies to be in Cozy magazine, which is because it is in a Home & Garden related category – the magazine seems to offer extra promotional benefits for lenses related to topics that it covers.

Feathers Everywhere! Avoid Common Down Comforter Care Mistakes

✏ Edit Title

Good news! ✕

You've created a lens on a topic that is eligible for inclusion in our Cozy magazine, powered by Squidoo. This means your lens gets a special look and feel, inclusion in a powerful promotion engine, and you basically get a dedicated publicist who wants to see your lens do well. But if you'd rather fly solo, click here to opt out.

Introduction, Contents & Discovery Tool ✏ Edit

Why not add a title?

Write something interesting here. Introduce people to your topic and give them a reason to keep reading.

Text Module #link ✏ Edit ✕

New Text Module

What else do you want readers to know about this topic? The more great content you write in this building block (or "module") the better your page will do.

This module is empty. Please click edit to start adding content to it!

Before I start building my lens, I want to edit some of the settings in the toolbar on the left. I'm going to click on **Topics & Tags** to start.

You can see here that my Bedding and Pillows topic selection is what landed me in the Cozy magazine.

Down below, you can also see the four tags that I initially set up for the lens. I can now edit those and/or add more tags. I would recommend having at least 10 total tags, but there is nothing wrong with entering more.

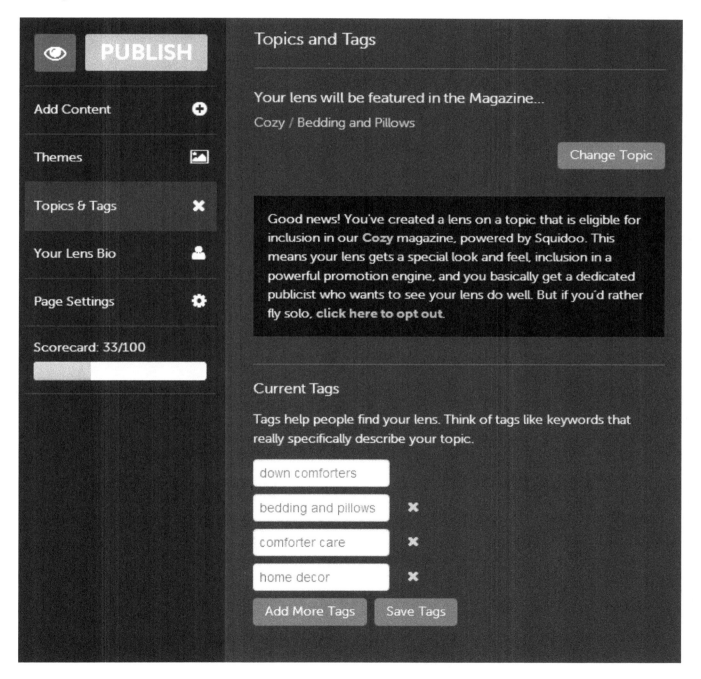

Just click on the **Add More Tags** button to create a blank text box for a new tag. You can continue to click that button again to produce more blank boxes until you have enough for the tags you want to enter. When you are done with your tag changes, be sure to click on the **Save Tags** button.

I've gone through and entered a decent list of tags for my lens, as seen below:

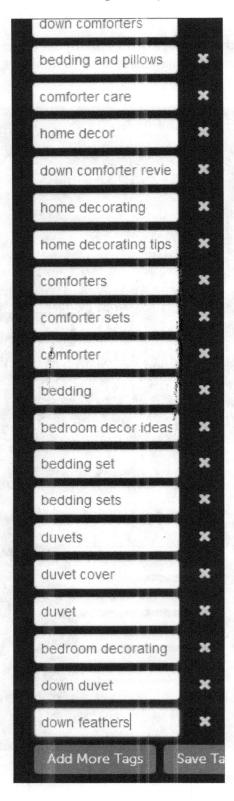

Next, click on the **Your Lens Bio** tab on the left. This shows your profile picture and biography information. I like to have a preset bio that I can easily make a few minor changes to for each of my new lenses that I create. This particular settings tab allows me to customize the bio for each lens without having to create a different Squidoo account each time.

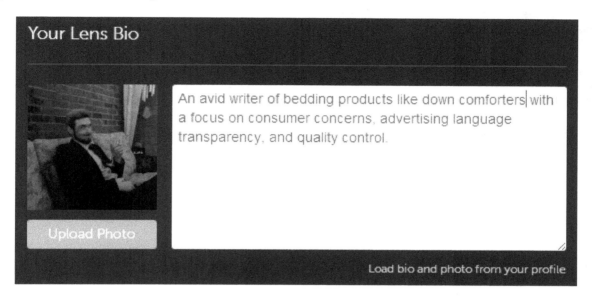

After I've done this, the progress bar at the bottom of the toolbar on the left now says 41/100 instead of 33/100. Simply click on that to open up a window with more information about this. Squidoo has some requirements for each page to create it, which are the items listed here in the scorecard. Simply proceed with your lens creation until you have this complete (at 90/100 – the last 10 is given when you publish).

Here are the relevant items for a lens:

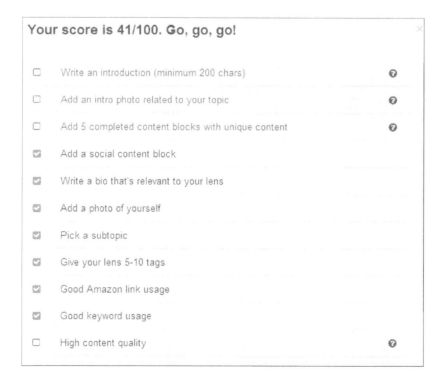

As you can see, the remaining tasks that I need to complete involve the content of my lens. Notice their emphasis on high quality, unique content. Make sure that all text you put into Squidoo is your own writing and not something reused from elsewhere (or even spun content).

I'm now going to start to create my lens content. Each of the modules listed down the center of the page has an Edit button in the top-right. Simply clicking on that allows me to edit the content for each module.

First I have the introduction. I'm simply going to provide a title and some text here that will summarize what my lens is about. I can also use a relevant picture here that will also help to capture attention.

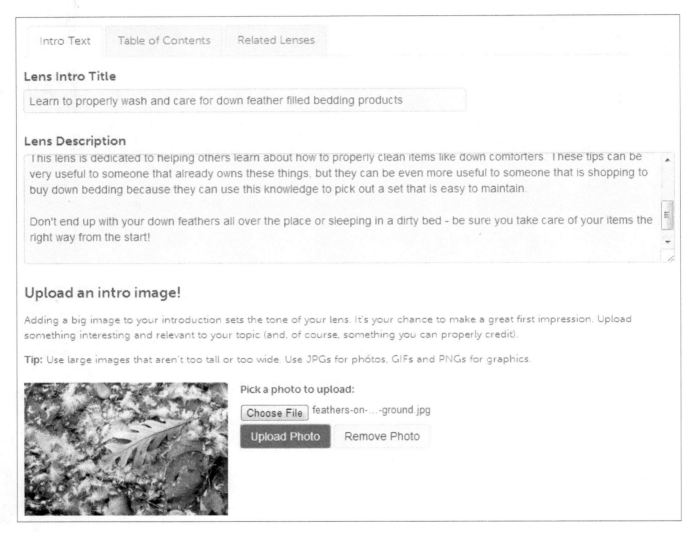

There are sometimes tabs available at the top of the edit page for each module. The Table of Contents tab here can be used to easily create links within your page that will jump visitors straight to specific modules of content in your lens.

Turn on the Table of Contents here, choose a layout, and specify which modules to show in the list (all will show by default).

You can see the settings I have selected for my lens below:

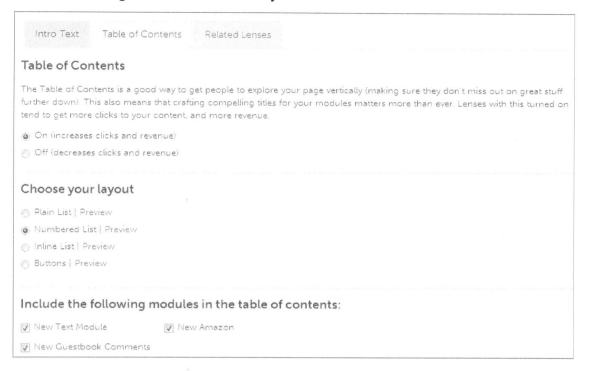

The third tab here is **Related Lenses**. This is where I enter the URLs for the related lenses from my research. Just put in the ending of the URL (leave off the initial squidoo.com portion of each link).

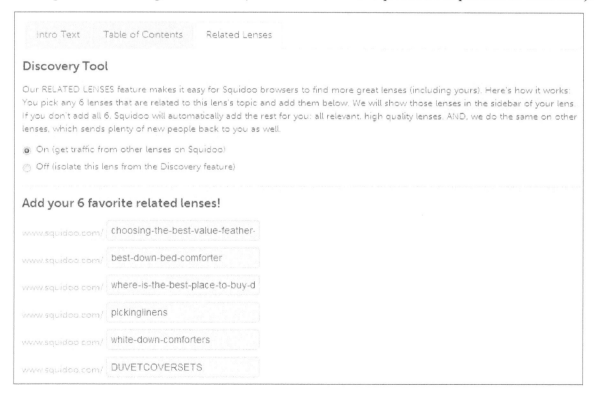

Turning this feature on here allows you to receive traffic from other lenses. If you do not specify all six related lenses, Squidoo will select for you based on your tags and content of your lens. I prefer to choose instead of letting them do it for me.

Squidoo automatically provides an Amazon advertising module on the lens, although it can be removed if you wish to keep all advertising on your site. At the very least, provide a title for the Amazon module.

Below that, you can search for and add the Amazon products to the module.

Search on the left, click the **Add** button for the products you want to use, and then set some custom text for each on the right.

The custom text is a great place to put a quick, personalized review for each product – something Squidoo recommends to do to increase sales.

There is also another tab for this section – **Display Options**.

This can be used to change the information that is shown with each Amazon ad in this module, although I typically leave the default settings.

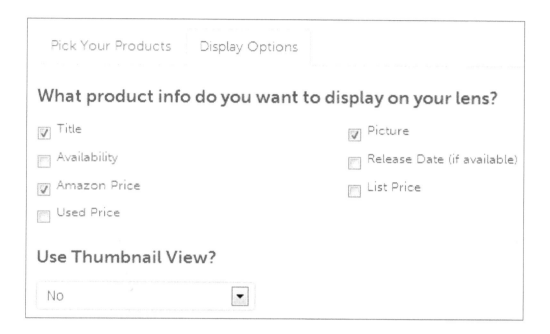

Next, I'm going to edit the Guestbook Comments module at the bottom.

This is where visitors of the lens can leave comments.

One of the ways you can increase lens rank on Squidoo is by getting more visitors to interact with things like leaving comments (but it can also be other things, like voting on polls).

I'm just going to set a quick custom title and description for this module.

I am going to leave comments set to automatic approval for now, assuming that I don't start receiving spam comments on this lens.

Despite the fact that I have left automatic approval for comments turned on, there is still something that I want to do here to try to protect myself from comment spam.

I am going to prohibit HTML on this lens with the very last setting available here – **Should HTML be allowed in comments?**

By at least having this setting set to **No**, people won't be able to drop comments on the lens that have HTML text links in them.

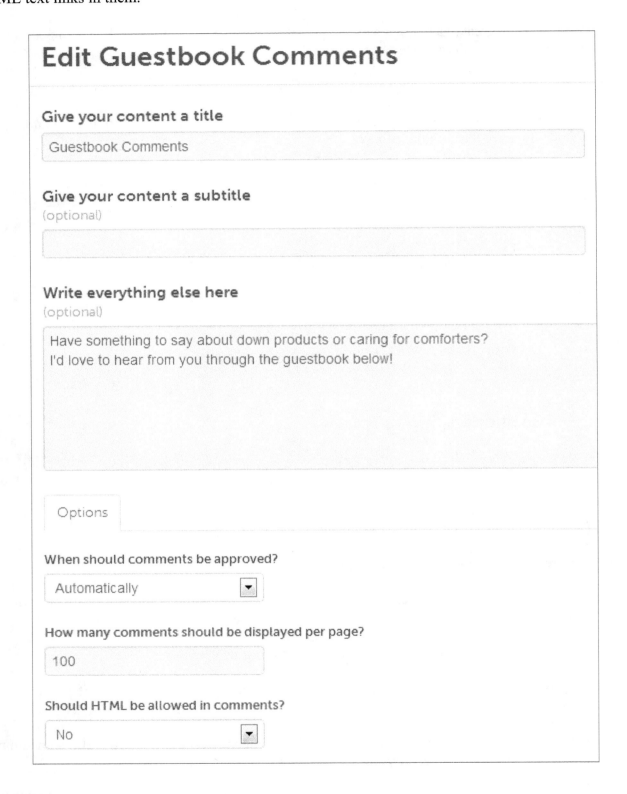

Squidoo requires 5 decent content blocks on each lens.

To create more of these, just use the toolbar on the left – click on **Add Content**.

This toolbar allows you to select from a variety of different content modules on Squidoo, which can be normal blocks of text content, Amazon ads, videos, and much more.

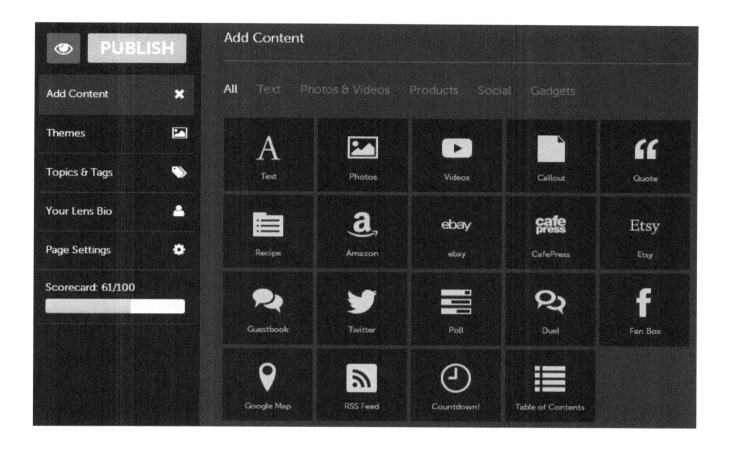

I'll be adding a number of Text modules, my most frequently used type, but I am also going to add a Poll to my lens.

I strongly encourage you to explore through the different types of content that you can add to your lens here because there are really a wide variety of options that may apply to different situations.

For example, if you are creating a page that is centered around some type of annual holiday, try using a countdown timer to show the amount of time left until that holiday on your lens – any creative extras you can use will help.

I'm just going to create a simple poll for my visitors to try to get them to interact with the page.

This is really just a basic example of one of the ways that you can get creative with your lenses and also try to encourage interaction with people that visit it.

I am also going to use it as a way to potentially help people decide what product they want to buy, so I am going to ask people if they prefer real down or down alternative.

This is just a simple question, but it is something that most people visiting this lens should either have a response to or be interested in how others have responded.

You can see the information I have provided to create this poll here:

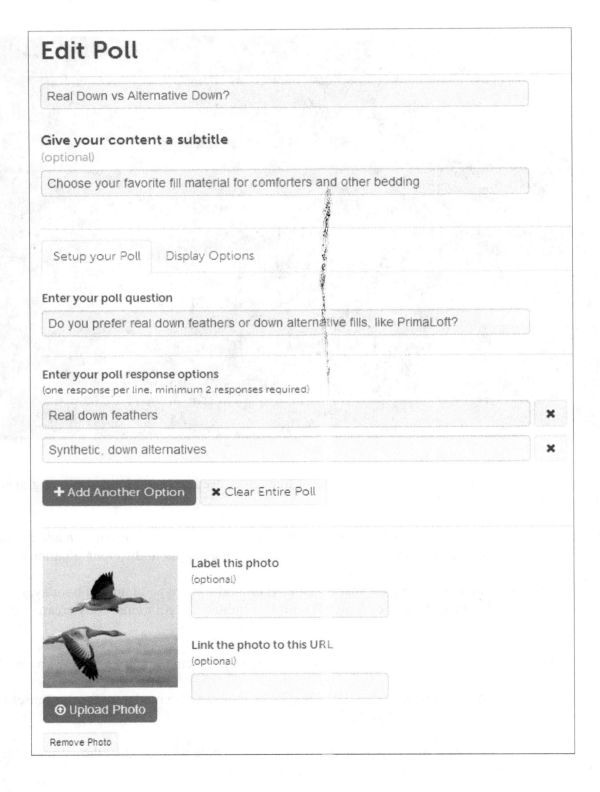

Next, I have created a series of text modules. However, I have not shown all of these in this guide that I created for the lens, but they can be seen in person on the live lens using the link at the end of this chapter.

One particular text module that I do want to show you here is one that does two things worth pointing out.

First, I have used HTML in the content to create an HTML list. This can be useful to provide a bit of variety in the look of your content, something I have previously recommended to you in the creation of your own site content.

Second, I have also placed an HTML link here to my own website and also to a relational page elsewhere (I picked Wikipedia, but it could be anywhere).

I've shown this module in edit mode below. In the large text box at the bottom, the HTML list is the large paragraph at the top (not all of this is pictured) and one of the HTML links is at the bottom.

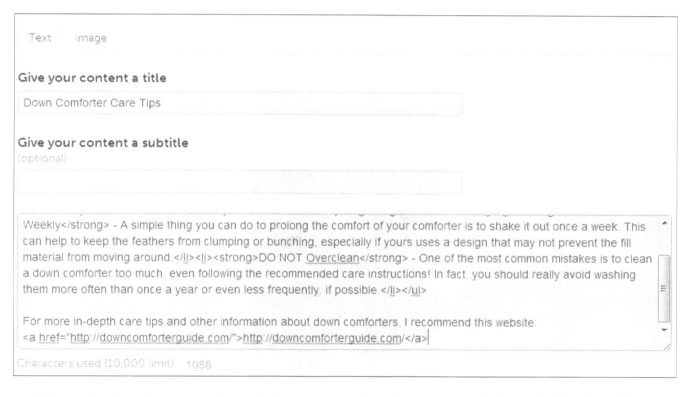

After saving the changes to this module, we can see how it is going to look on the live lens (pictured on the following page).

The HTML list helps to break up paragraphs of content, which is something I commonly use in articles on my own websites.

The links offer other helpful reading for site visitors. Obviously, one of these links is the link I want people to click. If someone trusts the information I provide here, they should proceed on to my website for more info and potentially to purchase a product through Amazon.

Down Comforter Care Tips

- **Follow Care Instructions** - All comforters and other bedding products will have a tag on them. Make sure you strictly follow the instructions provided there by the manufacturer. Most people ignore this information, but that is really one of the worst mistakes you can make with anything using down feathers.
- **Shake Weekly** - A simple thing you can do to prolong the comfort of your comforter is to shake it out once a week. This can help to keep the feathers from clumping or bunching, especially if yours uses a design that may not prevent the fill material from moving around.
- **DO NOT Overclean** - One of the most common mistakes is to clean a down comforter too much, even following the recommended care instructions! In fact, you should really avoid washing them more often than once a year or even less frequently, if possible.

For more in-depth care tips and other information about down comforters, I recommend this website: http://downcomforterguide.com/

You can also learn more about down feathers here: http://en.wikipedia.org/wiki/Down_feather

Once you are done with your content creation, you should see 90/100 in the Scorecard in the toolbar on the left:

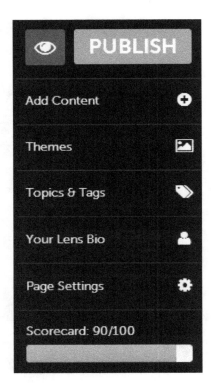

At this point, you can now click on the Publish button at the top to make your lens live.

You can see the completed lens from this tutorial here: http://www.squidoo.com/down-feather-comforter-care

11-4 SQUIDOO SEO TIPS

SEO applies to your Squidoo lenses in two different ways:

1. The content of your lenses can be optimized to rank it for various search engine keywords.

2. Lenses can be used to provide your site with targeted backlinks.

This setup is really a win-win for you.

Your lens gets search rankings and brings in traffic. That traffic can then navigate to Amazon through ads on the lens, to your own site through links on the lens, or even to other lenses of yours (through your profile or as related lenses that you've listed).

Even if your traffic doesn't reach one of your ultimate goals, you still earn a little bit from Squidoo, so it is really hard to view anything as a failure here.

SEO with your lens content itself really works the same way that it does with your website. You simply want to try to pick out a primary keyword phrase to target on each lens that you create, although you can also try to target a couple of secondary phrases within the content itself (just go for one phrase in your title though).

Make your lens content as rich as possible using a variety of media and also plenty of text content. Pictures, videos, lists, outgoing links, social polls, or anything else can be used – whatever works for your target subject.

Since one of the unique things about lenses is the in-depth nature of each page you create, don't be afraid to cover a few related topics in your content as long as it relates to your primary keyword phrase.

When it comes to the SEO benefits for your own website as a result of creating a Squidoo lens, those benefits come through the links that you create on the lenses. You can obviously get direct traffic to your site through those links, but they can also provide you with some SEO benefits as well.

The links that you create on Squidoo will be "nofollow" links these days unfortunately. However, that doesn't mean that you have to completely dismiss the SEO benefits of building those links.

Google wants to see some relational "nofollow" links to your site, so this is one great way to build them and make it appear to be done naturally as long as you are not overusing the links. In fact, Google has been using "nofollow" links more and more for their rankings lately, so they definitely do not ignore these links entirely!

Since the links will not provide you with a major SEO boost to your own site, keep your focus on driving traffic to the lens by optimizing the content to get great search rankings.

Lenses can easily get top ten rankings for decent keyword phrases.

Look in the 100-500 monthly search range or possibly higher if you can link together multiple lenses. For example, create 7 lenses all relating to your main website niche, and specify those lenses as the related lenses – this will put links on your lenses back to your other relating lenses. These links are actually NOT "nofollow", so they can pass search ranking power.

11-5 AVOIDING PROBLEMS WITH SQUIDOO

As of March 2013, Squidoo started cracking down on affiliates that are taking advantage of the network and not providing what the site is really looking for with their lenses.

I wanted to be sure to include a few notes about this in a separate chapter for easy reference because failure to follow this advice can result in the permanent removal of your lenses and potentially even your Squidoo account.

First of all, refer back to the first Squidoo chapter to see the notice displayed when you create an account. This summarizes the Squidoo mission statement, so be sure to adhere to it by creating unique content on their lenses.

Next, be sure not to overuse affiliate links – either your own links or even the ones that Squidoo provides. Ultimately, there is no point in loading a lens with Amazon links because it isn't going to be well received by Squidoo or your lens visitors, which completely defeats the purpose of building it.

Think about the things that I recommend with the creation of your own site. To be more specific, I'm talking about creating a useful site that doesn't depend on your advertising to exist. This same thing should be done with your lens. It shouldn't require Amazon ads to make sense.

To go a step beyond that, I also recommend to keep that same train of thought when it comes to creating outgoing links on your Squidoo lenses. They will actually limit you to 10 outgoing links to one site from one lens, but you should honestly not be using that many.

I am often looking to have a link on all of my lenses pointing back to my main Amazon site. However, I don't want Squidoo to think that the lens was only created for this purpose. This will definitely flag your lens and remove it for this reason alone, so be sure to be careful with this.

Just use a single link or possibly two on the lens back to your own site. Another tactic you can use is to link out to another website (preferably one that doesn't have advertising, like Wikipedia is one I like to use). Linking to another site and your own makes it less apparent that the lens just exists for a link to your site.

Remember, focus on content quality above all else, with your site, Squidoo, and even other sites for that matter, and all of the success you seek to find will follow. Getting greedy and overeager is the most common mistake you can make once you have the right knowledge that you need to actually do this type of work properly, so just keep calm and remain patient (things in the internet world don't always happen overnight, especially search rankings).

12 SITE FLIPPING

The final class in this series is completely optional but still something that many of you will find useful at some point in your affiliate site building career. This lesson teaches you a number of different tactics that you can use to sell completed and profitable Amazon affiliate sites. These same strategies could also be used to sell other kinds of websites. We will learn how to use forums, Flippa, and even private affiliates to sell these sites.

Primary Lesson Objective

☐   Sell Your Profitable Amazon Site (Optional)

Lesson Steps Checklist

☐   Pick a Site Flipping Method

☐   Gather Sales Records, Traffic Data & Other Important Site Info

☐   List Your Site for Sale

☐   Setup Site Purchase Through Escrow for Safety

☐   Transfer Site, Domain & Other Accounts to New Site Owner

Chapter Notes

Chapter Notes

12-1 SITE FLIPPING RECOMMENDATIONS

Before I actually get into teaching some specific tactics that you can use to sell your Amazon affiliate sites, I want to talk to you about site flipping in general as well as some of my recommendations for you.

First of all, this particular class isn't a requirement for all of your Amazon sites. In fact, some of you may never want to sell any of your sites, while others may want to sell all of them.

A completed Amazon affiliate site can really be sold at any time, but if you make sure to meet some requirements before you sell, you will be able to fetch a much higher price per site.

In general, if you want a good price for each site, make sure you meet ALL of the following:

1. Site construction is complete

2. At least one top 10 Google ranking

3. Daily traffic

4. Multiple sales within a single month

The following criteria can be considered optional, but the more of these you meet, the better price you will receive for each site:

1. Traffic records for multiple months with increasing traffic each month

2. Sales records for multiple months with increasing earnings each month

3. Active social networking accounts (YouTube, Facebook, etc) with followers

4. Traffic / Sales records for a minimum of one year

When To Sell Sites

Technically, you should be able to make more money from each Amazon site that you build by keeping them, but there are some situations where I would recommend to sell.

Selling sites allows for quick income, which can be desperately needed by some when they are first starting out. Even if a site could make more after keeping it for a year or two, some people may not be able to wait that long.

A downside to selling your sites is that it can create a never ending need to do so to keep your monthly income high enough, although this often only applies to people that are completely depending on their online income.

Whenever possible, keep a real job as long as possible and don't let a quick gain from selling a site lead you to believe that you can earn a full-time living that way. Yes, it can be done. However, it is a non-stop cycle of building and then selling sites.

When you keep a site instead of selling it and then move on to the construction of a new site, you give yourself the opportunity to build a passive income that grows with each new site.

If you do decide to sell a site and do not want to always be building and selling each new site, just ensure that you still have your normal source of income coming in on top of it.

This allows you to use that money as catch up money to recover previous investments you may have had to make to get to this point (possibly from other courses you've purchased that didn't work out). Then you can start fresh with building new sites to keep them to build a passive, recurring income.

Site Pricing

One of the most common points of confusion over selling sites is how to price them. A general rule of thumb to use is 18 times the monthly profit of a site, but that number could really depend on which criteria you have met for selling a site (discussed earlier in this chapter).

It could also depend on how you go about selling the site and/or how much interest there is in it. Selling a site on Flippa may not fetch as much for your site as some of the other methods I discuss, although a site that would attract interest from multiple buyers can actually do better there.

I have sold a site as early as six weeks after creating the domain. The entire site was completed in four days. The site got a top 10 Google ranking and made about $50 during the first full month, so it had some things going for it. I actually sold the site for 60 times the monthly revenue ($3,000), but this is definitely not something that most would consider ordinary or something you should expect to do with your own sites.

That particular site was one that I sold through the Warrior Forum, a strategy that I will discuss in the next chapter. However, I wanted to mention here that hyping up a site publicly is one possible way of getting much more for a site than the 18 times number.

Typically, to really get 18 times the monthly profit on a site like Flippa, you will want to have a years worth of traffic and income records. This may seem like a long time to wait, but you also have to consider that the income will likely increase during that year to make the site even more valuable.

If you are selling a site with just a couple months worth of records on Flippa, you may want to shoot for around 10 times the monthly income as your minimum bid amount. This gives you a decent price for the site if only one person bids and the potential to get a better price if it is desired by more than one person.

Prepare Before You Sell

One of the most common mistakes that people make when trying to sell a website is not taking the time to make it as appealing as possible to potential buyers. When someone is looking to buy something like an Amazon affiliate site, they are looking for an indication that the purchase will be a good investment.

A lot of people will never build sites and will simply buy them one by one off of sites like Flippa to build a recurring monthly income, so you want to try to appeal to these buyers as much as possible because they have the most money to spend.

The easiest way to appeal to that type of buyer is to provide as much proof as possible. Anything you claim about the site in terms of traffic or sales – back it up with proof in the way of screenshots (on Flippa, some of these can even be verified, like with Google Analytics stats).

Anything that is connected to the site, in the way of marketing that you still control, make sure you provide complete information and proof for those things as well. This could be something like YouTube Channels, Facebook Fan Pages or Groups, Squidoo Lenses, etc. Any of these properties included with the sale of the website will help to increase the value, especially when these other properties have subscribers, followers or additional earnings.

Also be sure to investigate whether you can transfer ownership of these additional properties. You don't want to include another account in the sale of your website if it cannot be transferred to the new owner. However, you may still be able to mention that it exists if it provides the new owner with some type of benefit, like ongoing traffic.

Whenever you are providing proof of traffic or income, make sure you break it down as much as possible. For example, with Google Analytics, don't just show them how much traffic you receive – show them where that traffic comes from (so they know it is free traffic that will keep coming). If you make money from Amazon and other sites, like Squidoo, make sure you break that income down so people know exactly where it is coming from.

Another thing to remember is to provide your proof for each month so people can see trends from month to month. If they can see a rising trend in your traffic and earnings, your site will be viewed as being more valuable.

If you happen to be building some type of seasonal website and not an evergreen website, you may actually have to wait a full year before selling the site so you and others can get a clear picture of how much income it will make in a year. Monthly income is only relevant as an average for a full year with a more seasonal type of site.

Make sure you also provide proof of any achievements for the site, like Google rankings for various keyword phrases. Dig up as many of these as you can because they will increase the value of your site. Figure out the keyword phrase and a ranking position for each phrase.

Finally, don't forget to talk about the website itself. If you build a site that is completely unique content, it will be much more valuable to potential buyers. If you build a site using any of my plugins, you can also mention that they get those commercial plugins for free to use on that site and get to upgrade to new versions for free – just add together the prices of those plugins to get a rough value that is essentially given to the new site owner as a bonus.

Remember, anything the new owner gets for free that you paid for can really be mentioned when selling the site – paid time on your domain name, for example, would get transferred to the new owner (website hosting doesn't usually apply here though, since you would transfer the site to the new owner and they would host it themselves).

12-2 FORUM SITE FLIPPING

The first site flipping strategy that I want to talk to you about is extremely powerful and can really be used for a wide variety of purposes.

The whole idea here is to essentially generate hype over a website and eventually find a buyer for it. However, you can really replace "website" with almost anything else that you want to sell or promote (like "product", "service" or "person").

Think about your target buyer – who is most likely to want to buy what you are selling? Then, find an online community where these people hang out.

For Amazon affiliate sites, other marketers and affiliates are your target buyer. For this reason, the Warrior Forum actually makes a good candidate: http://www.warriorforum.com/

This is the forum that I used for this tactic, but I also want to emphasize that this isn't the only option.

You can definitely look on Google to find other candidates, especially if you want to try this tactic to sell something other than a website (ie, you could actually use this same strategy to generate traffic for your Amazon site, but you would want a forum with your target niche customer for that purpose).

One single post on the Warrior Forum back in 2010 actually led to the sale of DogCrateSizes.com for $3,000 just six weeks after registering the domain name. In fact, this one post also led to me developing commercial WordPress plugins and coaching other Amazon affiliates, so I can honestly say that you wouldn't be reading this book right now if it wasn't for this post from four years ago.

The key is to use a forum that is popular and also allows you to have a link in the signature of your posts.

On the Warrior Forum, just follow these steps:

1. Find a popular thread about Amazon affiliate sites – the best ones were often created multiple days ago and are still near the top of the list because people keep posting to it (this just indicates it is an active thread).

2. Casually chime in to the thread with a useful post and simply share your Amazon site with others. This site should be something special that the average affiliate doesn't see – in-depth content or something else creative about it that helps it stand out.

3. Follow-up with responses on the thread. Assuming you get interest and some hype generated about the site, you can proceed to the final step.

4. Add a link to your forum signature. This should point to either a sales page for the domain or a page for them to contact you. Going for contact with the person can often be better, as this gives you a chance to sell the site to them by email, which can often be much more successful than with a direct sales page (especially since you can get interested buyers to contact you without disclosing a price in public).

The whole idea here is to share the site, generate interest in it among other Amazon affiliates, and eventually find one of those affiliates that is interested in buying the site directly from you.

With this tactic, you can likely sell a site for a nice price based on the monthly earnings, especially if there is something unique about the site. You may even get affiliates interested in learning more from you about your site building process!

If you decide to do something like this on a regular basis, you may even want to get people to sign up for a newsletter list to get in contact with you or to find out about other sites of yours.

You could simply ask people to join to find out about future sites you have to sell. This allows you to build a newsletter list of potential buyers that you can continually grow with each new site being sold, which will often make it easier to sell future sites since you will have a list of customers that you can promote the sale to.

You can see that post in person by visiting the link below:
http://www.warriorforum.com/main-internet-marketing-discussion-forum/220802-amazon-affiliates-you-seriously-making-money-10.html#post2803972

This particular post has received almost 119,000 views to date, although that number obviously didn't view this thread before my site had sold (it was in the 40,000 view neighborhood then):

		Amazon Affiliates - Are You Seriously Making Money? (1 2 3 ... Last Page) waken		03-21-2011 12:15 AM by ryansjones	865	118,778	Main Internet Marketing Discussion Forum

Notice how I didn't even chime into this thread until the 10th page, but I certainly got a lot of people talking about my site after that point.

So you can see exactly what I said, just in case something should ever happen to the Warrior Forum or that post (very unlikely still), I have at least included my initial post on that thread on the following page.

phpnetpro
WP Plugin Developer
War Room Member

Join Date: Nov 2008
Location: SC, USA
Posts: 308
Thanks: 32
Thanked 239 Times in 64
Posts

Re: Amazon Affiliates - Are You Seriously Making Money?

I don't think I have chimed in on this thread yet.

I do think there is a lot of merit to these websites. I personally run a number of them myself and still actively make new ones that make good money.

Depending on what type of niche you get into, you may have more work cut out for you. Some of the people make it seem easier than it really is, although that may be because they outsource nearly everything. It is a lot of work, but once you can get a site running and marketed properly, it will often not require much attention. You should keep your sites updated once a month or so at the very least though, just so they don't become stagnant in the eyes of the search engines.

I like to get very specific with my product targeting, especially with Amazon products. I try to make a site based on just a couple of products or a small line or products.

I will grace all of you with one decent example of my work in this area. I know most people won't spill their niche secrets, but I don't mind sharing one. Don't try to join in on this niche because there is not much left for decent keyword domains - just use this as an example for your own niches.

I have recently (in the last two weeks or so) made a new site promoting amazon products for a particular niche: dog crates.

My site and keyword:Dog Crate Sizes

Although the site is extremely new, I already have a Google top ten ranking for "dog crate sizes". I make much simpler sites than this one, but the 20-30 pages for this site do help to make it a bit more powerful with search engines. I put this site together, from scratch, in about 4 days. I have been doing a bit of marketing every day or two since I made the site live. I get daily traffic to the site, all of it is free traffic. I send daily traffic to amazon. I haven't had sales every day but I have had over $400 in sales just since it started.

The key is to make a site that may actually be useful to people and at least somewhat unique for a search engine. Figure out what they are looking for, give it to them and them pass them along to the next step (which, for us, we prefer to be the buying stage). You can target certain products and buying keywords, but you can also have quite a bit of success if you target the markets that people look at immediately BEFORE they will buy something. This allows you to insert yourself as the middleman ☺.

Amazon Affiliate Marketing - How to Find a New Niche

Increase Your Amazon Affiliate Cookie Duration from 24 Hours to 90 Days!

My high quality and affordable Amazon WordPress Plugins

First of all, even if this tactic fails to sell the site, you're still building a targeted backlink that Google will pick up when you link to the site in your post. Use your primary keyword phrase, the name of the site, or even a short keyword for your product niche (I could've used "dog crates" for my link text).

At the bottom of that picture, you can see my signature links. The one that I used to sell the website is not pictured here, since I removed that years ago right after the site sold. However, I simply put a text link that said "Want to own DogCrateSizes.com? Click here to learn more.".

It was such a simple yet clever text link. With my post and the posts of others in the thread, I easily built name recognition for my site among those that were reading the thread. Then, they see the text link and are obviously drawn to it because who wouldn't want to own the awesome Amazon site that everyone is talking about in the thread?

Once you get someone to click on your signature link, I recommend landing them on a page on your own website that will give them some brief information.

Something like "Since my Amazon product website, DogCrateSizes.com, has received such an overwhelming response from other internet marketers I have decided to give one lucky person the chance to OWN DogCrateSizes.com!". Then, proceed to give them a summary of how the site is doing – traffic, sales, Google rankings, etc. You could then provide a contact form to reach you to get more information, or you could also add a newsletter sign up form here and provide more info including your contact info to those that join the newsletter.

I highly recommend that you browse through the link that I provided above for that post. Read through the thread starting with that post to see how people reacted to my site and also see my responses.

I originally made that first post on November 1st, 2010. I didn't post the offer to sell the website until December 1st, 2010, and I had a completed sale with $3,000 in my Paypal account on December 3rd, 2010!

What I actually did on December 1st to generate even more interest for the site was to make a standalone post with that link in my signature.

Here is a link to that standalone post:
http://www.warriorforum.com/adsense-ppc-seo-discussion-forum/294342-how-find-niche-market-guide-finding-new-amazon-product-niche-markets.html

This extra attention for the site also contributed to me becoming a product developer for other marketers, since I realized then that a lot of people could benefit from the knowledge that I have learned over the years after this post.

This particular post has received almost 24,000 views to date and even gets random posts to it still because it gets Google traffic now:

		How to Find a Niche Market - A Guide to Finding New Amazon Product Niche Markets ([] 1 2 3) phpnetpro	04-17-2013 10:32 AM by Bunnytale []	131	23,885	Adsense / PPC / SEO Discussion Forum

Although I decided to include this particular strategy because it can help you sell an Amazon site, there is really much more that this strategy can do.

I would encourage you to read through my posts on those threads to get a better sense of how to pull off something like this on your own and potentially for something completely different from selling Amazon sites. You can honestly build followers and customer lists using this method for basically any niche.

12-3 SELLING SITES ON FLIPPA

Flippa is somewhere that you can go to sell pretty much any website.

The downside to using this marketplace is that you will pay extra fees, but it can also deliver buyers to you without you having to find them yourself.

In general, if you want to fetch a decent price for your site, you will need a lot going for it to get it from a buyer on Flippa.

The buyers in this marketplace are often seasoned site buyers, so they are looking for something particular and want it at a price that gives them the best chance of making a profit.

If you can find buyers for your sites using any of the other methods I discuss in this guide, I would recommend using those strategies instead.

One exception to this is if you have a site that you believe will have multiple buyers interested in it, since the bidding on Flippa can drive the price higher.

If you do not have an account on Flippa and wish to sell a site there, you need to create an account.

Get started by visiting the Flippa website:
http://flippa.com/

To begin creating an account, click on the **Sign Up** link at the top of the page:

Now you just need to proceed through a series of steps to create your account and also verify it. The entire process is fairly quick and simple though.

First provide a username, email and password for your account:

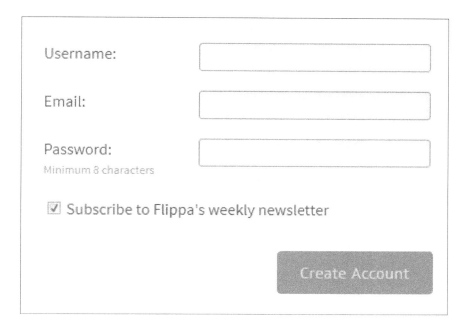

After you click on the **Create Account** button, they will send you a confirmation email. You will need to click on the link in that email to verify your account before you can begin using it.

Flippa has a phone number verification system that you will then need to complete to be able to buy or sell sites.

Hi rsplugin, Welcome to Flippa!

Congratulations! Your account has now been created.

You can now access all **logged-in features.** You can **see hidden listings,** you can **save searches** to be emailed to you later and you can create draft listings.

However, before you can buy or sell, you need to verify your phone number. It's a quick, automated process which takes less than two minutes and costs you nothing.

Once you have completed their verification process with a phone number, you will see a green **Sell** button in the top-right of the Flippa website:

Just click on it to start creating a listing to sell a site. This takes you to a page where you simply enter your domain to get started.

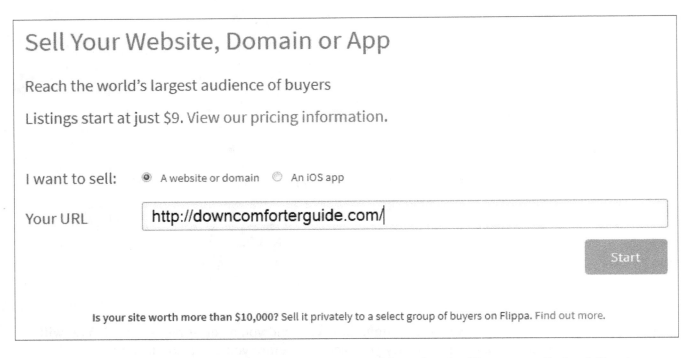

Unlike the other classes that I have taught throughout this series, I will not actually be following through with this particular step with DownComforterGuide.com because I do not wish to sell the website. However, I am going to at least use the domain so I can get into this system to point some things out to you that are important when selling a site on Flippa.

Since I last sold a site on Flippa, they have actually changed their site listing interface. I am very thrilled about this because I found the old system to be very confusing to use. Typically, if something is confusing for me online, then the average user is completely lost.

Everything is now simplified into 5 steps. The first is shown below:

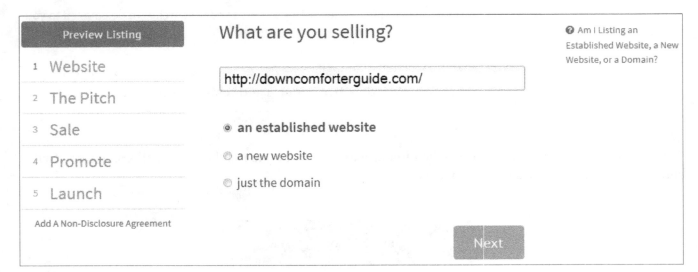

As long as you have traffic and/or sales on a site, you will want to select **an established website** for this first step.

With **a new website**, you would also sell a complete website and domain name, but you would not be able to claim any traffic or income from the site in the listing (this is used for people that sell template/auto websites in most cases).

Notice the five steps listed on the left.

The required information to enter is in the center of the page.

On the right, you can find a text link that goes to a help page, in case you have more questions about one of these steps.

Once you click on the **Next** button, the number of steps actually changes for some reason. It appears as though the first step, Website, really has a few parts to it.

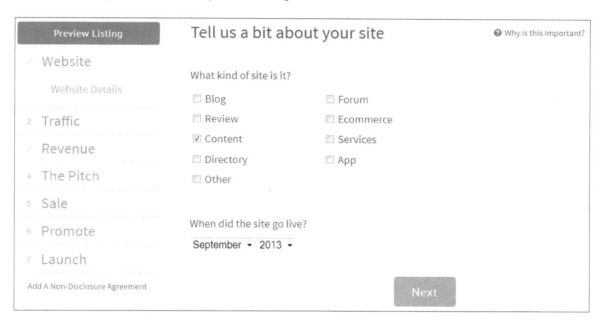

I list my Amazon sites as **Content** sites, although you could also classify some of them as **Review** sites.

You can actually select both options here, as long as your site fits both site types. Beyond selecting what kind of site you have, you just have to provide a month and year when the site went live, so this steps is pretty straightforward.

Next, we need to provide traffic information.

You can simply list the number of unique visitors and pageviews per months here, or you can just connect the listing with Google Analytics to have verified information in your listing (highly recommended).

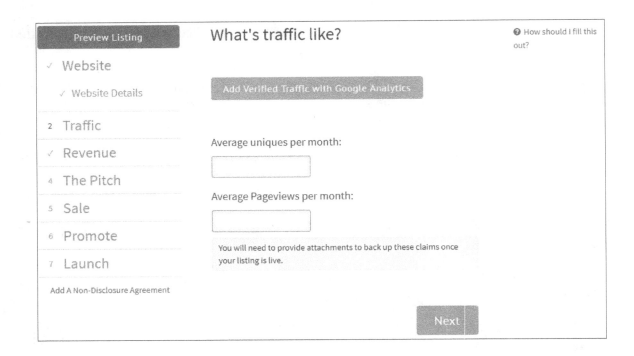

Just click on the green **Add Verified Traffic with Google Analytics** button. This will take you to Google and show you the page below:

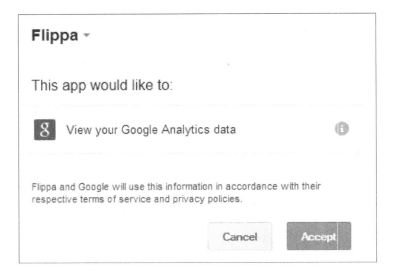

Simply click on the **Accept** button – this will automatically add verified traffic information to your listing.

Next, just specify how you monetize the site (click all that apply). This will just be Amazon for this type of site.

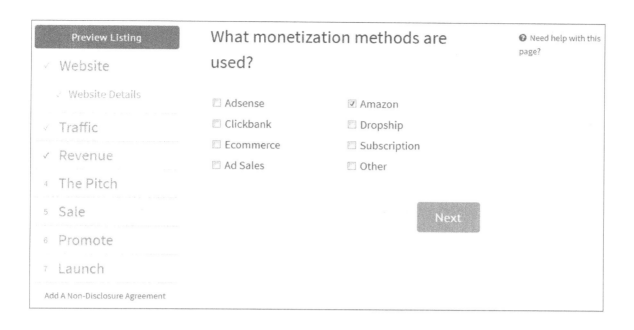

Now you finally get to create the actual listing:

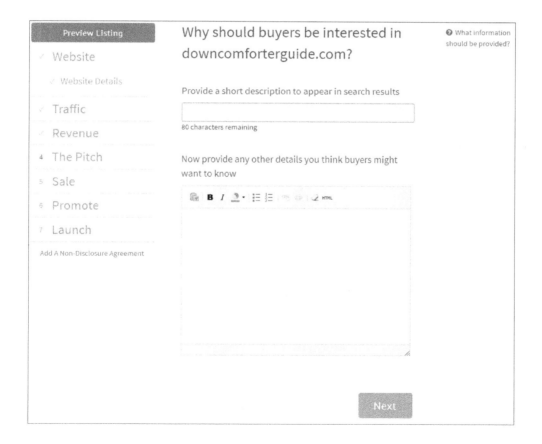

For **The Pitch** you need to provide a short description and then your full listing text, which can also include HTML.

The description will show up with your domain name in search results and other listings on the Flippa website, so this should be something that will grab the attention of those that will be interested in your site.

Try to summarize the most appealing aspects of your site in this description – this could be the traffic, income, niche, and even the fact that it is an Amazon site.

The full listing text needs to be made as complete as possible to give you the best shot at selling your site.

You don't need to write a sales page for your site. Instead, just give a brief summary of the site and talk about the important and appealing aspects of it.

Be sure to include all of these in your site listings:

1. Whether a site is custom content

2. When the site was built

3. How a site was built (ie, WordPress)

4. How you monetize the site

5. Everything included with the sale with as much detailed information as possible (ie, Site, Content, Domain, Facebook, YouTube, etc).

You will not be able to edit this information once your listing goes live, so be sure to make this complete the first time. However, you will be able to go back and upload file attachments to your listing and add additional information through comments on the listing.

Next, you need to set the price. I previously talked about setting the price of a site. The minimum price that you would be happy selling the site for should be put as your reserve price (the second text box here).

The first text box is for the opening bid. You could set this as the same amount, but you could also set it to a lower number to encourage early bidding on your listing.

As long as a reserve price is set, your site will not sell for less than that amount, but you should still set your opening bid to a number that hints at your reserve price (ie, don't set a reserve at $2000 and make the opening bid $10 – go for $1000 or more in that situation).

Flippa now has a site value calculator built into their system. However, I have not seen this before today, so I cannot reliably say how good of a job it does in calculating a recommended price or how that price compares with my recommendations. I would still recommend seeing what their recommended price is to ensure that you are in the same ballpark though.

Shorter listing times work best for most sites that are not going to sell for a ton of money (under a couple of grand).

Flippa recommends 5 day listings, but you can go higher if you wish. If your site is well established and you want a premium price for it, you may need to give people longer than 5 days to make a decision.

Here is the **Sale** page on Flippa for this step:

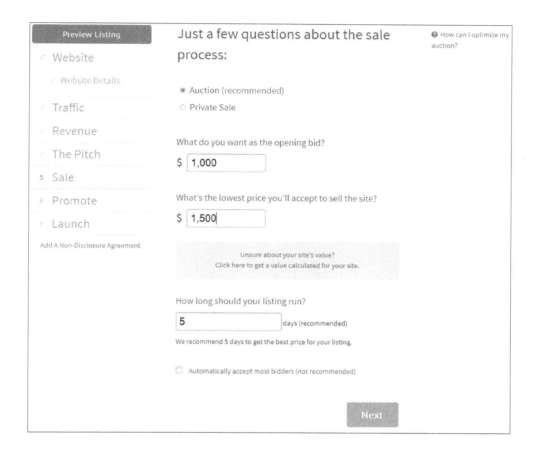

The next to last step is **Promote**. This is where you select the options for your listing on Flippa.

For this type of site, the lowest listing fee is $29 for a Standard listing. If you think your site can fetch $1,000 or more, it may be worth going for the Stand Out option at $49 to get more people to look at your listing (this gives you a screenshot of your site next to your listing, among a few other tweaks to help it stand out from Standard listings).

The Show Off option is $99. I would really only recommended this for sites that you want to get $2,000 or more from – these should be well established sites with long-term proof of income and improvement in traffic and earnings.

Here is the **Promote** screen with the options at the top:

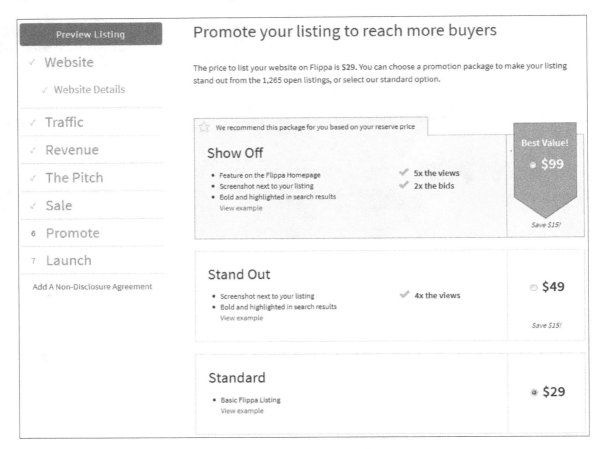

Below those options are a series of additional promotion features that you can add to your listing:

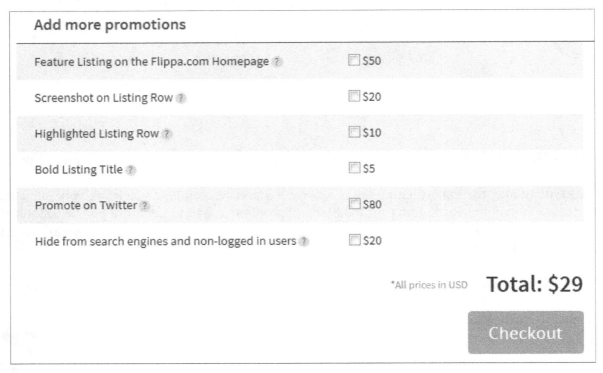

These additional promotional features will vary depending on the package option that you selected. All but the last two are included in one of the packages, so you may be better off upgrading to a better package if you want any of the first four features listed here.

The last two features, Promote on Twitter and Hide from search engines, are really only used for special cases. Promote on Twitter is $80, so this should only be used for the best of sites to generate a lot of interest for them.

The last option is really only used when you want to do a private sale – this prevents the listing from being indexed and even seen on Flippa except for by logged in users (useful when you use an NDA and don't even want to share the website name with people unless they are interested and pass your approval).

The final step of the process is to pay for your listing, which makes it go live on Flippa. When you pay for the listing, you are paying a listing fee, so this is no guarantee that the site will sell. However, if the site does not sell, they allow you to list it again for free.

When a site does sell on Flippa, you also have to pay an additional fee of 5% of the final sale price. Here are their exact terms on this additional fee:

Success Fee

☐ I accept that if my auction is successful, I will pay the success fee, which is 5% of the sale price, capped at a maximum of USD $3,000, and a minimum of USD $10.

When you actually run a Flippa auction listing, be sure to keep an active eye on it. Respond to any comments/questions people may have. Whenever you can get involved in a conversation with someone about your site listing, you have a much better chance at completing a sale.

One last thing about Flippa. Be careful who you approve to place a bid on your auction once it tops the reserve price.

If someone with no review ratings drops a nice bid on your auction and never communicates a single word with you, it is a great indication that it could potentially be the start of a fraudulent purchase (there are Flippa scammers, so be sure to follow all Flippa recommendations and even use escrow to complete sales).

12-4 PRIVATE SITE SALES WITH AFFILIATES

The last strategy that I want to talk to you about can be one of the easiest ways to sell your sites, although it may actually be the least profitable. However, if you need to sell a site fast, don't have the time to do it yourself, or need help with the whole process, then this may actually be the best way to go.

The idea behind this strategy is simple: just contact an Amazon product developer to sell your site for you. You may actually be able to get a complete service from it so all you have to do is collect the paycheck.

Think about these different aspects of selling a site to consider whether this option would work best for you.

Can you do the following?

1. Collect information needed to sell a site

2. Write some type of sales letter/page/information to attract interest

3. Find potential site buyers

4. Transfer a website to a new hosting account

5. Transfer domain name DNS

6. Transfer domain name ownership

7. Transfer ownership of additional properties included in the sale

8. Potentially provide short-term guidance/support for the new owner

If you cannot do all of these things, you may want to consider this option and go for someone that can do all of these things for you and find a buyer for your site for a single price.

Personally, I would be willing to do something like this for anyone that has gone through this course. Just submit a support ticket to me to talk more: http://ryanstevensonplugins.com/support/

As long as the person selling the site is going to collect at least a few hundred dollars from a sale, they would likely be willing to devote at least one promotion email to it. For additional services like handling the sale for you, transferring the website itself to the new owner, etc, you would likely need to go up a bit higher.

For a site that would sell for $1,500, paying a third to the affiliate is reasonable, although there will be a lot that will simply want 50% just for sending an email to sell it.

The main thing to consider is what you benefit from the deal and also whether it is worth it to the Amazon developer to promote it. Even someone with an average newsletter size like mine can make $500+ from a single email, so a site sale that would only pay $100 would really not be very worthwhile for myself or other Amazon developers (go for Flippa for cheaper sites).

Getting paid from a deal like this could potentially be tricky, especially if you do not necessarily know or trust the person who is selling the site for you. You have to consider whether you will be accepting the payment from the buyer and paying the seller their commission or the other way around. Then, you also have to consider what will happen if the buyer decided to file a chargeback or dispute on the purchase.

One option to avoid payment issues is to use an affiliate network for the sale. This will eat up more of the profits in fees, but it can be worth the peace of mind.

For an affiliate network, I would recommend JVZoo for this purpose. You could set up a listing for your site and simply not have it shown in the live marketplace. In fact, you could probably just get the Amazon developer to handle this part of it for you, since they would likely already have an account there and be familiar with how to create a listing. You could then just be the "affiliate" and have the developer promote with your link.

RESOURCES

Watch The Coaching Videos & Amazon Advertising Software

The live coaching series for these 12 classes was recorded and is available for online viewing. There are 12 HD videos where you get to see this strategy being put into action – more than 26 hours worth of video training.

This book and the videos both feature (in class #8) the use of five WordPress plugins that create various types of advertisements for Amazon affiliates.

Those plugins are plugins that I have personally developed for use on my own Amazon affiliate sites and also make them available to my trainees to help them build advertisements for their own sites.

Although the ads could technically be built manually, I highly recommend the use of these plugins.

The coaching students of the live series received these plugins for free with this course. However, I am unable to do that with customers of this book because of the major price difference (live trainees paid up to $497 for this complete series).

The videos, plugins and also digital copies of the lessons from this book can all be obtained by purchasing option #3 of my home-study course for this series.

Visit my website below to get access to these videos and plugins:
http://ryanstevensonplugins.com/azon-coaching/

Free Training & Ongoing Updates

Pick up my original Amazon affiliate training course and stay informed of updates to this book, new training courses, and new software by joining my email newsletter.

Join my newsletter here:
http://supertargeting.com/

Contact Me

I would love to hear from you about successes that you may have as a result of this course. I also welcome any other questions, comments or suggestions you may have for me.

Contact me here:
http://ryanstevensonplugins.com/support/

Techie Master Class

I ran an introductory training class to teach people how to manage their websites and do basic web design and even programming on their WordPress sites. This was a five-part series that included an ebook guide and an HD video from the live class. This is useful information for all of you, so I wanted to include it for you for free.

Get my Techie Master Class ebooks and videos (nothing to buy here):
http://ryanstevensonplugins.com/tmc/